Profile in Silver

Books by J. Neil Schulman

From *PULPLESS.COM, INC.*

Novels
Alongside Night
The Rainbow Cadenza

Nonfiction
The Robert Heinlein Interview and Other Heinleiniana
The Frame of the Century?
Stopping Power: Why 70 Million Americans Own Guns
Book Publishing in the 21st Century,
   Volumes One and Two

Short Stories
Nasty, Brutish, and Short Stories

Omnibus Collection
Self Control Not Gun Control

Collected Screenwritings
Profile in Silver and Other Screenwritings

J. Neil Schulman's

Profile in Silver
and Other Screenwritings

PULPLESS.COM, INC.
10736 Jefferson Blvd., Suite 775
Culver City, CA 90230-4969, USA
Voice & Fax: (500) 367-7353
Home Page: http://www.pulpless.com/
Business inquiries to info@pulpless.com
Editorial inquiries & submissions to
editors@pulpless.com

Copyright © 1999 by J. Neil Schulman
All rights reserved. Published by arrangement with the author. Printed in the United States of America. The rights to all previously published materials by J. Neil Schulman are owned by the author, and are claimed both under existing copyright laws and natural logorights. All other materials taken from published sources without specific permission are either in the public domain or are quoted and/or excerpted under the Fair Use Doctrine. Except for attributed quotations embedded in critical articles or reviews, no part of this book may be reproduced or utilized in any form or by any means, electronic or mechanical, including photocopying, recording, or by any information storage and retrieval system, without written permission from the publisher.

This collection is fiction. Names, characters, places, and incidents either are products of the author's imagination or are used fictitiously. Any resemblance to actual events, locales, or persons, living or dead, is entirely coincidental.

First Pulpless.Com™, Inc. Edition August, 1999.
Library of Congress Catalog Card Number: 99-62026
ISBN: 1-58445-102-5

Book and Cover designed by CaliPer, Inc.
Cover Illustration by Billy Tackett, Arcadia Studios
© 1999 by Billy Tackett

Paperless Book™ digital editions of this and all other Pulpless.Com™ books are available worldwide for immediate download 24-hours-a-day every day from the Pulpless.Com, Inc., web site, either for a small charge, or *free* with commercial messages.
Please visit our Catalog on the World Wide Web at
www.pulpless.com

Continuation of copyright page

"Profile in Silver" (First and Second Draft Stories and Teleplays)
Copyright © 1985, 1999 by J. Neil Schulman

"Timeshare"
Copyright © 1999 by Kate O'Neal & J. Neil Schulman
Used by permission of the co-writer.

"To Err Is Humanoid"
Copyright © 1999 by Kate O'Neal & J. Neil Schulman
Used by permission of the co-writer.

No Strings Attached was originally published as a paperless book™ by Cadenza Communications, Inc., and electronically distributed by SoftServ Publishing Services, Inc., September, 1990.

"No Strings Attached"
Copyright © 1986, 1999 by J. Neil Schulman

To
Alan Brennert
and
Victor Koman
Writers To Whom I Give My Highest Literary Praise: Envy

And to Kate O'Neal
Two out of three ain't bad, kiddo.

Table of Contents

	PAGE
But It's In The Script: Foreword by Brad Linaweaver	11
Author's Preface	15
All the King's Horses	19
Profile In Silver	85
First Draft	99
Second Draft	141
Colorblind	185
Timeshare	227
No Strings Attached	251
The Mars Story	423
Figure 8	435
To Err Is Humanoid	441
About J. Neil Schulman	503

But It's in the Script
Foreword
by Brad Linaweaver

J. Neil Schulman has done two amazing things.

The first is to write, sell and see produced one of the very best episodes of the revived *Twilight Zone*, perhaps the best episode.

The second is not to have a career in television afterward.

Mutual friends often ask me how this is possible. I've never had a good answer.

This book proves one thing. It ain't about the scripts.

Hollywood is the most dishonest criminal enterprise in the world. Everybody knows it. Think about the humor of it.

How many times have you seen movies where the hero walks away from money at the end?

Remember when Dustin Hoffman doesn't bend over to pick up a single diamond at the end of *Marathon Man*? Olivier, the Nazi dentist, is dead and his ill gotten diamonds are all over the place. Dustin could pay for many things with that money: a nice funeral for his brother, publish the book he is writing to vindicate his father, even pay for his own dental bills. But in a Hollywood movie the hero is honored for walking away from money.

Or consider the maniac heroine of *Titanic*, who sits on a jewel for years that could be used to help shipwreck victims or do some other kind of charity work, and then drops it in the drink at the end. All Hollywood ever does is moan and groan about how not enough is done to help the poor, but let a character in a movie choose between charity and walking away from money and she'll walk away from the money to prove she's got heart.

The point is that the real Hollywood wouldn't walk away from a penny to save its soul. Hollywood would sell its grandmothers to the Arabs for a three-picture deal. Hollywood has yet to rise to the level of being venal.

There is only one good thing about all this. Where there are no artistic standards, there is no bias against quality any more than there is a bias against crap. Something good has as much chance of being made as something bad, because the decisions are based on anything but the quality of the script.

If there were justice in this town, J. Neil Schulman would not have been allowed to stop doing scripts for television after "Profile in Silver." They would have hunted him down and forced him to write against his will. His second script for *Zone* was not produced on that show but would have been just fine on another program of similar quality for network or cable. But where was that series?

The *Star Trek* script Neil did with his wife for *Next Generation* was finished after "Profile in Silver" had been on the air to rave reviews. But this is Hollywood. They weren't even allowed to come into the *Trek* production offices to pitch ideas. The irony here is that the Schulman & O'Neal script did the first example of Ferengi as positive capitalists instead of rotten money lenders. So naturally Neil and his wife received the typical Hollywood reward. They were completely ignored.

Much later the idea of good Ferengi showed up on *Deep Space Nine*.

Then there's the movie script about the British Royal family. Neil predicted the future on that one. So naturally it couldn't be allowed at the time. And when it all comes true, it's no longer relevant. Except that someone better placed in Hollywood, politically, could have made the movie before, during and after the divorce that barely shook the world.

The greatest crime of all is in what happened to *No Strings Attached.* Anyone who can read Neil's history of this script, and *not* doubt the honesty of Hollywood, is qualified for a successful career in Hollywood.

The stores are full of books on how to write scripts. None of these books tell you how to sell scripts. There's a damned good reason for that, as this book demonstrates.

But if you want to see samples of first-rate screenwriting, you'll find it in this book. And if you hadn't been told which of these scripts got on the air, you'd never be able to figure it out. Because they *all* were more than good enough to be produced.

At least Neil got to pick up the money.

Brad Linaweaver, March 28, 1999

Author's Preface

This book contains the outlines for, and two drafts I wrote of, my teleplay "Profile in Silver," which, after a "polish" and production, was first aired on the CBS television network program *The Twilight Zone* at 8:00 PM ET March 7, 1986.

It also contains "Colorblind," a second, unproduced screenplay I wrote on commission for *The Twilight Zone*; and "Timeshare," a spec short script for that series which I co-wrote with my (now-ex-) wife, Kate O'Neal.

Also in this collection are *All the Kings Horses*, a feature-length 1983 screen treatment I sold to Vista Films but which was never produced; *No Strings Attached*, an unproduced full-length "spec" screenplay I wrote in December 1986; *The Mars Project*, a short treatment for a never-produced CBS TV movie I wrote on commission in 1987 for McDermott Entertainment; and *Figure-8*, a never-submitted spec movie treatment I wrote in March, 1988—a project on which I had intended to co-write the screenplay with author Léon Bing.

Last in this collection is "To Err Is Humanoid," a never-sold spec script for *Star Trek: The Next Generation* which I co-wrote with Kate O'Neal in May, 1989—and the only "episodic series" script in this collection.

From the publication of my novel *The Rainbow Cadenza* in June, 1983 to the publication of my short story "The Repossessed" in Carol Serling's anthology *Adventures in the Twilight Zone* in September, 1995, I published no fiction—and that short story had actually been written February 26, 1984.

Further, my book *Stopping Power: Why 70 Million Americans Own Guns*, published in June, 1994, was my first book length work seeing print since *The Rainbow Cadenza* eleven years earlier.

Aside from several Op-Ed pieces, anyone following my writing could easily assume I had given up writing as a career ... or at least fiction writing.

I hadn't given it up. I simply could not get the books I wanted to write published or the screenplays I was capable of writing produced. People who don't like my writing can conclude that it was time for me to choose another line of work: the market had spoken.

Readers more sympathetic to my efforts can look to the quotation from *Ecclesiastes 9:11* that

> the race is not to the swift; nor the battle to the strong, neither yet bread to the wise, nor yet riches to men of understanding, not yet favor to men of skill; but time and chance happeneth to them all.

I have my own thoughts on why my career stalled. If I were to tell it here it would seem to a lot of people to be whiny, paranoid, and self-serving. So, I'll give it a rest for the time being. Let's leave it for now that this book collects the bulk of what writing I was working on during the "missing" years.

Writing dramatic scripts and treatments is like writing literary short stories and novels in that both tell stories about fictional characters—or at least fictionalized characters. They are unlike literary short stories and novels in that the dramatic form only lets you know what can be seen and heard. You are not usually privy to the characters' thoughts, or to the writer's—unless the writer cheats by putting in a "voice over" narration, or some cute device such as subtitles, like Woody Allen did for one scene in *Annie Hall*.

Because of these dramatic limitations, the screenwriter must count on the production company, director, cast, and crew to bring the story to life. Without that help, screenwriting demands that a reader use even more imagination than is required from readers of literature.

That is probably why books containing screenwriting are usually of interest only to aspiring motion picture and television professionals. It also helps to explain why a lot of good scripts never get produced and a lot of bad ones do. The above quote from *Ecclesiastes* applies as much to the business of making movies and TV shows as it does to the career paths of its personnel.

If you are not familiar with reading screenplays, there are a few technical terms you need to know.

THE SHOT is what is seen and heard on the screen. In a screenplay it is indicated by material all CAPITALIZED, beginning at the script's left margin. "INT" means an interior shot—indoors; "EXT" means an exterior shot—outdoors.

Material under the shot header using the full margins describes the scene and actions.

Material in narrower margins under a character's name is dialogue that character is saying. And, parenthetic material ( ) in dialogue margins is not spoken but indicates intent or directions.

"CUT" is an abrupt change of camera shots.

"DISSOLVE" is a slower change, usually indicating passage of time.

"B.G" is shorthand for "background."

"O.S." means off-screen (not visible on camera).

A "beat" is a dramatic pause.

Some of this terminology also finds its way into the screen "treatment," which is how a story is told in the movie-making business before a screenplay is written.

I hope you're able to get past the unfamiliar formats of screenplays and screen treatments to enjoy the stories. This is some of my favorite storytelling.

And, to prove I never give up: if you happen to be a producer interested in making any of these, my agent is still Joel Gotler. The number's in your secretary's autodial.

—J. Neil Schulman, March 28, 1999

All the King's Horses

When I wrote *All The King's Horses* in 1983, the fairy tale romance between Charles, the Prince of Wales, and Princess Diana, was in full bloom, and no one in the press had yet expressed any indication that there was trouble brewing in Kensington Palace—trouble that would not become public for another decade.

But while I foresaw that the glare of attention would place unbearable pressures on the new Princess, I did not write my story as the tragedy it became, with her death while running away from that attention. I wrote a happy ending for the Princess of Wales—one which, we see now, she did not have the power to write for herself.

What you're about to read is virtually a full-length script. All the scenes that would be in a screenplay are there, and so is most of the dialogue.

All The King's Horses was my first film sale. I was working at the time as an assistant to Joel Gotler, whom I'd originally met as my screen agent, and our friendship had grown to the point that when he started his own agency, we had a comfortable enough relationship for him to continue representing me and for me to work in his office.

The core idea for the story came out of an idea I tossed off during a discussion of the British royal family I'd been having with my friend, Samuel Edward Konkin III, libertarian publisher and editor. I wrote up the idea as a four-page outline and the next morning brought it in to Joel. Joel said, "I can sell this"—and within an hour, he had set up a meeting with film producer Herbert Jaffe of Vista Films, and his son, Robert Jaffe. Together they'd produced several successful features, including *The Wind and the Lion*, *Demon Seed*, and one of my favorites, the H.G. Wells-as-time-traveller movie, *Time After Time*, with Malcolm McDowell and Mary Steenburgen. Robert had also written and directed a very amusing send-up of slasher films called *Motel Hell*, a movie that's worth seeing if only for the dueling-chainsaw sequence.

That meeting resulted in a contract for me to write a fifty-page treatment, but under Robert's guidance, the treatment kept on growing so that by the time I turned it in, it contained every scene you'd need for a full script, and the treatment ran over one hundred pages.

(A personal milestone: with the first money I got for writing *All The King's Horses*, I bought my first computer, an Osborne Executive, a transportable CP/M machine with a built-in monitor and bundled software including the best word-processing program for the time, Wordstar. It had a single-sided 5-1/4" floppy drive for disks that could hold 180K, and 128K of RAM. It was on this primitive machine that I wrote *All the King's Horses*—but as primitive as it was, it was fantastically better than using a typewriter. I wrote all my *Twilight Zone* scripts on it. It was the computer I was using when I first logged onto a computer BBS, and was the computer on which I wrote my first essays on electronic publishing. I still have my Osborne Executive in my closet. It still works, too.)

My original draft of *All the King's Horses* used the real names of the British royal family. That decision was Herb and Rob's; they thought it made the project more commercial. A few months later when I decided to submit the project for novel sale, I decided to fictionalize the names. That is the draft of the treatment I have included in this book. So when *Twilight Zone* executive Alan Brennert and I discussed "Greek-Tycooning" "Profile in Silver" (that story will be in my introduction to the "Profile" scripts, later in this book), I'd already had experience doing just that.

Apparently, using the real names, or the fictionalized names, didn't make any difference for Vista Films in trying to get a studio to finance its production. I never found out the reasons for its failure to be produced—the writer rarely does—but from remarks Robert made to me in passing, I gather that Anglophiles among studio executives didn't want to risk ticking off their British counterparts.

After selling the film rights for this story to Vista Films, I was surprised that I couldn't sell it for a novel, even after writing several sample chapters.

But, perhaps you'll gain some appreciation of the idiotic rejection letters one has to put up with when—after winning a literary award for my second novel—one New York publisher rejected the possibility of a novel based on the following 100-page treatment, writing that I was a screenwriter and they had no confidence I could make the transition to novel-writing.

This is the most commercial story I ever wrote. That it was never produced or sold as a novel is a testament to the failure of the American revolution completely to wipe out the American gentry's affection for the British monarchy—affection that may even exceed that of the British tabloid press, judging how they've exposed the British royal family to ridicule since I wrote this.

In reading back over this screen treatment after seeing the British monarchy fall into scandal then tragedy, I think I understand the real reasons why the marriage of the Prince and Princess of Wales failed. These people have an impossible job to do. They have to convince people that just because of your ancestry, you can be brought up to live to a higher standard than anyone else.

Monarchy may be a silly idea...but giving a royal family all the headaches of being royal, and none of the powers that make the offices meaningful, may be even sillier.   JNS, 1999

All the King's Horses
A Screen Treatment
by J. Neil Schulman

We open in the contemporary-day Court of QUEEN VICTORIA II of Wittland during a routine Investiture at Buckminster Palace. With the Queen smiling happily to the hundreds of court spectators, the LORD CHAMBERLAIN makes a long-hoped-for statement: "We are pleased to announce the engagement of His Royal Highness Prince Arthur, the Prince of Caterwaul, to Lady Susan Herbert."

As the court spectators react with enthusiastic applause, their applause is echoed outside Buckminster as a crowd gathers in the hope of seeing one of the most attractive royal couples in recent memory. A military band strikes up the song, *Congratulations*.

OPENING TITLES BEGIN:

As we see the strikingly handsome ARTHUR, PRINCE OF CATERWAUL and the strikingly blonde, blue-eyed Lady SUSAN, soon to be the PRINCESS OF CATERWAUL, greeting crowds of waiting admirers ... while a schoolboy kisses Lady Susan's hand ... as they answer questions on a WBC interview show ... appearing together at the opera ... and walking hand-in-hand through "home country" crowds, winning the affection of the local people.

We watch, on the eve of the wedding, the magnificent Royal Fireworks Display (to Handel's *Music for the Royal Fireworks*) and immediately jump into the Royal Wedding, watching their vows to the ARCHBISHOP OF CRANBERRY, both at Appalled Saint's Cathedral directly, and repeated live on 3/4 billion televisions in homes, department stores, and bars throughout the world. We see the royal couple's carriage parade through the streets of Lipton after the wedding and their train departure to meet the royal yacht *Wittannia* for their honeymoon.

TITLES PAUSE for a second official announcement. This one is a traditional handwritten notice, framed in wood, secured by a COURT OFFICIAL to the gates of Buckminster Palace. A MAN in the front row of eagerly awaiting onlookers reads it aloud: "'Er Royal 'Ighness," the Man shouts to the thousands behind him, "was safely delivered of a son at 8:23 PM today. 'Er Royal 'Ighness and 'er child are both doing well."

Someone shouts out, "God Bless the Prince and Princess of Caterwaul!" and to the sound of the crowd singing *For He's a Jolly Good Fellow* we cut to the front of Quaint Merry Hospital as the Princess and Prince leave with their new infant son.

We watch the christening by the Archbishop of Cranberry of the second-in-line to the Wittish throne, PRINCE JOHN RICHARD PAUL GEORGE.

TITLES CONTINUING, we attend the blond, blue-eyed Prince John's four-year-old birthday party...and his sixth, where he is given a pony ... and his eighth, where he is given a micro-computer.

Finally, as an Official Photographic Portrait is being taken ("Say 'cheese'!") of Prince Arthur, Princess Susan, and eight- year-old Prince John, we FREEZE FRAME and OPENING TITLES END.

CUT TO:

The Prince and Princess of Caterwaul, dressed to kill, in their box at the Royal Filbert Hall, watching a performance of The Asian Liberation Ballet.

Prince Arthur is enjoying the performance tremendously.

Princess Susan is bored silly, and keeps nodding off, then jarring herself awake each time her head starts drooping forward.

This occurs several times, until the performance finally ends and everyone applauds.

Susan is *most* enthusiastic in her applause—she's applauding the performance's *end*.

A few minutes later, the Prince and Princess (accompanied by DETECTIVE BODYGUARDS) emerge from the Hall, heading toward their limousine, and having to cross picket lines by HUNDREDS OF DEMONSTRATORS with SIGNS carrying ANTI-TOTALITARIAN SLOGANS.

As soon as the Demonstrators see the Prince and Princess, there is immediate JEERING and BOOING at them, with shouts of, "*Whose side on you on, anyway?*" and "*You've watched those bastards dance while they dance on the graves of the innocent!*"

WITTISH BOBBIES dressed in crowd-control gear clear a path for the Prince and Princess through the picket lines, and the two of them brave their way into the back of their limousine.

SUDDENLY, a DEMONSTRATOR *lobs* a RAW EGG at the Royal Couple, and the egg *hits* the Princess square in the face.

Immediately, the OTHER DEMONSTRATORS start pulling the EGG-THROWER back, and THE BOBBIES start rushing toward him to make an arrest; The Princess and Prince's Bodyguards take the opportunity to get the limousine doors open and shove the Royal Couple into the back.

The Bodyguards jump into the front and the LIMOUSINE DRIVES AWAY.

INSIDE THE LIMOUSINE, the Princess of Caterwaul is obviously greatly upset by what's just happened. She's on the verge of tears and the Prince is trying to comfort her, taking a handkerchief and wiping the egg off the Princess's face.

"The bloody *coward*," Arthur says to his wife.

A VOICE from the front of the limo comes back over the intercom, "Sir, is Her Royal Highness all right?"

Princess Susan manages to nod.

"Yes, she'll be fine," the Prince says. "Thank you."

"The worse of it, Arthur," Susan says, "is that I'm on *their* side. Why did we have to go through all this tonight?"

The Prince sighs. "It was the Primal Minister's idea," he says. "It was thought our appearance would be conciliatory just before the summit."

"God," Susan says, "I *hate* politics."

Prince Arthur takes his wife by the hand. "You look as if you could do with a drink."

"Oh, that would be *lovely*," Susan says.

The Prince gets on the intercom again, "Barry," he says, "could you please drive us to Peccadillo?"

"Yes, Sir," the voice comes back.

Susan looks happy for the first time that night.

CUT TO:

THE LIMOUSINE pulling up in front of The Pink Panther, a night spot near Peccadillo Circus.

One of the Detectives opens up the back door so the Prince and Princess can get out. Prince Arthur gets out first, then extends his hand to help the Princess out—

When immediately several CARS rush up and a gaggle of RE-

PORTERS jump out. "Oh, bloody *hell*," Arthur says.

"Your Royal Highnesses!" ONE of the Reporters shouts. "Do you have any comment on—"

The Princess can't take it anymore. "Haven't you all done *enough* for one night?" she practically shouts at the Press. "Aren't we *ever* permitted just to be ordinary human beings?"

PEOPLE coming out of The Pink Panther and beginning to stop and stare.

The Prince sees that this is dangerously close to causing "a scene." "Darling, we'd better go," he tells the Princess.

Susan glares at her husband. "Whose side are *you* on, anyway?" she asks him, then jumps back into the limousine.

The Prince gets into the limousine, and the limousine drives off again.

INSIDE THE LIMOUSINE, the Princess glares at the Prince.

"Darling," the Prince says, "I was only just—"

"I don't want to talk about it," the Princess says, then clams up.

They drive on in silence.

CUT TO:

THE PHOTOGRAPHIC PORTRAIT that we saw Prince Arthur, Princess Susan, and Prince John posing for at the end of the Titles Sequence. We PULL BACK FROM the Portrait TO SEE:

The three of them near the end of breakfast in their Lipton estate, Kenspeckle Palace. The table they are seated at is just short of being ridiculously long. Prince Arthur is at one end, a stack of morning newspapers beside him. He picks up one headlined: 'Whose Side Are You On?' Princess asks Prince, and throws it down in anger.

At the table's far end, Princess Susan is flipping through a fashion magazine, and looks up when she HEARS the SPLAT! of Arthur throwing down the paper. They glare at each other briefly, then Prince Arthur picks up *The Times of Lipton* and begins reading an article on Wittish Relations with the Republic of El Arginine a decade after the Walkman Islands War.

Susan returns to her fashion magazine.

Midway between them, on the side, is Prince John, looking back and forth between his parents.

Except for the setting, this might be any family at breakfast: they are casually dressed; breakfast is bran flakes, milk, and toast; and there are no servants present.

That is, this might be any family at breakfast the morning after Mom and Dad have had a fight.

There is an interminable silence. Finally, John can't take it any more. "May I be excused?"

Princess Susan looks up from her magazine, concerned. "You haven't touched your breakfast."

"I don't feel at all hungry," John says.

"You're not coming down with a fever just before we leave, are you?" Susan reaches over to feel John's forehead.

"Leave the boy alone, for Heaven's sake," Prince Arthur says. "It's likely that he just doesn't 'feel at all hungry.'"

Susan glares at her husband, who turns back to his newspaper. "You're excused," she tells John, "but you'd better change straight away—your father's taking us to the airport in just forty minutes' time."

John gets up, but pauses. "Daddy, why don't you come to America with Mummy and me?"

"There's nothing I'd like better," Arthur says, "but I'm afraid I'm tied up here with business—'the firm's business,' as your great-grandfather used to call it."

John accepts this with a resigned shrug. His attempt at diplomacy has failed.

After he leaves, we pause once more on the Prince and Princess of Caterwaul as they studiously, and silently, ignore each other at the breakfast table.

Prince John's bedroom is a dialectic between the old and the new—the royal and the ordinary—and reinforces our impression that prince or not, this is, above all, a modern eight-year-old boy. Perched on an ornate four-poster bed is a Teenage Mutant Ninja Turtle surrounded by comic books; hanging on the wall next to a portrait of a royal ancestor is a framed *Terminator IV: The Beginning* poster. A marble chess table holds, instead, a game board with assorted miniature magicians and monsters. A model of the shuttle *Discovery* is suspended from a Victorian fixture and an arcade-size video game sits upon a thick Persian rug.

A state-of-the-art computer (the one we saw being given to John on his last birthday) sits on a desk made when "state of the art" meant an abacus.

John decides to spend a little time before departure working on a favorite program.

He is not very far along when his governess, ANNE MacINTOSH, breezes in. Anne is the 1980's edition of the traditional Wittish Nanny—Mary Poppins in a jogging outfit. Mid-fortyish and wholesomely attractive, she is stern when necessary, indulgent when it suits her—of necessity, she is Prince John's best friend. But at the moment, duty before friendship: "Time to change into your travel clothes, John."

John looks up from his computer. "Is that how *you're* going?"

She looks down at her own jogging outfit, but there's no getting past *this* woman. "No one will be looking at *me, Your Royal Highness*"—and we know she only calls him this when she means business. "Nevertheless, when I return in ten minutes' time, we'll *both* be properly attired."

She turns to leave, but John calls to her, "Annie?"

Anne turns back.

"They're going at it again," John says.

Anne sighs; she doesn't need any explanation. "Perhaps this trip will be good for them. They always say that absence makes the heart grow fonder."

John ponders this. Even at eight years old, he's not sure that the adage holds true. CUT TO:

Prince John changing his clothes when there's a knock at the door. "Yes?" he says.

"It's Daddy," comes Prince Arthur's VOICE from behind the door. "May I come in?"

John finishes tucking in his shirt then runs to the door and opens it.

Prince Arthur walks in, arms clasped behind his back.

"I just wanted to tell you," Prince Arthur says to his son, "that it's very important how you behave on this trip. Everything you say and do is going to be a reflection on the entire country. Do you understand?"

"Yes, Sir," John says.

"And while you're on this trip, I want you to take care of your mother for me."

"I will, Daddy."

Arthur softens up a bit. He looks over, notices the Space Shuttle model, and points to it. "That one is new, isn't it?" Arthur asks.

"Annie and I just finished putting it together," John says. "Daddy, can I be an astronaut when I grow up?"

Arthur smiles. "When you grow up, John, you're going to be the King."

"Oh," John says. "Then can I be the King *and* an astronaut?"

Arthur looks uncomfortable and doesn't answer.

Properly attired—with Prince John carrying his birthday computer along in an attache case—the young Prince and his governess rendezvous with Prince Arthur again, Princess Susan, and their travelling companions on an open stretch of estate lawn. In most families the statement "Your father will be taking us to the airport" means that Dad will be driving the family Ford. The "family Ford," in this case, is instead a military helicopter that Prince Arthur will be piloting.

As soon as the entourage—Princess Susan, her LADY-IN-WAITING, her LADY'S MAID, Prince John, Anne MacIntosh, and two DETECTIVE BODYGUARDS are strapped in, Prince Arthur lifts the helicopter off for their flight to Heathcliff Airport.

One might expect that a helicopter flight with one's father piloting would be exciting for an eight-year-old boy, but this is nothing out of the ordinary for Prince John, and the flight is as commonplace for him as a drive in the family Ford would be for most children. So, to pass the time, John opens his attache case to resume programming on his new computer, but his father stops him. "You'll have to put that away," Prince Arthur tells his son.

"Why, Sir?" John asks.

"Regulations don't allow the use of electronics gear anywhere near aircraft—there's the possibility that it might interfere with navigation."

John shrugs and closes his attache case again; then joins the rest of his companions in watching the scenery below.

As usual wherever members of the Royal Family go, mobs go also; a reception committee of well-wishers, camp followers, reporters, and chaparoned groups of children—behind police lines—surround the supersonic Discorde jetliner that Princess Susan and Prince John will be taking to New York. It is Wittish Airways' scheduled 10:30 AM flight, not a private charter, but because royalty are to be aboard, the other 75 passengers have already been boarded and the Discorde taxied to a spot where the Princess and her son can make royalty's usual dramatic departure.

IN RAPID SEQUENCE:

—The other travelling companions climb the movable staircase into the Discorde ahead of Princess Susan and Prince John—

—Prince Arthur tells his wife and son, "I'll telephone you each day," then kisses them goodbye, on both cheeks in the Continental manner—

—Princess Susan and Prince John climb to the top of the movable staircase, then turn to wave at Prince Arthur, still at the bottom. Arthur waves back to them——And WE HEAR from the crowd what sound like SEVERAL GUNSHOTS.

Immediately chaos erupts. There are SCREAMS. DETECTIVES begin scanning the crowd with their guns drawn—

—Prince Arthur *tries to climb* the staircase to protect his wife and son, but his BODYGUARDS surround him, making it impossible for him to move. He locks eyes with Princess Susan, but all she sees is his complete *helplesssness*, not his efforts to get to the two of them—

—From her VANTAGE POINT at the TOP of the STAIRCASE, Princess Susan SEES the cause of the disturbance: A SMALL BOY who managed somehow to smuggle a TOY CAP PISTOL past airport security has discharged it at another small boy—and Susan STARES IN HORROR as she sees a DETECTIVE spotting what he thinks is a real gun and aiming his own weapon at the Boy—

Susan shouts out, "*No, please don't!*" but of course in the NOISE no one can hear her. She is certain that she is about to witness a tragedy ... when just in time, the Detective realizes that it *is* only a small boy with a toy, and TAKES his FINGER off the TRIGGER without firing.

We FOCUS a moment on the Prince and the Princess of Caterwaul—each with feelings of frustration and helplessness—then they lock eyes once more before Princess Susan regains her composure enough to guide Prince John aboard the aircraft.

The door closes. Prince Arthur looks on, wistfully, as the staircase is pulled back and the plane taxies away to take off.

Aboard the Discorde in flight. The FLIGHT ATTENDANTS have their hands full keeping upper-class AUTOGRAPH SEEKERS away from Princess Susan and Prince John.

A BOY about John's age tries to come forward to meet the Prince. They smile at each other and John waves to the other boy to come forward and keep him company. But before the boy can come forward, a STEWARDESS chases him, "Back to your seat where you belong."

With a sigh, John resigns himself to a flight without anyone his own age to talk to, with his mother preoccupied by something, and without his computer ... until Anne MacIntosh, in the seat in front of him, hands him a book—one of fantasy writer C.S. Lewis's classic Chronicles of Narnia, *Prince Caspian.*

Happily, for once, John opens the book and begins to read.

WE SEE:

The Discorde's landing at JFK International Airport.

WE HEAR:

A HIGH SCHOOL MARCHING BAND playing the Wittish Royal Anthem—and playing it badly out of tune.

Princess Susan and Prince John deplane and wave to the crowd waiting for them. Next to the marching band, a line of OFFICIAL GREETERS stands along a red carpet laid to the plane's staircase.

Princess Susan manages to conceal her distaste for the out- of-tune playing rather better than Prince John, who's had less experience repressing his feelings in public. But Anne manages to kick him before his laughter causes an international incident.

Thus begins Princess Susan and Prince John's official goodwill tour of the United States.

(For the duration of the tour, in addition to their personal entourage, AMERICAN SECRET SERVICE AGENTS wearing gray suits and distinctive lapel pins will never be far away from Princess Susan and Prince John.)

A SERIES OF SHOTS connected by THEME MUSIC in the style of Handel's *Water Music* takes us to:

—A ticker-tape parade through New York City (stock footage intercut) for the Princess of Caterwaul and her son—

—The World Trade Center, where the MAYOR OF NEW YORK presents Princess Susan and Prince John with the Key to the City and—"So you'll feel like *real* New Yorkers"—gold-handled pooper scoopers for their corgis—

—Midtown New York's fanciest toy store, where the STORE MANAGER is giving Prince John the Grand Tour—by the numbers. Prince John stops and actually tries to play with a game, but the manager hurries him away—to a better photo location for the assembled reporters—

—Philadelphia, where the MAYOR OF PHILADELPHIA presents Princess Susan and Prince John with a replica of the Liberty Bell and with the Key to the City—

—A luncheon reception with the "Descendants of the American Revolution" in front of a huge banner that reads:

WE DIDN'T REALLY MEAN IT!—

—The Washington Monument, where the MAYOR OF WASHINGTON D.C. presents Princess Susan and Prince John with a box of red tape and with the Key to the City—

—The official Wittish Embassy Reception where the WITTISH AMBASSADOR, LORD DAVID WILSON, Princess Susan, and Prince John are on a receiving line meeting AMERICAN DIGNITARIES, SENATORS, REPRESENTATIVES, and the United States SECRETARY OF STATE, DR. HENRY WERFNER. Prince John is having trouble staying awake—

—A luncheon at the White House, THE PRESIDENT and FIRST LADY hosting. While the President is giving his welcome address, this time *Princess Susan* is having trouble staying awake, and Prince John is kicking her under the table to look alive—which she does, just before she's supposed to thank the President—

—A Garden Party where a MOTHER is pushing her FIVE-YEAR-OLD DAUGHTER forward to give a bunch of flowers to Princess Susan, and the frightened-to-death little girl bursting into tears. Her own mother is too embarrassed to care about the little girl's distress, leaving Princess Susan to make, "There, there, Sweetheart, don't be afraid" sounds—

—Dallas, where the MAYOR OF DALLAS presents Prince John and Princess Susan with Ten Gallon Hats and the Key to the City—

—Sacramento, where the GOVERNOR OF CALIFORNIA presents Prince John and Princess Susan with California Avocados and Certificates of Honorary Citizenship of the State of California—

—Los Angeles, where the MAYOR OF LOS ANGELES presents

Prince John and Princess Susan with a Map to the Stars' Homes—and the inevitable Key to the City: "I hereby declare you *Angelenos*"—

—And finally, as THEME MUSIC ENDS, Princess Susan and Prince John are let into their suite of rooms at the Beverly Wilshire Hotel.

As soon as Prince John sees a bed, he collapses onto it, fully dressed and face down.

Later that night. Princess Susan, now in an elegant bathrobe, is watching television with Anne MacIntosh—also robed, though somewhat less elegantly. Princess Susan's Lady-in-Waiting and Lady's Maid have already gone to bed.

ON TELEVISION, a late-night Network Special, *Royalty in America*, is recapping Princess Susan and Prince John's ceremonies that day with the Governor of California and with the Mayor of Los Angeles—"I hereby declare you *Angelenos*." "I think," Princess Susan says, "that if I ever receive the key to another city, I shall *scream*."

"The Royal Goodwill Tour," says ANCHORMAN, TED SINGER, "ends in Los Angeles, with Princess Susan and young Prince John flying back to Wittland tomorrow morning. We'll be back with the coverage of that departure and a retrospective of the entire two-week visit, tomorrow night. This is Ted Singer. Good night for ABS News."

Princess Susan takes the opportunity of the commercial break to check in on the now-fast-asleep Prince John. She tucks her son in, kisses him on the cheek, then ducks back into her own suite. Anne has changed the TV channel; in the background, one of the cable stations is playing an old episode of *Father Knows Best*.

"Is he asleep?" Anne asks Princess Susan.

"Fast asleep, looking just like an angel," Susan tells Anne. "Poor thing—this trip hasn't been any fun for him at all."

"He hasn't complained once," Anne says.

"No, of course he wouldn't," Susan says. "He's exactly like his father." Susan looks over to the television and notices, for the first time, the program. A typical *Father Knows Best* scene with a happy, communicative family—an *ordinary* family of the type she longs for and can never have. "Oh, do please put something else on," Susan says to Anne. "I can't *bear* this sort of thing."

Anne changes the channel again. *The Tonight Show* is on—JAYVID LENOMAN is behind his desk. "My next guests," says Lenoman, "are the co-authors of the bestseller, *Not With My Son, You Don't!*"

"*That's* more like it," Susan says.

"F. Melvin Michaelson," Lenoman continues, "is the precedent-setting attorney who has defended heiress-bank-robbers, accused cult murderers, and errant multimillionaire husbands—"

"Has he ever defended you?" a celebrity guest quips.

The telephone rings—not on TV, but in the hotel room. Anne gets it. "Trunk call from Lipton," she tells Princess Susan. "His Royal Highness."

ON TV, Lenoman continuing: "Michaelson's client, in what turned out to be another landmark case, was network news commentator, Grant Heller, host of the weekly program, *Heller's Journal*. Mel Michaelson's and Grant Heller's collaboration on this bestseller—"

Anne hands the phone to Susan then ducks out discreetly.

Susan lowers the TV SOUND; we SEE but NOT HEAR, F. MELVIN MICHAELSON and GRANT HELLER joining Leno on the set.

WE INTERCUT:

PRINCE ARTHUR, at the breakfast table, holding a cordless telephone. "Good morning," he says.

"Good night, you mean," Susan says.

"How was your day?" Arthur asks.

"Bloody exhausting."

"I saw you on the telly," Arthur says. "You and John have handled everything splendidly. I'm very proud of you both."

"I'll be sure and tell John you said so."

"I can tell him myself, if you'd like."

"He's fast *asleep* at the moment. It's almost *midnight* here."

Arthur doesn't let this get to him. "Well, you'll be back home tomorrow and I can tell him then."

Susan does *not* say anything.

"You sound odd," Arthur says. "Is everything quite all right?"

"I'm just so *tired* of all this—" Susan stops. She doesn't want to get into an argument again—over long distance. "I'm just tired."

"Well, then," Arthur says, "get some sleep. Everything will be back to normal when you get home."

"I'm sure," Susan says.

"See you tomorrow," Arthur says.

"Good night," says Susan.

Susan hangs up ... and looks as if perhaps she might start crying. She goes over to the TV and turns up the SOUND again.

Grant Heller is a New Yorker in his mid-to-late forties with a hound-dog face. F. Melvin Michaelson is aristocratic looking, sixtyish and silver-haired. We hear their conversation with Jay Leno as we focus in on Susan, the emotional tension coming to the surface.

"The main problem we had in Grant's case," Michaelson says, "was preventing his wife from abducting Grant's then-five-year- old son before we could get a custody hearing in California—"

"And, you see, Jave," Heller cuts in, "we were up against the clock because I split up my time between L.A. and New York, and California had a six-month residency period before I could even *file* for divorce—"

"That was the big victory in your case, wasn't it?" Lenoman asks.

"That's right, Jave," Michaelson answers. "The California Supreme Court has just upheld the Appellate Court's decision to stop defining residency by the number of months lived in the state and county, and rely instead on various other criteria—"

Anne MacIntosh comes back into the suite to find Princess Susan crying in front of the television set. The governess takes the Princess into her arms to comfort her.

The discussion of divorce on TV has pushed Princess Susan past the point of no return.

"Anne," Susan says, "I've decided to leave Arthur."

The governess nods understandingly.

Daybreak, the next morning. An American SECRET SERVICE AGENT is manning a security desk in the hotel corridor between the elevators and the royal suite. Anne MacIntosh comes out of her room and begins chatting up the agent, taking out a cigarette and asking, "Got a light, darlin'?"

Almost like a Bugs Bunny cartoon we see, first, Prince John—carrying his computer—then Princess Susan, sneak across the hallway into the fire stairs while the agent is being distracted by Anne.

As soon as Susan and John are into the stairwell, Anne calls for the elevator and rides it down to the lobby.

Anne has the hotel doorman summon a taxi for her, then takes it about a block's distance from the hotel and tells the cabbie to stop.

Princess Susan and Prince John check to make sure that no one can see them, then get into the taxi with Anne. The cab speeds off.

Ten AM or so. The Princess's Maid rolls a breakfast cart down the hotel corridor to the Princess's suite. The television is still on from the night before. The Maid leaves the cart in front of the television then goes into the Princess's bedroom to wake her. But the Princess's bed has not been slept in and the Princess isn't there.

The Maid checks into Anne MacIntosh's room—the bed likewise fresh—then checks into John's room. No prince.

At this point, the Maid panics then goes running down the hotel corridor to get the Princess's Lady-in-Waiting.

A short while later, a meeting is in progress in the Princess's suite (the TV still on in the background) with the Lady-in-Waiting, the Maid, the two Wittish Detective-Bodyguards, and the American Secret Service Agent. "And I tell you," the Secret Service Agent says, "that no one got in here and Their Royal Highnesses never passed my desk."

"Do you think we should telephone the Prince?" one of the Detectives asks.

The Lady-in-Waiting shudders visibly at the thought.

She is saved of having to make a decision by the TELEVISION taking the foreground with a SPECIAL BULLETIN:

A perky Asian woman stands outside the Federal Building in Westwood holding a microphone: "This is CONNIE DATSUN with a live Supercam report from the Los Angeles offices of the United States Immigration and Naturalization Service ... are we ready with that tape?"

She goes VOICE OVER a TAPED REPLAY:

"This is the scene just a few minutes ago ..."

ON TELEVISION, we see Princess Susan and Prince John, surrounded by reporters and television crews, as they emerge from the Immigration and Naturalization Service offices, battle their way down the corridor past reporters throwing questions at them, then dogtrot out of the Federal building toward a waiting taxi which Anne MacIntosh is holding for them. They manage their way in and the cab speeds off.

Connie Datsun, live again: "... Susan, Princess of Caterwaul, and her eight-year-old son, Prince John of Caterwaul, have requested this morning that the United States grant them a visa for permanent residency in this country. So far, we have been unable to get any statement from official sources, other than confirmation from the District Director of I.N.S. for Los Angeles that a request *has* been made, commenting on this—uh—*unusual* turn of events. This comes only hours before the Princess and young Prince were to return home—"

The dumbstruck expressions of the Princess's Lady-in- Waiting, her Maid, the two Wittish Detectives, and the American Secret Service Agent confirm everything we are already thinking.

This time, it's *really* going to hit the fan.

A few minutes later in Wittland. It's evening. Prince Arthur is in his office at Kenspeckle Palace, doing paperwork at his desk, when his personal secretary, GROUP CAPTAIN RONALD CHESTERTON, ducks his head in. "Trunk call from America for you, Sir. Lord Wilson."

"Thank you, Chess," Arthur says. Chesterton ducks out again and Arthur picks up. "David? So good to hear from you. How's Washington treating you? ... Could you speak up? This connection is bloody awful ... What? ... *What*? ... No ... Nobody even knows where they've gone? ... No ... No, thank you ... I'll be all right ... Thank you for calling, David."

Prince Arthur holds the receiver in his hand without hanging up. He pauses, silently, then punches a number into the phone.

The phone answers on the first ring. "Hello, Gwen—Arthur. I must speak to the Queen at once ... I don't care if the Primal Minister *is* with her, let me speak to my mother!"

There is another pause.

Then Arthur, in an altogether different—*higher*—voice: "Hullo, Mummy?"

"This is a Gift From The Lord!"

We HEAR this VOICE OVER a look at New York City, mid- morning, focusing in on a glass skyscraper on Third Avenue. Then, inside, the plush editorial offices of the largest-selling weekly supermarket tabloid in America, *The Inquisitor*.

Practically the entire STAFF of the publication is crammed into the conference room. Around the room on walls are framed front pages of the tabloid with various screaming headlines regarding Michael Landon's Ghost, the Kennedys, UFO's, Miracle Diets, and Dead Idols Who Overdosed on Drugs and Whose Bodies May Be Exhumed Because Their Fans Don't Believe They're Dead.

The tabloid's MANAGING EDITOR, SAMANTHA FRIENDLY, is holding forth:

"This is a *Gift From The Lord*!" she repeats—and we are reminded of Aimee Semple McPherson at her most pious. She stabs a finger toward a male reporter, JEFF JEFFRIES. "Jeffries—this is Michelle Phillips and Kim Bassinger oferring you a threesome—and you can't get it up!"

The staff laughs.

She points to a photographer, ROY PETERSON. "Peterson—this is a visit from Madonna giving you a million dollars tax free, on the sole condition that you don't reveal that she's had a tummy tuck—and you couldn't resist selling me a picture of her scars!"

More laughter.

She gestures grandly to everyone. "This is a *bonus* of six months' salary to the reporter who finds out 'The Real Reason Princess Su Left Prince Artie'—the same to the reporter who gets me 'Exclusive Pix of a Tearful Princess Su and Prince Jack'—and I'm throwing in *another* three months' salary if *The Inquisitor* is in the racks with this before *The Star Chamber* gets it. And *you* people are telling me that you don't even know where they *are*?"

"Nobody's seen them *any*where since they left the Federal Building in Los Angeles, three days ago," a REPORTER says.

"With a six-month salary bonus up for grabs, that's *your* problem."

She turns soft, for a moment: "Look, boys and girls, this story is our bread-and-butter for the next two, three—maybe *five*—years. I don't want to have to rely on free-lancers and wire services for this. Hire detectives, if you have to. We'll pay any royal servants enough to *retire* on, if you can get them to talk. Don't worry about libel—this time, we've got figures who are so public they *can't* sue us. I want charges, I want counter-charges, I want venom—and I want it *now*. Don't tell me you can't find them! Pretend you're reporters, for Chrissakes. Check hotels, airports, friends, city land records—but get me the story!"

Jeff Jeffries lights a cigarette and turns to Roy Peterson. "Whadd'ya say, Roy?" he starts, sounding like a real yahoo. "You and me, the next 'Woodstein'?"

An AERIAL VIEW of Camp David, Maryland, mid-afternoon. A golf cart driven by Secretary of State Henry Werfner, and carrying the Wittish Ambassador, Lord David Wilson, is chasing three joggers.

When the cart gets close enough, we see that one of the men jogging is the President.

The President shakes hands with the Ambassador. "David, good to see you." The President introduces the other two joggers: "My aide, DENNY HODEL. The ATTORNEY GENERAL, BARRY COMPTON."

"Lord Wilson," the Attorney General responds, shaking his hand.

"Mr. President," the Ambassador continues, "I'll get right to the point. Her Majesty's Government wants the Princess of Caterwaul and Prince John of Caterwaul back. We have cancelled their passports and wish you to return them at once."

The President looks over to the Attorney General, who shakes his head. "Your Excellency," Compton says to Wilson, "legally speaking, Princess Susan and Prince John are simply tourists who have requested a change in visa status. At the moment, that status is 'Case Pending'—which means they may remain, at the very least, until their case is resolved. They are in the country legally, have broken no laws, and we have not been informed of anything that would classify them as 'undesirable aliens.' Of course, if your government is prepared to bring criminal charges against them and extradite—"

The Ambassador looks like he might have a stroke from apoplexy. "Bring criminal charges against members of the Royal Family? Ridiculous!"

The Attorney General shrugs helplessly.

The Ambassador's blood pressure climbs another notch. "Henry," he says to Werfner, "perhaps *you* can explain the situation?"

The Secretary of State clears his throat. "David tells me it is the Primal Minister's position that in allowing the Princess and Prince to remain here against the wishes of Her Majesty, we are granting political asylum to members of the Royal Family against their own nation—and against the nation that has been our closest ally for a century-and-a-half."

"Mr. President," the Ambassador says, trying to gain some control of the situation. "Two men can be the best of friends all their lives, but if one of them runs off with the other's wife, that friendship can be strained past the breaking point. This is such a situation."

"David, that's all well and good," the President says. "But I *can't* force them to leave. It would be political suicide—for me, for my entire party."

"We have polls, letters, phone calls, telegrams," Hodel explains. "From the mayors of New York, Philadelphia, Washington, Dallas, Los Angeles. From the Governor of California. From the National Organization for Women. From the Descendants of the American Revolution, of all groups. But all these merely confirm what we knew three days ago. My wife follows Princess Susan more closely than she watches *Cheers*."

The Ambassador winces at the comparison.

"My wife," the Attorney General says, "informed me that if I send them back, I can forget about my sex life until after the election—when I'll be back in private practice."

The Ambassador frowns. "And I suppose you've heard from the First Lady, Mr. President?"

"Oh, I wouldn't worry too much about what Betsy would do if I deported them," the President says. "I *do* have the Secret Service protecting me."

The Ambassador is not amused.

In front of an office tower in Century City, mid-morning.

A taxi pulls up to the curb. A woman, wearing dark glasses, emerges from the taxi and looks around. "The coast is clear," says Anne MacIntosh.

Also wearing dark glasses, Princess Susan gets out of the cab. Then, carrying his computer, follows a much-shorter member of the Royal Family. He's also wearing dark glasses.

As the cab speeds off, the three of them stroll casually—a little *too* casually—into the building.

Princess Susan checks the building directory. She sees a listing for The Star Chamber—Editorial Offices ... 18—gasps, as she realizes she's smack in enemy territory—then backs up the directory to find what she's looking for:

Law Offices of Michaelson, Chase & Speakman ... 23.

Susan, John, and Anne get into the elevator—alone—and Susan gives a little sigh of relief as she punches "23."

The elevator doors start to shut when a VOICE from the lobby SHOUTS, "Hold that elevator!" and an ARM is thrust in to hold it.

Five more people—carrying cameras, microcassette recorders, and notebooks—get in, talking animatedly. Obviously, these are reporters and photographers for *The Inquisitor*'s chief competitor, the weekly supermarket tabloid called *The Star Chamber*.

One of the reporters punches "18."

"Still no sighting?" a REPORTER asks a PHOTOGRAPHER.

The Photographer shakes his head. "We've staked out every hotel in the area, and no sign of Their Nibs. They must be staying with friends. Or maybe they left L.A. entirely."

The Photographer takes out a cigarette and starts lighting up.

"Excuse me," says John, tugging at the Photographer's sleeve, and speaking with an undeniably *Wittish* accent, "but I thought you should know. There's a notice forbidding smoking in the lift."

Anne rolls her eyes heavenward. Susan bites her lower lip.

"I don't see any Bobbies around to stop me, kid," he replies.

The other photographer and reporters begin laughing.

"Hey, you're all Wittish, right?" the Reporter asks Susan. "What do you think about your Princess pulling a disappearing act like that?"

"Terribly irresponsible, I should think," Susan says dryly.

The elevator doors *finally* open at "18" and the Reporters and Photographers get out at the *Star Chamber* editorial offices and walk off talking, without even looking back.

The elevator doors close again.

Susan and Anne look down at Prince John as if to strangle him.

Facing the elevators as they emerge on "23" is a RECEPTIONIST looking as if she's off the latest cover of *Cosmo*.

"May I help you?" she asks, somewhat officiously.

Without removing her sunglasses, Susan says, "We're here to see Mr. Michaelson, if you please."

"Do you have an appointment?"

"No ... no, I'm afraid we don't. We didn't dare risk it."

"Mr. Michaelson doesn't see *anybody* without an appointment. But if you'll have a seat, I'll get his secretary so you can make one."

"Confidentially?"

"Naturally," the Receptionist says.

"Very well."

"Who shall I say is here?"

"Susan."

"Susan what?"

The Princess of Caterwaul removes her sunglasses. As she does, so do Prince John and Anne.

The Receptionist's jaw drops. "Holy sh—" She manages to bite off the last word. The Receptionist tries punching a number into her phone.

About the fourth time, she manages to get it right.

"Delores," the Receptionist says. "You know that case the Boss has been yammering about for three days? The one he says he'd kill for?"

Later. Prince John and Anne MacIntosh are in the law office conference room, waiting. John is playing with his computer. Anne is watching television—a network newsbreak.

An ANCHORMAN, CARL OSBORNE, is sitting behind a desk, a slide of Princess Susan and Prince John behind him. Osborne says: "The tempest caused by the request of the Princess of Caterwaul to take up permanent residency in the United States with her son continues, with Wittish Foreign Secretary, Colin Oglesby, calling the United States—quote—'rash and irresponsible for creating a dangerous rift between two traditional allies in a world never more than one step away from international chaos'—unquote. The Administration has so far been unavailable for comment on Oglesby's charges—"

We PULL SLOWLY AWAY from the television to a nearby closed door, with F. Melvin Michaelson etched on it.

Behind that door, we find Princess Susan in consultation with Michaelson.

Michaelson is seated at his desk, listening. Susan is talking, looking out the twenty-third story window to Century City at noon.

"So, you see," she says, "I really don't see that I had any other choice. I want to lead an ordinary life again. I want my son to grow up as an ordinary boy. If, when he's grown, he wishes to accept the awful restrictions of a Royal Life, that will be *his* choice."

"What you've been telling me for the last hour," Michaelson says, "is that you want a divorce."

Susan looks at him. "It's not that I wish to divorce Arthur. It's the *Prince of Caterwaul* I must divorce."

"Arthur might be willing to give that up for you," Michaelson says. "There *is* precedent."

"No!" Susan surprises him with her vehemence. "He couldn't live without it. It's the only life he's known. It's the life he *has* chosen."

"If this gets to court, his lawyer will argue that it's the life *you* chose also."

"My God, I was a silly nineteen-year-old Wittish girl—raised on fairy tales about Prince Charming—and the Prince of Caterwaul was in love with me and asking me to *marry* him. What girl wouldn't have been swept off her feet? By the time the reality behind the fairy tale hit me, our honeymoon had left me pregnant with John."

"That's why you never had any other children," Michaelson says.

Susan nods. "I had no desire to bring yet another child into such an insane existence."

"Are you in love with your husband?"

Susan looks miserable. "How can I ever know? His every move is conditioned by what other people think is proper for him. He never does *anything* of importance without permission. Just with what, precisely, am I supposed to be in *love*?"

Michaelson taps his fingers together.

"Your case presents—well—unique difficulties," Michaelson says. "Protection for you and your son. Schooling for John. Controlling publicity. Oh, yes. My fee. You *can* afford to pay me, can't you?"

Susan smiles for the first time. "I thought this was a case you'd 'kill for.'"

"Fine. Who do I have to kill to get paid?"

"Don't worry. I've managed to save out of the household money."

Michaelson smiles. "The law requires that we show 'evidence of permanent professional, business, social, and civic ties consistent only with California domicile'—"

"What?"

"Nineteen-forty-nine, *Penn Mutual Life Insurance versus Fields*. You must live, work, and have friends here before you can file suit."

"We've been living in a house I've taken in Brentwood since the day we left the hotel. And—I must take a job?"

Michaelson nods. "Something for which you have 'special skills'—that part's for your immigration case, if push comes to shove. As for 'civic ties,' I suppose you can join the P.T.A."

"Would it count that the Governor of California has made us 'honorary citizens' and the Mayor of Los Angeles has declared us 'Angelenos'?"

Michaelson laughs. "It might. It just might."

"Which leaves just 'social ties,'" the Princess says.

Michaelson picks up the phone and punches in a number. "Are you free for dinner tonight?" Susan nods. "I've got a friend who might be a big help to us in a number of ways. Have you ever seen a television show called *Heller's Journal*?" Before she can answer, the phone is picked up. "Grant? Hi. Listen, there's someone I want you to meet, but this has got to be strictly off-the-record ..."

That evening. A suburban house in Santa Monica with a station wagon parked in the driveway.

Inside the house, Grant Heller is in his study, a pipe in his mouth producing clouds of smoke, working at a word processor. The evening news is on TELEVISION in the background, Connie Datsun anchoring.

After a VOICE OVER report SHOWING FILM of "Today's demonstration in front of the White House by several thousand women demanding that the Princess of Caterwaul and her son be allowed to remain in the United States," we return to Connie Datsun at her desk and a SLIDE of Prince Arthur comes up behind her. "The Prince of Caterwaul," Connie Datsun says—and at this, Grant stops typing and gives the TV his attention, "has continued his official duties without commenting on the crisis surrounding him. Today he continued his inspection tour of working conditions in Wittland. With that report is Lipton correspondent, ALLEN AVERY."

A TAPED REPORT comes on—Grant Heller watching closely.

Avery is standing in front of the Lipton department store, Marx & Spinoza, holding a microphone. "The Prince of Caterwaul is keeping a 'stiff upper lip' regarding the break-up of his marriage," Avery says, "and his only statement on the subject has been that he will continue his duties as usual. This was evident today as he talked with department store sales personnel."

The TAPED REPORT CUTS to Prince Arthur—surrounded by reporters and cameras—talking to a SALES CLERK in the television department. "What exactly do you do here?" the Prince asks the man.

"I'm in charge of the tellys, Sir," the Clerk says.

"Keep you busy here?" Arthur asks.

"It's been a little slow lately, Sir."

"Pay you enough, do they?"

"Be better when business picks up, Sir."

"That's the spirit!" Arthur says, and moves on to another clerk.

The TAPE CUTS BACK to Allen Avery in front of the department store. "How much longer the Prince of Caterwaul will be able to keep his *own* spirits up is another question entirely. This is Allen Avery reporting from Lipton."

As the TELEVISION NEWS moves on to another story, Grant resumes typing.

OUTSIDE Heller's house, Melvin Michaelson's Cadillac—with Princess Susan, Prince John, and Anne as his passengers—pulls into the driveway next to Grant's station wagon.

INSIDE again, Grant's son, BRAD—now Prince John's age—comes into Grant's study and says, "Dad, they're here."

AT THE FRONT DOOR, Michaelson introduces the visitors to Grant and his son. There is an instant connection between the two eight-year-olds, who immediately head off to BRAD'S ROOM to play computer games.

BACK IN THE LIVING ROOM, Heller says, "Listen, Mel's call caught me on deadline for Sunday's show, and I didn't have a chance to shop for supper. I guess we're going to have to eat out."

Susan is charmed by Heller's informal approach and his unselfconsciousness around her, but realizes a problem. "I'm not sure that's a very good idea," she says. "We've been ducking the press the past three days—Oh, sorry. No offense meant."

"Don't worry about it," Heller says. "I have a feeling Mel brought me in on your side to prevent me from hounding you to death. As for keeping my colleagues away from you while we dine out, I have an idea ..."

CUT TO: The six of them piling into Grant's station wagon, and as the station wagon pulls out, we CUT TO:

The Place Your Order Here counter inside "TACO HEAVEN."

Susan is ordering: "... that's one green-chile *Burrito Ambrosia*, three *Taco Gigantica*'s, three *Burger Grande*'s ..."

Mel Michaelson is shaking his head slowly at Grant's *declasse* tastes, but Prince John—and Princess Susan—couldn't look happier.

A few minutes later, the six of them at a brightly colored table surrounded by greasy paper and full mouths—but otherwise alone.

"So you see," Grant says between bites, "I don't think you'll have a lot of trouble with Uncle Sam—not with public opinion on your side the way it is—but I'd be worried about some kind of action by your own government."

"But you think we're safe for the moment," Susan says.

"Only as long as nobody knows where you are," Grant says. "The minute anybody knows your address, you'd better have that security system—TV cameras, ultrasonic motion detectors, alarm system hooked up to a private patrol company. I'll take care of it first thing in the morning."

"That's frightfully good of you," Susan says.

Heller puts on a Texas accent. "Happy to be of service, Ma'am."

John picks a piece of avocado out of his *Taco Gigantica* and holds it up. "What's this *green* thingie?" he asks suspiciously.

"That's avocado, dear," Susan says. "The Governor of California gave us a crate of them, remember?"

"Well, it looks *disgusting*," John says. "Get it *away* from me."

"John!" his mother says sharply. "You're not being polite."

"Why must I be polite?" John asks. "I'm not going to be a prince anymore."

"Ordinary people have to be polite as well," Anne says.

John decides "ordinary people" would know about this. He looks to Grant Heller for confirmation. Grant nods. John looks to Mel Michaelson. Mel nods. Finally, John looks to the other eight-year-old.

Brad Heller nods. "They get you no matter *who* you are," Brad says.

Later that night. With "Good nights!" all around, Michaelson drops his new clients off at their equally new address in Westwood. Michaelson checks to see that the street in front of the house looks deserted before he drives off. But as soon as the Cadillac drives away ... Jeffries and Peterson pop out from behind a bush.

"Hold it!" Peterson shouts, and a series of flashes—interspersed by motorized film advances—goes off in their faces.

The three of them are scared almost out of their wits; John grabs on to his mother.

"How dare you!" Susan begins. "Stop that!" she says to Peterson.

"Don't give us that, Princess," Jeffries says. "You know we were going to catch up to you sooner or later."

"Who the devil are you?" Anne asks.

"Jeff Jeffries, *The Inquisitor*, at your service," he says. "This is my sidekick, Roy Peterson."

Peterson stops shooting long enough to bow slightly.

"Well, Mr. Jeffries ... Mr. Peterson," Susan says. "We are no longer public figures, so I'll thank you to leave us alone. Good night."

She motions Anne and John to start into the house again.

"Give me a break, Princess," Jeffries says, blocking her for a moment. "There are a billion people wondering why you ditched Artie. Think of the public service I'm doing."

"I don't give a damn for your 'public service,'" Susan says angrily. "This is precisely the sort of thing I'm trying to get away from—get my son away from. *Good night.*"

She pushes past him and begins unlocking the front door.

"Say, Roy," Jeffries says loudly. "You get the license number off that Caddie?"

"Yep."

"Okay. I'll have Sarge run it through the Motor Vehicles computer in the morning. Might be a new boyfriend."

John and Anne precede Susan through the front door.

"You people make me sick," Susan says—and she slams the door.

As soon as the door slams, Jeffries and Peterson walk a dozen paces down the street, then stop.

Jeffries pulls out a microcassette recorder, zip-squeals in reverse, then begins the playback.

"I don't give a damn for your 'public service,'" Susan says again.

Jeffries chuckles and shuts off the recorder, pocketing it as they continue down the street.

Inside the house. There's little furniture so far, which makes the instrument in the middle of the living room floor immediately visible as they enter. "They've installed the telephone," Susan says.

"Mummy," John asks, "may we call Daddy?"

"It's almost eleven," Anne tells John, "—way past your bedtime."

"Perhaps this *would* be a good time," Susan says. "Arthur will just be getting up." She turns to John. "Very well," she says. She turns to Anne. "Would you put through the call for him, please?"

Anne looks at Susan with concern, then nods.

Anne punches in the call, direct, and a few seconds later it's answered, "Kenspeckle Palace."

"The Prince of Caterwaul, please," Anne says. "Prince John of Caterwaul is calling."

"One moment, please."

Anne hands the phone over to John. WE INTERCUT:

Prince Arthur, just out of a bath and in his robe. "Hello?"

"Hello, Daddy. This is John."

Arthur's face lights up. "John! How are you?"

"I'm fine, Daddy. How are you?"

"I'm well, except ... I miss you terribly."

"I miss you, too," John says. "When are you coming to join Mummy and me?"

"Where are you?"

"We're still in California."

"Did your mother tell you I'd be joining you?"

"No," John says, "but you will, won't you?"

"I'll have to talk to your mother about that," Prince Arthur says. "Is she there?"

"Daddy wants to talk to you," John says.

Susan hesitates a moment. "Say good night to your father. Then off to bed with you."

"Mummy says I have to go to bed now. Good night, Daddy."

"Good night, John. You be a good boy and do what your mother tells you."

"I will, Sir."

John hands the phone over to Princess Susan, then heads for his bedroom, his governess in tow.

Susan waits until they're out of earshot.

"Hello, Arthur," she says wearily.

"I'm afraid you haven't explained this very well to John," Arthur says. "Nor to me, for that matter."

"It's not an easy subject to get into—with either of you."

"You could have at least told me, instead of leaving me to hear it from David Wilson."

"I was afraid if I called, you'd talk me out of it. And I didn't want that to happen."

"I'm going to try it, now," Arthur says. "Susan, we've had our difficulties before. And when you ran into trouble, you used to turn to me for protection against the world. Now you've turned to the world for protection against *me*."

"I saw things very clearly for the first time," Susan says, "when that toy pistol was shot off at Heathcliff Airport on our departure. What I saw is that you *can't* protect me from the world, Arthur. You're like a lion who's been raised in a zoo—they've manacled you and clipped your claws. They've trained you never to roar too loudly lest you frighten the children. But I know what it is to be free, and I can't live in your cage anymore—and I don't want our son to grow up in a cage, either."

"Susan, let's stick to the facts," Arthur says. "I'm your husband, whom you promised to 'love, honor, and cherish.' You've let me down, you've let our families down, you've let the country down. I *could* speak of my love for you, but I think it's more important that I speak of the duty you've promised, and the honor involved in keeping that promise."

"Duty! Honor!" She almost spits the words across the Atlantic. "Don't you realize those are the words they've used to cage us?"

"You're asking the impossible," the Prince tells her. "You are the *Princess of Caterwaul* and your son will someday be King of Wittland. Do you think the world is going to forget that fact simply because you choose not to live in a palace? You wish us to live by the rules of ordinary lives ... but we are *not* an ordinary family, no matter what our personal desires."

Susan begins crying.

"I was right not to call you before this," the Princess says ... and hangs the phone up.

This time, Susan sits on the empty living room floor and cries alone, without Anne MacIntosh to comfort her.

A few days later, back in Wittland. Prince Arthur is making an inspection tour of a factory (what it manufactures, we're not sure) and is being escorted around by a group of the factory's EXECU-TIVES. All of them are wearing business suits topped by industrial hats and eye protectors.

The factory MACHINE NOISE is horrendous.

Arthur stops at a WORKER operating a piece of power machinery. "What exactly are you doing?" Arthur asks the Worker.

"I'm sealing the managram fartlers, Sir," the Worker shouts.

"Ah," Arthur says, as if he understood this. "Keep you busy here?"

"Not as busy as I'd like, Sir. Laid off three weeks last March."

"Pay you enough, do they?"

"The wife and I could always use more, Sir, what with another little one on the way."

"Well, keep up the good work and I'm sure there will be," Arthur says, reassuringly.

As Arthur and the Executives move off the floor, through a set of double doors to a somewhat quieter area, Arthur asks the Supervisor, "Just what *are* 'managram fartlers,' and why must they be sealed?"

The Supervisor shrugs. "Is that what he said? I thought he said he was *stealing* them."

Arthur ponders this as the group emerges from the factory and is confronted by the usual gaggle of reporters.

"Are there any questions for His Royal Highness?" the CHIEF EXECUTIVE asks.

The REPORTER from the *EXPRESS-MAIL* gets in the first question. "Sir, do you have any comment on the story just published in the American weekly, *The Inquisitor*?"

Arthur is caught off guard. "I'm afraid I haven't seen it."

"I just happen to have a copy, Sir," the Reporter says, handing it to Arthur.

The Inquisitor is headlined:
PRINCESS SU ON THE RUN:
"I Don't Give A Damn For Public Service—
You People Make Me Sick!"

There is a PHOTO of an Angry Princess Susan below the headline.

The factory's Chief Executive intervenes, "I was calling for questions regarding industrial—"

"No, I'll answer this," Arthur intervenes, tapping the Chief Executive on the shoulder gently.

The Prince pauses a moment, then goes on:

"First," he says, "I can assure you unequivocally that the Princess of Caterwaul has been misquoted, or quoted out-of-context. Such remarks are just not her style. Nevertheless, if she *had* said something of the kind, could she be blamed? The tour I have been making today has been to study working conditions in this factory. Any worker—given intolerable working conditions—would be accorded the right to strike his employer, or quit. From before our marriage, you ladies and gentlemen of the press have tailed Susan mercilessly, making her feel that she is on exhibit in a zoo. You maintain that you have done this as representatives of the public. If you are, then the public must share responsibility for your actions. And since the public has imposed intolerable working conditions on the Princess of Caterwaul, then the public should not be surprised that the Princess of Caterwaul has quit. If I had not gained a greater tolerance for the pressures attendant on this job, by growing into it, I might well have done the same."

The *DAILY AUTOGRAPH* REPORTER: "Sir, are you saying that you approve of the Princess's actions, and will do nothing to bring the Princess of Caterwaul and Prince John back?"

"I will do everything within my power," Arthur says, "to bring my wife and son back. Do not, however, be surprised if I fail, since you've left me little power with which to make an attempt."

Amidst a dozen shouts of "Sir!" and "Prince Arthur!" from the Press, Arthur says goodbye to the factory's Executives and leaves.

In front of the office tower housing Melvin Michaelson's law firm—mid-morning.

A Jeep CJ7 with the roof off pulls up to the curb. Half-a-dozen other cars pull up behind it.

Princess Susan—looking like a charging rhino—gets out of the Jeep's driver's seat, followed close order by Prince John, Anne MacIntosh—and two additions to her coterie: *the two Wittish Detectives assigned to her and her son as bodyguards who—upon finding them—have resumed their duties.*

REPORTERS and PHOTOGRAPHERS jump out of the other cars and immediately begin besieging them with questions and shooting pictures.

Princess Susan is clutching, tightly, a copy of *The Inquisitor*—the one with her on the cover.

Susan, John, and Anne march to the nearest elevator and Susan punches for her floor. The Wittish Detectives are holding everyone else out until two staffers for *The Star Chamber* protest, "But we *work* in this building!"

The Detectives allow these two on, holding everyone else back.

It is the same Reporter and Photographer who were on the elevator with them last time.

"Are you filing for divorce?" the Reporter asks.

Susan doesn't answer.

"Are you going to sue *The Inquisitor*?" he tries again.

Susan remains silent.

The Reporter and Photographer shrug to each other.

The Photographer takes out a cigarette and starts lighting it.

Prince John looks up at his mother and Anne. "*Deja vu?*" he asks them, then tugs at the Photographer's sleeve. "Excuse me," he says to the man, "but I thought you should know. There's a notice forbidding smoking in the lift."

"I don't see any Bobbies around to stop me, kid," he replies.

This time, John nods to one of his Detectives, who takes the cigarette out of the Photographer's mouth, and grinds it out.

John gives a very "Stan Laurel-ish" nod of the head.

The elevator doors open, the Reporter and Photographer follow the Royal Entourage out ... and realize they're on their *own* floor—"18"—the editorial offices of *The Star Chamber*.

Susan walks up to the receptionist as the astonished Reporter and Photographer watch.

"Would you please tell your Managing Editor, Mr. Malcolm," Susan says, "that the Princess of Caterwaul is here for her job interview?"

The receptionist puts through the call. The Reporter and Photographer look as if they're about to faint.

The front page of *The Star Chamber*—and two hands holding it. Over Prince Arthur's PHOTO:

"The Inquisitor Has Lied About My Wife!"

Over a PHOTO of Princess Susan:

Meet *The Star Chamber*'s New Fashion Critic—
THE PRINCESS OF CATERWAUL!

We PULL BACK to SEE the tabloid being read by Managing Editor Samantha Friendly in her office at *The Inquisitor*.

Her intercom buzzes. "Yes?"

"Jeffries and Peterson," her secretary says.

"Send them in," Friendly says.

Jeffries and Peterson come into her office. "Have a seat," she tells them as they come in.

The two men sit down across from her desk, and smile. "Another assignment for 'Jefferson' so soon?" Jeffries asks.

"'Jefferson'?" Friendly asks.

"Like 'Woodstein.'" Peterson explains. "Jeffries, Peterson—'Jefferson.'"

"How ... clever," Friendly says, exuding warmth. "No, I called you in to give you your bonus checks in person. That's nine months salary extra, for each of you."

She hands them their envelopes.

The two men open their envelopes and grin widely at the checks.

"Beautiful!" Peterson says. "Want me to get a shot of you handing Jeff his check?"

"That won't be necessary, she says. "That's all. You can go."

The two men are taken aback by her abruptness, but rise to leave.

"Oh, 'Jefferson,'" she says, as an afterthought. "Have you seen the issue of *The Star Chamber* hitting the racks today?"

They shake their heads.

"You might want to pick up a copy on your way home," she says.

"All right," Jeffries says. They turn to leave again.

"'Jefferson,'" she calls again, "just one last thing."

The two men turn back.

"You're fired," she says.

Early afternoon, OUTSIDE the Wittish Consulate General in Los Angeles at 3701 Wilshire Boulevard, TO ESTABLISH, then:

INSIDE, in a plush conference room in the east wing, Wittish Ambassador, Lord David Wilson is seated around a conference table with SIX MEN dressed in SAVAGE ROW suits. These men are AGENTS of the WITTISH SECRET SERVICE.

Wilson is speaking: "The two paramount considerations in this operation are *the absolute safety* of the Princess of Caterwaul, Prince John of Caterwaul, and Miss MacIntosh; and *absolute secrecy* regarding this operation. *Not one hair* on Their Royal Highnesses' or Miss MacIntosh's persons are to be put at risk, under penalty of Her Majesty's *extreme displeasure*."

ONE of the AGENTS: "The Americans know nothing of this?"

"Nothing," Wilson says. "Nor can the Primal Minister guarantee your safety if word of this operation gets out. If you succeed in returning the Princess of Caterwaul, Prince John of Caterwaul, and Miss MacIntosh to Wittish soil, the Primal Minister will issue an official statement that Their Royal Highnesses were suffering from homesickness, and decided to return home. If the Princess doesn't cooperate, there will be another official statement shortly about Her Royal Highness's need to recover from stress."

The Agent: "And if we fail?"

"Then," the Ambassador says, "it is unlikely that the Primal Minister will be able to do *anything* on your behalf, since there's quite a good possibility the scandal will bring down the government with calls for immediate elections."

Another Agent: "Are we likely to encounter any extraordinary security precautions?"

"Their Royal Highnesses' Detectives report that they haven't been shown any, so I wouldn't worry about that. Any other questions?"

The Agents remain silent.

"Very well," Lord Wilson says. "The operation is set, then, for three tomorrow morning. That's all."

In front of Princess Susan's house in Westwood, early evening.

It is no longer a deserted village street. LOS ANGELES POLICE have set up sawhorses along the sidewalk to keep back REPORTERS, PHOTOGRAPHERS, TV CAMERAS, LOCAL CHILDREN, STREET PEOPLE, TOURISTS, MIMES, and SOUVENIR DEALERS.

Inside the house (there's more furniture now), Susan looks out her front window, holding back a curtain slightly so she can see without being seen herself. She shakes her head sadly. "Arthur was right," she says. "I thought it was only *royalty* that interests them. It seems that someone trying not to *be* royal anymore interests them even more."

"Do you think it will always be like this?" Anne asks.

"I've asked myself that a dozen times in the past few days. It's all been rather pointless if I've simply exchanged one pack of foxhounds for another."

Susan walks over to a coffee table, on which are lying several Wittish newspapers, and begins flipping through them, looking at their HEADLINES for what must be the tenth time.

The Times of Lipton: Prince of Caterwaul Defends Princess's 'Right to Strike'

The Daily Looking Glass: 'Intolerable Working Conditions,' Declares Prince Arthur

The Sin: Prince Arthur Tries to Patch Things Up

"When I spoke to Arthur," Susan says, "I accused him of not being able to protect me from the public ... and here he is doing it."

"You've decided to go back home, haven't you?" Anne asks suddenly.

Susan looks up, astonished. "How did you know?"

"You've been looking dreamily at those newspapers since I bought them," Anne says.

"Do you think I've been very foolish, Anne?"

"I don't think you've been foolish at all," she says. "The purpose of a walk-out is to let the company know how much they need you. I think you've won your point."

Susan looks at her watch. "It's the middle of the night back home, and I'm too exhausted to wait up," she says. "I'll telephone Arthur the first thing in the morning and let him know we're on our way back."

Susan and Anne hug each other.

WE RETURN OUTSIDE to the street scene in front of the house—everyone milling around as if at a carnival—then CUT TO:

THE SAME SHOT of the house—3:00 AM that night—and the street is deserted again. The police sawhorses remain, but even the police are gone.

TWO BLACK ROLLS ROYCES pull up in front of the house.

The six Wittish Secret Service Agents get out.

One of the Agents takes out a police MagLite and FLASHES it three times at the front house window Susan was looking out earlier.

Quietly, they all walk up to the front door. It is opened *from inside* by the two Wittish Detectives who'd rejoined Susan and John as their bodyguards.

The six Agents enter the house, are joined by the two Detectives, and all eight men silently begin climbing the stairs.

The two Detectives directing the others by hand gestures, they break into three teams: two for Prince John's bedroom, three each for Princess Susan's and Anne MacIntosh's bedroom.

A few seconds later, Prince John, Princess Susan, and Anne are being carried—kicking but not (their mouths are covered) screaming—down the stairs—

WHEN BRIGHT LIGHTS and SIREN suddenly turn on throughout the house, the lights blinding the Intruders. They stop in their places—

—The Agents let go of Princess Susan, Prince John, and Anne to make a run to the front door—where they are met by BEL AIR PATROL GUARDS with their GUNS DRAWN.

(At Grant Heller's suggestion, Princess Susan had refrained from telling her Detectives about the automatic security system Grant had installed—and the Wittish have fallen into the trap that Grant had set for a Wittish abduction attempt.)

CUT TO:

A TELEVISION MONITOR showing THE ABDUCTION ATTEMPT IN PROGRESS. We PULL BACK from the MONITOR to SEE:

That we're in a TV STUDIO CONTROL BOOTH. A DIRECTOR says, "Tape ending ... Three, two, one ... Back live—Camera two!"

—And we're on the Studio Set of *Heller's Journal*—with Grant Heller seated opposite Princess Susan, Mel Michaelson, and U.S. Attorney General, Barry Compton.

Grant Heller lights his pipe and says, "Mr. Attorney General, now that you've seen the tape made by Princess Susan's security cameras, do you have any comment?"

Compton looks as if he's sitting in an electric chair.

"Well, Mr. Heller ... you see ... of course the Department of Justice will conduct a very *thorough* investigation of this—er—incident—"

"I believe," Susan says, "the word you're searching so hard for is 'kidnapping.'"

"Well, Your Royal Highness," Compton says, "whether this—uh—'abduction' attempt is legally kidnapping is the very point under investigation. It's a knotty problem in 'Conflicts of Law' which may very well have to be settled by the Supreme Court, or possibly even the United Nations—"

WE are now VIEWING the PROGRAM on a PROJECTION TV SET.

"—particularly since, in this case, the custody of the child in question has never been ruled on by an American Court—"

"That will be corrected shortly," Mel Michaelson interjects.

Heller turns back to Princess Susan: "Then you *are* intending to remain in Los Angeles and file for divorce?"

And as Susan answers, "Yes," we PULL AROUND to a REVERSE VIEW to SEE:

THREE MEN in their TWENTIES and a GIRL about NINETEEN— all of them wearing fashionable looking outfits reminiscent of military fatigues—watching *Heller's Journal* on a top-of-the-line projection television in an expensively appointed living room. On the wall, there is a framed photograph—clipped from a newspaper— showing the destruction in the Walkman Islands War of the Arginian cruiser *General Belligerent.*

"But, as I understand it," Heller says, puffing on his pipe, "you *were* intending to return voluntarily when the abduction attempt took place?"

"That's also correct," Susan says. "The kidnapping attempt showed me what my true position is."

STILL ON TV, the four Arginians watching:

"Regardless of the custody status of Prince John," Heller says to the Attorney General, "that wouldn't affect the legality of an abduction attempt on the Princess of Caterwaul and Miss MacIntosh, would it?"

"I don't think I'd better comment on that at this time," Compton— ON TV—says. "We have not yet decided whether to prosecute the Wittish Agents, inasmuch as they may very well have been acting upon the lawful orders of a traditionally friendly government—"

ONE of the Arginians—CARLOS—speaks to the GIRL—ANA—in Spanish. What he says, if translated, is: "Them, they won't prosecute. All this supposed tension between the Wittish and the Americans is nonsense—they've been in bed together all along."

Some days later. It is late morning, in the Wittish countryside. Prince Arthur is on horseback—wearing dress shirt and cutaway frock, breeches and boots—along with a rather large contingent of similarly mounted and dressed characters, in the middle of a fox hunt.

The foxhounds are sniffing aound—trying to pick up the scent again—when suddenly the fox is spotted, and the hounds start chasing it, the riders following the hounds close order.

As Arthur rides after the hounds, ANOTHER RIDER—*not dressed for the hunt*—pulls his horse alongside, and starts shouting, "Sir! Sir!"

Without slowing down, Arthur looks over to the man. "You're not with the hunt," Arthur shouts, "so who the devil are you? Anti-Blood-Sports League? Press?"

"PROCESS SERVER!" the man shouts—and sticks his hand out with an envelope.

"Oh, no you don't!" Arthur shouts. The Prince digs his heels into his horse and gallops away into the countryside with the Process Server in full pursuit of *him*.

Prince Arthur, underwater in full SCUBA gear, with a group of divers.

ANOTHER DIVER paddles his way up to the Prince and tries to hand him an envelope wrapped in plastic. Arthur looks at the diver—sees that behind the mask it is the Process Server again—and goes swimming off, the Process Server swimming after him in a torrent of bubbles.

Prince Arthur wearing a jumpsuit and parachute and standing with other jumpsuited men in an open airplane obviously set up for skydiving.

After several SKYDIVERS jump out, Arthur follows.

We see Arthur majestically freefalling toward earth—then another figure—also freefalling—drops in next to him, and tries to hand him an envelope.

Arthur looks closely and recognises—at the same time we do—the Process Server.

Arthur immediately pulls his ripcord—and the Process Server quickly drops below as Arthur's parachute catches air.

A formal dinner at Kenspeckle Palace. Prince Arthur in full evening dress, greeting lords and ladies, dukes and duchesses, cabinet ministers, and foreign dignitaries.

A now-familiar man—in waiter's uniform—walks up to the Prince of Caterwaul.

It is the Process Server.

The man says, "Roses are red, violets are blue, dinner is served"—he hands the Prince an envelope—"and so are you."

As his guests attempt to suppress laughter, Arthur looks as if he'd like to have the Process Server sent to the Tower of Lipton.

Los Angeles International Airport. A Royal Air Force VC 10 jet is coming in for a landing.

There are no brass bands or red carpets this time as Arthur, Prince of Caterwaul; his private secretary, Group Captain Ronald Chesterton; and the usual VALET and DETECTIVE BODYGUARD deplane down a movable staircase. Then, they walk a few feet to a BELL JET RANGER HELICOPTER, board, and with Arthur at the controls, take off. CUT TO:

THE BELL HELICOPTER landing on the helipad atop the Downtown Los Angeles Westin Bonaventure Hotel. Press and TV are behind POLICE LINES atop the hotel as Prince Arthur gets out, is met by Lord Wilson, and the party walks inside, ignoring the media's shouts of, "Prince Arthur!"

One Hundred Eleven North Hill Street, downtown Los Angeles—the Los Angeles Superior Courthouse. EXTERIOR VIEW, morning. There is a mob of REPORTERS, PHOTOGRAPHERS, SIGHTSEERS, and TELEVISION CREWS.

Ted Singer, the Anchorman for the late-night *Royalty in America* report, is standing in front of the Courthouse, speaking to a TV Camera:

"It was a storybook romance like other storybook romances," he says, "a storybook wedding like other storybook weddings, a storybook marriage like other storybook marriages. But like half the storybook romances, weddings, and marriages in the modern world, the Bride and the Bridegroom did not live happily ever after. The wife ran away from her husband's house with their eight-year-old son, and has filed for divorce and child custody. There is only one not-so-slight difference between this case and hundreds of thousands seemingly like it. This time, the Petitioner is the Princess of

Caterwaul, the Respondent is the Prince of Caterwaul, and the child being fought over is next-in-line after his father to be King of Wittland someday.

"This is Ted Singer reporting from the Los Angeles Superior Courthouse, Friday, August thirty-first."

Newswoman Connie Datsun is making a similar report to a TV Camera:

"Three-quarters-of-a-billion people around the world are reported to have watched the Royal Wedding on television," she says. "In a few minutes, they will have the chance to see the arrival of the Prince and Princess of Caterwaul for the Royal Divorce ... and here comes the first limousine—'limousine'?—now."

Princess Susan's Jeep pulls up, and Susan gets out, walking the press gauntlet into the Courthouse.

Almost immediately, a limousine arrives with Prince Arthur.

INSIDE the Courthouse, the corridor in front of Department 2B. News media have been kept outside the Courthouse so it is empty except for the lawyers waiting for their clients.

Michaelson begins the introductions: "Susan, this is Arthur's lawyer, Former California Attorney General, RALPH BARTOK."

"How's it going?" the Princess says, shoving out her hand to shake.

Bartok shakes her hand.

The Prince is taken aback at the informality, but tries not to show it.

"Your Royal Highness, F. Melvin Michaelson," Bartok introduces in return.

"How do you do?" the Prince says.

Susan takes a granola bar out of her handbag and begins peeling it open, offering it for a bite to the others. "They're fantastic," she says.

None accept, and she bites into it herself.

"The Judge," Michaelson says, "denied all *in limine* motions in the pretrial meeting, so we're going directly to trial in a few moments."

"Also," Bartok says, "the Judge didn't at all like the idea of litigants in an American Court being addressed by an honorific greater than 'Your Honor,' so for the duration of this trial, you are simply 'Mr. and Mrs. Windsong'."

"Very well," Arthur says.

"Shall we go in?"

"I'd like a moment with Her Royal Highness, if I may," Arthur says.

The two attorneys look nervous, but both nod.

The lawyers go in and Prince Arthur turns to Princess Susan. "I only wanted to say that I knew nothing whatever about the abduction attempt until it was all over," Arthur says.

"I knew that, Arthur," Susan says, almost tenderly. "But don't you see? That just makes it worse because they didn't even see fit to consult you."

Arthur sighs. "How is John?"

"Taking this as well as can be expected," Susan says. "Grant Heller and his son have taken John to a science fiction convention to take his mind off all this."

There's a long moment of silence.

"We'd better go in," Susan says.

Susan and Mel Michaelson are at one table. Arthur and Ralph Bartok are at the other.

A COURT CLERK is at a table attached to the Judge's bench, working. A COURT STENOGRAPHER is preparing his machine. A BAILIFF is standing, waiting.

In the gallery, Anne MacIntosh is seated with other WITNESSES.

A WOMAN—attired as a Judge—enters the Courtroom from the judge's Chambers and starts toward the bench.

The Bailiff says, "Remain seated and come to order. Court is now in session, THE HONORABLE GLORIA ROSENSTEIN, Judge Presiding."

Judge Rosenstein takes the bench.

The Clerk hands her a sheaf of papers. She studies them for a moment, signs one of them, then hands it back to the Clerk.

She looks up. "The first matter on today's docket," she says, "is Case Number 602357, *In Re Dissolution of Windsong Marriage*, and related Case 602621, *Windsong versus Windsong*." She turns a page. "State your appearances."

Michaelson gets up. "Your Honor, Michaelson, Chase and Speakman, F. Melvin Michaelson appearing, representing the Petitioner, Susan Windsong."

Michaelson sits down.

Bartok gets up. "Bartok and Tannen, Your Honor, Ralph S. Bartok appearing, representing the Respondent, Arthur Windsong."

Bartok sits down.

Judge Rosenstein flips through some more pages. "I see that Petitioner has temporary custody of the child John by order of this Court dated July 8th, on Petitioner's *ex parte* Motion to Show Cause alleging an abduction attempt by the father's agents in violation of California's *Domestic Violence Act*. I don't see the boy in the courtroom, or his name on either of the lists of witnesses. Is he available if we need him?"

Michaelson stands up. He's in Anaheim, Your Honor, and we can produce him anytime after an hour or so recess."

"Very well, Mr. Michaelson. Do you wish to make an opening statement?"

"Yes, Your Honor."

"You may proceed."

"Your Honor," Michaelson says, "the issue in this case revolves more around values in conflict rather than personalities in conflict. It is the Petitioner's contention that the life of Royalty is too laden with restrictions and obligations to be imposed on anyone without full informed consent. When Susan Herbert married the Prince of Caterwaul at age nineteen, she was too struck by the glamour of the situation to be able to make a reasonable appraisal of the life she was about to enter. We maintain, therefore, that since nineteen was too young, then her eight-year-old son must be allowed the right to grow to his full majority before deciding whether he wishes such restrictions and obligations to be thrust upon him. We are maintaining that the two rights we wish upheld in this case are the right of a woman to be free from her husband's will—no matter *who* he is—and the right of a boy to grow up free to choose his own destiny. It is to defend these rights that we petition not only for dissolution of this marriage, but for custody of eight-year-old John as well. Thank you, Your Honor."

Michaelson sits down.

"Mr. Bartok," Judge Rosenstein says, "do you wish to make an opening statement?"

"Your Honor," Bartok says, "we'd prefer to reserve our opening statement to the beginning of Respondent's arguments."

"Very well, Mr. Bartok. Mr. Michaelson, call your first witness."

"Your Honor," Michaelson says, standing again. "I call to the stand Her Majesty, Queen Victoria the Second of the Unified Kingdom of Great Wittland."

There is a stir in the gallery, and several heads turn to look back at the doors.

Michaelson is not, however, one of those looking back.

Nobody enters.

After several seconds' pause, Judge Rosenstein says, "Mr. Michaelson, as a court of inferior dignity, is there any point in my finding the Queen of Wittland in contempt for ignoring your subpoena? You must be aware that I have no way of enforcing such a finding on a foreign head of state."

"That is all the notice I was asking for, Your Honor."

"Let the record state," the Judge says, "that the Queen of Wittland has been subpoenaed to testify in this Court and has declined to appear, with no penalty that can be imposed. Call your next witness, Mr. Michaelson."

"Your Honor, I call Miss Anne MacIntosh."

As Anne takes the stand and is sworn in by the Clerk, Arthur leans over to Bartok and whispers, "Why call the Queen to testify, since he knew beforehand she wouldn't appear?"

Bartok whispers back, "He just got into the record proof that any custody order issued by this Court is not enforceable in Wittland. He'll use that to try and get Judge Rosenstein to rule against any custody arrangement that involves John ever visiting Wittish soil."

Arthur whistles silently.

"State your name and occupation," the Clerk says to Anne.

"Anne MacIntosh. I'm the governess to Prince John of Caterwaul."

"Miss MacIntosh," Michaelson begins. "How long have you been in the employ of the Prince and Princess of Caterwaul? ..."

Outside the Courthouse, about five that evening. Mel Michaelson says to Susan, "I'll see you back here Tuesday morning," then Princess Susan and Anne MacIntosh brave the Press back to the Jeep. Susan picks a parking ticket off the windshield, she and Anne get in, and Susan drives away.

A few seconds after the Jeep pulls away from the curb, a YELLOW VAN pulls into traffic behind them.

INSIDE THE YELLOW VAN, we see the four Arginians.

A SHOT of the Jeep on the freeway, still being tailed by the Yellow Van, then a CUT TO:

THE JEEP on Harbor Boulevard in Anaheim as it passes the Anaheim Convention Center, the Convention Center's giant display announcing:

WELCOME WESTERN SCIENCE FICTION CONVENTION.

Susan pulls the Jeep into one of the major hotels adjacent to the Convention Center, and parks.

The Yellow Van pulls into the hotel also.

As Susan and Anne enter the hotel, they walk into an atmosphere somewhere between a Teamsters Convention and Alice in Wonderland. SCIENCE FICTION FANS are wandering throughout the hotel lobby—riding the escalators, sitting in the bar and coffee shop—and many of them are wearing ELABORATE COSTUMES. Many of the costumes are original, but a good many are handmade reproductions of costumes taken from popular media: we see many *Star Trek* Data's and Counsellor Troi's, several skinny teenagers wearing padded American Gladiators costumes, and even an old-fashioned robot or two.

One of the Arginians—EDUARDO—follows Susan and Anne as they weave their way through the hotel past convention events in progress: past a Panel Discussion on the Industrialization of Space, past a film room showing *The Day the Earth Stood Still*, past an Author's Reading, past an Autograph Session with an "s-f" Author, until Susan and Anne reach the hotel elevators.

Princess Susan is counting on nobody ever *dreaming* that the Princess of Caterwaul would show up at an event like this for her not being recognized, but while she's waiting for the elevator, a FAN WEARING WITTISH REGENCY COSTUME notices her and does a double take.

We can see a moment on the Fan's face—an expression equivalent of "It *couldn't* be!" then we HEAR a SHOUT of, "Hey, it's Ray Bradbury!" and a stampede in the direction of that s-f luminary begins. The Regency Fan hesitates for just another second—then, with a shake of the head meaning, "Nah!"—joins the crowd following Bradbury.

Eduardo waits with Princess Susan and Anne for the elevator, and when it arrives, he gets on it with them.

After Susan and Anne get out of the elevator at their floor, Eduardo lets the doors begin to close—then presses the elevator's STOP button.

After waiting a few seconds, Eduardo gets out of the elevator in time to notice which room Princess Susan and Anne are going into.

INSIDE the hotel room, Grant Heller, Brad Heller, and Prince John are waiting for Susan and Anne.

OUTSIDE, in the corridor, Eduardo waits ...

THE CORRIDOR, as Princess Susan, Prince John, the Hellers, and Anne emerge.

Here we have a demonstration of the principle that parents going through a divorce pay for their guilt by being extra indulgent with a child. Princess Susan has agreed to enter the masquerade competition with Prince John, that evening at the Convention Center.

The Princess is wearing a costume—a reproduction of the "Rebel Alliance" uniform from *Return of the Jedi*.

Prince John is in a Teddy-Bearish "Ewok" costume from that film.

A helmet is part of the Princess's costume, and she is putting it on as she emerges from the hotel room; when on, it conceals her face.

But Eduardo, waiting near the elevators, *sees her* put the helmet on.

And, when the elevator takes them all down to the hotel lobby again, Eduardo waves to his compatriots to follow them.

The Convention Center has been set up with several thousand chairs, surrounding a runway and stage, for the Convention Masquerade—a competitive parading of all the best costumes and skits fans have been working up for the past year.

In a Prepping Area, MASQUERADE PARTICIPANTS are putting the final touches on their costumes, taking pictures of each other, and being given final tips for their presentations.

Grant Heller and Anne MacIntosh are taking pictures of Princess Susan and Prince John in their costumes.

(Both Princess Susan's and Prince John's faces are concealed by their costumes.)

Elsewhere in the prepping area, we see FOUR IMPERIAL STORMTROOPERS, also from the *Star Wars* films.

One of the Arginians, Carlos—wearing a rubber E.T. mask and holding an Instamatic camera—goes up to ONE of the Imperial Stormtroopers and says to him (with a heavy accent), "May I take a photograph of the four of you? For my little boy."

"Sure," the STORMTROOPER says. "Hey, guys, line up."

"No, it is too crowded in here," Carlos says. "Please, in the hallway?"

"Well ... okay. C'mon, fellows." the Stormtrooper says.

The four Stormtroopers follow Carlos out into the hallway.

"Around the corner will be good," Carlos says.

They follow him around the corner ... and the other three Arginians—also wearing rubber masks—are waiting.

Eduardo points a gun at the Stormtroopers.

"Hey, you're supposed to have that thing peace-bonded," the Stormtrooper says.

"This is no toy," Eduardo says. "Please, don't cause me to prove that." The Arginian gestures with the gun toward a nearby door. "The four of you ... in there, please."

The Stormtroopers do as they're told.

Carlos makes sure no one sees them, then follows the others through the door, slamming it.

BACK in the MASQUERADE PREPPING AREA. Brad Heller says to his father—still taking pictures—"Dad, we better get out there before all the good seats are gone."

"Break a leg," Grant Heller says to the costumed Susan and John—then Grant, Brad, and Anne head out to the audience to grab some seats.

The Masquerade. After seeing several other costumes on parade—each presentation announced—we hear, "We have an entry in the 'Media Costume' category—from *The Return of the Jedi*, Princess Leia Organa and Friend."

One of the Masquerade Organizers starts a tape recording and—to John Williams's "Ewok" theme music—The Princess and Her Ewok come out onto the runway and present themselves to the audience.

To receptive applause, "That presentation is by Johnny and Susie Windsong," the ANNOUNCER says—and there is some laughter, as several members of the audience recognize the names and assume it's a joke—"Wait, what's this?"

FOUR IMPERIAL STORMTROOPERS run on stage and *grab* the costumed Princess and Prince, dragging them off the runway into the back.

The audience laughs, hoots, and applauds loudly.

Even Grant Heller and Anne are applauding loudly until Brad says to his father, "Dad, that's *not* part of their presentation."

Heller's not sure whether to take his son seriously, until he sees the concerned expression. It *could* be a last-minute impromptu skit ... still ...

"Anne," Grant says, "would you keep an eye on Brad? I just want to make sure everything's okay."

"Of course, Grant," Anne says.

Grant trots out of the masquerade toward the area where Masquerade Participants are supposed to waiting for the judging. He looks around and doesn't see Susan and John.

Heller trots out to the parking lot, NIGHT:

AND HE SEES the Imperial Stormtroopers dragging Susan and John into the Yellow Van.

Grant doesn't waste a second. He runs to his own station wagon—manages to get into it and the engine running in time—then, as discreetly as possible, begins following the Van out of the parking lot and onto Harbor Boulevard.

Grant follows the Van onto the Northbound Entrance of the Santa Ana Freeway—Interstate 5.

And keeps on following them ... while he picks up his mobile telephone (he *is* a TV journalist) and says, "Operator, I need the number of the Westin Bonaventure Hotel in downtown L.A. ..."

While we're waiting for him to get that number, we SEE that his GAS GAUGE is reading *awfully* LOW ...

INSIDE THE YELLOW VAN, on Interstate Five Northbound. The Arginian girl—Ana—is driving while the third of the Arginian males, ANDRES—having removed his own stormtrooper costume—is helping Ana to remove hers—holding the steering wheel for her as necessary to keep the van in its lane.

In the BACK of the van, Carlos and Eduardo have taken off *their* stormtrooper costumes, and are tying up Prince John (his "Ewok" mask now off) and Princess Susan (her helmet off, also).

PRINCE ARTHUR'S SUITE in the Bonaventure Hotel.

Prince Arthur is watching television in the suite while eating a room service dinner with his personal secretary, Ronald Chesterton. Since he isn't going out that night, the Prince has let his detectives and valet off for the evening.

The room telephone rings. Chesterton wipes his mouth with a napkin, then gets up and takes the call.

"Yes?" Chesterton covers the mouthpiece. "Sir, it's a Mr. Grant Heller for you."

"Oh, that's the broadcaster, Susan's friend," Arthur says.

"Shall I tell him you're indisposed?"

"No, I'd better take it ... he's been with John all day." Arthur takes the phone from Chesterton. "Yes, Mr. Heller?"

WE INTERCUT:

Grant, in his station wagon on the freeway.

"Your Royal Highness, listen to me very carefully," Grant says. "I'm calling from my car on the freeway. I'm tailing a van with four characters who just kidnapped the Princess of Caterwaul and Prince John."

"What?" Arthur says. "Mr. Heller, if this is some bloody legal tactic that Mr. Michaelson has put you up to—"

"Listen, dammit!" Heller says. "I'm trying to save your wife and son's lives! But I called you first to make sure that it's not another abduction attempt by *your* people."

"I know nothing about such an attempt, Mr. Heller—but then, I knew nothing the first time as well."

"Can you find out? Because if it *isn't* your people—"

"Mr. Heller, can you hold? I'll find out directly." Arthur turns to Chesterton. "Go to the other telephone and get me the Primal Minister *at once.*"

A few minutes later, Arthur on the phone in the other bedroom: "You're absolutely positive? No, don't do anything except to keep this quiet—I'll handle everything from here. And, for Heaven's sake, don't worry the Queen with this yet! Goodbye."

Arthur hangs up, trots back to his own room, and takes the phone back from Chesterton. "Mr. Heller, are you still there?"

INTERCUT AGAIN:

"Yeah," he says.

"It's not any of our people. I'm sure. Do you still have the kidnappers in sight?"

The van is several cars in front of Heller's station wagon, in the Number Two Lane. "Right in front of me," he replies.

"You haven't notified any of the authorities yet?" Arthur asks.

"No," Heller says, "I was waiting until I talked to you."

"Then *don't*," Prince Arthur says. "I'm interested in getting my wife and son back safely, not capturing criminals."

"I got you," Grant says. "What do you want me to do?"

"I've got a helicopter at my disposal on the roof," Arthur says. "How can I rendezvous with you?"

"Is there a telephone in the helicopter?" Heller asks.

"I'm never without one," Arthur says.

"Good," Heller says. "As long as we don't change freeways, I'll be passing through downtown L.A. in about fifteen minutes. Once you're above the hotel, look for the freeway entrance signs. As soon as you're airborne, call me and I'll tell you which freeway I'm on. My mobile telephone number is ..."

And, as Grant gives Prince Arthur the number, we focus in again on the station wagon's GAS GAUGE, which now has its WARNING LIGHT ON.

Back at the Convention Center in Anaheim, in a hallway. Four TEENAGERS—wearing T-shirts and cut-offs—are reporting the theft of their Imperial Stormtrooper Costumes to CONVENTION SECURITY—also Teenagers, who are wearing futuristic military uniforms and carrying walkie-talkies. Nearby, Anne MacIntosh is on a payphone standing with Brad Heller, repeating Grant's mobile telephone number, which Brad is giving her, to the Operator: "Yes, Operator, that number is—"

ONE of the Teenagers is saying, "And the next thing we knew, this Hispanic guy in the rubber mask—I saw one just like it on sale in the Huckster's Room—was waving that gun in my face and saying, 'Get out of those costumes, *now!*' Then it got *really* bizarre 'cause he gives us each *five hundred bucks* for the costumes—and he says these are *deposits* in case he can't get them back to us!"

Anne, on the telephone to Grant: "Very well, Grant. I won't call anyone, if that's what Arthur wishes."

INTERCUT: Grant, in the station wagon.

"Just meet Arthur's private secretary at the Bonaventure."

"Brad and I are on our way," Anne says.

Grant hangs up.

Anne hangs up and turns to the teenager. "Is there anything else about them you can remember?"

ON THE ROOF of the Bonaventure Hotel, the same Bell Jet Ranger Helicopter that they took in from LAX is ready and waiting on the helipad.

"Sir," Chesterton says, "we should call the F.B.I. It's not your *place* to risk your Royal Person this way, and they're professionals—"

"No," Arthur says firmly. "I've had it up to here with 'professionals' of the sort that got us into this mess in the first place—and I'm *certainly* not going to leave this to the Americans, with things the way they've been lately. This is my *wife* and *son*, Chess—and it *is* very much my place to risk my life for them, as any man would."

"But you're the *Prince of Caterwaul*, Sir—not James Bond!"

Arthur pats Chesterton warmly on the shoulder. "My wife doesn't seem to be impressed by the Prince of Caterwaul very much. Perhaps she'd like being married to James Bond more."

"Sir, at least let me come with you—"

"I need you *here*, Chess, to coordinate communications for me. If a phone call comes in from the kidnappers, you're to forward it to me on the mobile telephone directly."

Arthur climbs into the helicopter, makes preparations, and starts the engine.

Chesterton crouches, cups his hands, and shouts, "Be *careful*, Sir!"

Arthur waves back.

Chesterton moves out of the way and the helicopter lifts off.

Nighttime AERIAL SHOT of traffic on Interstate 5, north of Burbank and still heading north. We are about 1,000 feet up and can see moderate-to-heavy traffic—mostly shadows and headlights of vehicles—below. It's almost ten o'clock, but this *is* a holiday weekend.

INSIDE THE BELL HELICOPTER. Prince Arthur is wearing a headset.

"Heller, this is Arthur again," he says.

INTERCUT:

Grant Heller, in his station wagon, speaking on the mobile phone. "Yes, Arthur."

"Just precisely how am I to locate you, Heller?"

"Can you see a freeway interchange where the Five Freeway crosses Highway One-eighteen?"

"Yes," Arthur says, seeing an interchange ahead.

"I'm coming up to that in a few seconds," says Heller. "I'll flash my lights as I'm coming past the interchange."

"Super," Arthur says.

Arthur flies to a spot just north of the interchange and hovers; a few seconds later he SEES a FLASH of HEADLIGHTS from below.

"I've got you spotted, Heller," Arthur says.

"Great," says Heller, "because I don't have *you* spotted, and if I don't, *they* don't. Do you see a yellow panel van a couple of cars ahead of me?"

"Yes."

"That's them," Heller says. "I'm going to try passing to get a closer look."

Heller pulls his station wagon from the Number Two Lane into the Number One, and begins passing cars. He puts his telephone down so it won't be seen, then pulls dead even with the Yellow Van and LOOKS IN.

He SEES Ana driving. Ana senses someone looking at her and LOOKS into the station wagon, SEEING Grant. There's no way for Grant to know it, but Ana was watching him on *Heller's Journal* and if she *recognizes* him, the tail could be blown.

Grant pulls a little farther ahead of the Van to give him a rearview mirror angle into the back. But it's too dark for him to see anything back there.

However, in the BACK OF THE VAN, Prince John CAN SEE a *by-now familiar* station wagon just ahead and to the left. John is about to *say something* about it, when Princess Susan *also* sees Grant's station wagon, and *catches her son's eye* in time to shake her head.

Carlos *sees* Susan, shaking her head—and Susan immediately starts rotating her neck around. "I've got a crick in my neck," she tells him.

Carlos buys it.

When nobody else is looking again, John nods to his mother.

Grant completes his pass of the Van without being recognized by the Arginian girl.

When Grant is several car lengths ahead of the Van, he picks up his phone again. "Arthur, are you with me?"

From above, Arthur says, "Yes, Heller."

"I could see a girl driving the van, but I couldn't see into the back."

"You're certain they haven't stopped anywhere?"

"Sure as shootin'," Heller says.

"I hope it doesn't come to that," Arthur says.

Inside the Hotel Office at the Bonaventure. Chesterton is talking with the SWITCHBOARD OPERATOR. "So I'll need a speakerphone up in the room directly," he says.

The Operator, "And if a call comes in for the Prince," she says, "you'll give me a signal, and I'm supposed to forward it to his mobile telephone?"

"That's correct," Chesterton says. "And be sure not to tell anyone about this."

The Operator nods.

Chesterton leaves. As soon as he's gone, she punches "0" on her board, and says, "Operator, would you please get me the F.B.I.? This is an emergency."

Back on Interstate 5, northbound. Heller's station wagon is now several hundred feet ahead of the Van.

FROM HIS VANTAGE POINT in the helicopter, Arthur sees the YELLOW VAN begin PULLING RIGHT before an exit.

"Heller," Arthur says, "I think the van is about to take the exit."

"State Highway Fourteen," Heller says, "leading into Kern County."

Heller starts pulling his station wagon right—still well ahead of the Van—and takes the exit.

A few seconds later, THE VAN EXITS also.

"What's up ahead of us?" Arthur asks from the helicopter.

"The Mojave Desert," Arthur HEARS Heller answer. "Edwards Air Force Base is up there—I've covered the Space Shuttle landings."

"My son tells me that he wishes to be an astronaut," Arthur says.

"So did I," Heller says. "For a while, I planned to go into the Air Force and try for the astronaut corps."

"Why didn't you?" Arthur asks.

"It turned out I was three inches too tall," Heller says. "But I haven't given up yet. They're going to be taking up journalists again soon."

"Somehow," Arthur says wistfully, "I think it's going to be a while before they take up princes."

The station wagon below and the helicopter above continue on into the night-blanketed desert.

Back at the Bonaventure. Anne MacIntosh has put Brad Heller to bed in Arthur's suite, and is waiting by the phone with Chesterton.

Suddenly, there's a LOUD KNOCK at the door.

Chesterton answers it.

A young F.B.I. AGENT flashes his identification. "Special Agent Powers," the Agent says, with a deep Southern accent. "I understand there's been a kidnapping?"

Chesterton hesitates a minute between personal loyalty to the Prince and his sense of duty, then nods and lets the Agent in.

CUT BACK TO:

Grant's station wagon. He passes a sign that says:

ENTERING KERN COUNTY and seconds later, THE STATION WAGON'S ENGINE begins to COUGH and DIE.

"Shit!" Grant says. Grant begins pulling his station wagon over to the right.

INSIDE THE VAN in the back, Susan and John SEE the station wagon pulling over and rolling to a stop. They look *worried*.

ARTHUR, from *his* vantage point in the helicopter, SEES Grant maneuvering his car over to the side. "Heller, what's wrong?"

Heller manages to pull his car all the way over to the right and rolls to a stop on the shoulder.

Then Heller sees his Fuel Empty light on.

"Arthur, I'm out of gas," Heller says. "Go on without me."

"No, I'll need you," Arthur says. "Be right down to pick you up."

CUT TO:

THE BELL JET RANGER landing. Heller gets in, and the helicopter TAKES OFF AGAIN. CUT TO:

THE HELICOPTER, back up to 500 feet.

Arthur flying ahead, sees a yellow van below. "There they are!" he says.

"Are you sure?" Heller asks.

"How many yellow vans are we likely to encounter this time of night on this highway?" Arthur asks.

CUT TO:

THE YELLOW VAN as it pulls into a Country & Western bar in the town of Rosamond.

Arthur pulls down low enough to see into the parking lot.

A MAN—looking like he punches cattle for a living—gets out from the driver's side.

"At least two," Heller answers Arthur's question, belatedly.

They've lost them.

INSIDE A DARK ROOM, as Carlos flips on a dim light then guides in Princess Susan and Prince John, still wearing their costumes and their hands still tied.

There is some equipment in here, but it's not easily recognizable.

Carlos unties Princess Susan and Prince John's hands, and motions Princess Susan to take the one chair in the room.

She takes it, and Prince John sits on her lap, looking exhausted.

"What are you going to do with us?" Susan asks Carlos.

"Ah, *Senora*—or is it now again *Senorita*?" Carlos asks.

"At the moment," Susan says, "it's still *Your Royal Highness*."

"As you wish," Carlos says. "Do not worry. No harm will come to you. It is bad enough that the world must see that we take you away by force. We do not need the world to see also that we hurt a woman and a child."

"How can I believe that," Susan says, "since you've allowed us to see your faces?"

"It does not matter," Carlos says, "because in a few days my sister, brothers and I will be known to the world as national heros."

"Who *are* you?" Susan asks.

"I am Carlos Rodriguez. The others are my younger brother, Andres, my still-younger brother, Eduardo, and my sister, Ana. We are from the Republic of El Arginine."

"And you expect money for our ransom?"

Carlos laughs—it is not an unpleasant laugh. "Senora—excuse, please—*Your Royal Highness*. We have no need of money. We have plenty money of our own. What we do, we do to honor the memory of our father, a naval officer killed ten years ago when your government sank our ship, *General Belligerent*, in what you call the 'Walkman Islands War' and we call the 'War to Liberate the Maltreated Islands.' We return you when the Wittish return the Maltreated Islands to our country."

"You must be *mad*," Susan says. "What makes you think the Wittish won't bring reprisals against your government for this?"

"Our government knows nothing of this. We do this on our own, for our people. We will tell the world this fact in a few days."

"You don't understand the Wittish mind," Susan says. "They would *never* pay such a ransom."

"In that case, Your Royal Highness," Carlos says, "then for a long time El Arginine will have a Princess and young Prince of its own."

Susan doesn't say anything.

Prince John lifts his head off his mother's shoulder and asks, "Do they have *avocados* in El Arginine?"

Carlos looks surprised. "Yes," he says.

Prince John wrinkles his nose. "Then I don't want to live there," he says.

At just about the same time, Arthur's helicopter is sitting on a strip of sand just off Highway 14, engine off. Prince Arthur and Heller are sitting. Waiting. And depressed as hell.

There is a long silence, which Heller finally breaks.

"What exactly does the Prince of Caterwaul do?" Heller asks him.

Arthur shrugs. "The truth be known, I'm little more than a glorified public relations man, most of the time."

"Ah," Heller says. "Keep you busy?"

"Too busy during the days," Arthur says, "often not busy enough at night."

"Pay you enough, do they?" Heller asks.

Arthur starts to answer ... realizes he's been caught with his own game ... and smiles.

His smile does not last long. His telephone rings.

He answers it, "Arthur."

WE INTERCUT:

Prince Arthur's Suite at the Bonaventure, Chesterton standing with Anne and several F.B.I. agents, next to a speakerphone. Special Agent Powers nods to Chesterton.

"Sir, this is Chesterton," the private secretary says. "We've got *them* on the line."

"Can you put them through to me?" Arthur asks.

"Yes," Chesterton says. "Stand by, Sir."

There is a long and terrible period of light static before the Hotel Operator puts the call through. The connection is made while Powers signals to begin tracing the call.

We HEAR Carlos on the phone: "Hello?"

"This is the Prince of Caterwaul. To whom am I speaking?"

"That does not matter now," Carlos says. "All you need to know is that we have the Princess and the young Prince."

"What do you want?" Arthur asks.

"We want what is rightfully ours," Carlos says. "You tell your mother the Queen to give us the Maltreated Islands back. We give you your Princess and Prince back."

Arthur hesitates a moment; this next statement is tricky. "I'll need proof that they're still alive," he says. "Let me speak to them."

"Wait," Carlos says.

There is another long moment of static; then: "Arthur, this is Susan."

"Have they hurt you?" Arthur asks.

"No, we're unharmed. We—"

The phone is pulled away. "That's enough," Carlos says.

"Now, my son," says Arthur.

A few seconds later: "Daddy?"

"John, how are you?"

"I'm well, Daddy, but I wish I had my computer, though they probably wouldn't let me use it around here anyway—"

The phone is pulled away again.

Carlos gets on again. "Stay at the Bonaventure. We will call you again on Monday."

The line disconnects.

We focus in on Arthur, sitting there trying to figure out what to do next. Heller is watching him, expectantly.

"'They probably wouldn't let me use it around here anyway,'" Arthur repeats.

"Use what?" Heller asks.

"His computer," Arthur says.

"He has his computer with him?" Heller asks.

"No, but he wishes he did, though he says 'They probably wouldn't—' Good heavens!" Arthur says, "I think that's *it*!"

"What's it?" Heller asks.

WE FLASHBACK to THE SCENE of Prince Arthur flying the helicopter with Prince John, Princess Susan, and the rest of their entourage to Heathcliff Airport for the trip to America. But *this time*, we WATCH THE SCENE from PRINCE ARTHUR'S POINT OF VIEW in the PILOT'S SEAT.

John opens his attache case to take out his computer, but Prince Arthur stops him. "You'll have to put that away," he tells his son.

"Why, Sir?" John asks.

"Regulations don't allow the use of electronics gear anywhere near aircraft—there's the possibility that it might interfere with navigation."

John shrugs and closes his attache case again.

BACK IN THE PRESENT, Arthur in the helicopter on the ground with Heller.

Arthur begins rummaging through a map box. "There *must* be a Sectional Chart for this region in here," he says—and he finds it: A Los Angeles Sectional Chart.

Arthur unfolds it. "There!" He points on the chart to Heller. "That's the only airport with a long-enough runway for a jet aircraft that they could have reached in the time period since we lost them."

Mojave Airport. A former military field.

"Why a jet?" Heller asks.

Arthur starts up the helicopter engines again.

"What would *you* use if you were about to abduct someone to South America?" he asks.

The helicopter rises again into the night sky.

BACK AT THE BONAVENTURE. Special Agent Powers on the telephone: "You got a trace on them? ... A pay phone at Mojave Airport. ... All right, *let's move it!*"

Special Agent Powers hangs up, then runs up to the hotel roof, where an F.B.I. helicopter is waiting for him.

Mojave Airport, Kern County, California.

It is close to midnight. The airport is dark and empty.

Almost empty, that is.

IN A GARAGE at the airport, Eduardo and Andres are breaking into a fuel truck with JET A written on the side. Eduardo is hot-wiring the engine while Andres is cutting the fuel valves with a bolt cutter.

Andres gets the valves cut just seconds before Eduardo gets the truck's engine going. Then Andres joins his brother in the truck and they drive it across the field to a HANGAR.

INSIDE THE HANGAR, as Eduardo drives the truck in, Ana is waiting with a LEAR 35 EXECUTIVE JET—about a six passenger job.

Andres and Eduardo jump out of the truck, and Andres begins fueling the jet.

Ana and Eduardo get into the jet, Ana in the pilot's seat, Eduardo in the co-pilot's seat.

Ana *inserts a key* into the console—they are *not* stealing the jet—then Ana and Eduardo—speaking Spanish—begin going through a preflight checklist.

Andres finishes fueling the jet, and turns the truck's engine off.

Eduardo gets out of the plane and says to Andres (in Spanish but subtitled English), "How much fuel?"

Andres (in Spanish) tells him.

Eduardo repeats the figure to Ana, then takes *American* money out of his pocket, counts out some and hands it to Andres.

Andres takes the money, puts it in an envelope, and *tapes it to the fuel truck's dashboard.*

Eduardo and Andres open the hangar doors.

Then the three of them get into the Lear 35 and Ana begins taxiing the jet across the field.

Carlos is returning Princess Susan and Prince John to the dimly lit room after the ransom call. Prince John is nearly sleep-walking in.

Susan looks pretty exhausted herself.

Carlos says to her, "Your Royal Highness, soon we will be on the airplane and we *all* will be able to—how you say?—'catch thirty winks.'"

"'Forty' winks," Susan says.

All the King's Horses

Carlos is quick; he shakes his head. "The seats are not *that* comfortable."

Susan smiles weakly.

A SHOT of the Lear 35 Jet taxiing to a halt near the AIRPORT CONTROL TOWER. A DIM LIGHT is VISIBLE in the tower.

FROM THE HELICOPTER with Prince Arthur and Grant Heller, WE SEE an AERIAL VIEW of the Tower. "That's odd," Arthur says. "The chart shows Mojave Airport as an uncontrolled field, yet there's a light on in the tower."

Then Arthur SEES the Lear 35 Jet taxiing to a halt near the tower and three DIMLY LIT FIGURES getting out of the plane.

Arthur lowers the helicopter enough for us to see that the three figures are Ana, Eduardo, and Andres.

Heller points at Ana. "That's the *girl* I saw in the van!" he tells Arthur.

"That's all I need to know," Arthur says.

Arthur flips on a powerful SEARCHLIGHT and begins swooping down toward the Arginians. "Heller, keep that *light* on them so they can't *see*," Arthur says.

ON THE GROUND, Eduardo sees the helicopter swooping down. He takes out his pistol and *begins shooting* up toward the light.

IN THE HELICOPTER. "They're *shooting* at us!" Heller says; but Arthur is already PULLING THE HELICOPTER up again.

A bullet whizzes through the helicopter, by providence not hitting anything vital.

Arthur *ignores* the bullet and hands Grant a microphone. "I need an American voice," Arthur says. "Tell them to surrender or we'll shoot them."

"We don't have any guns!" Heller says. *He* finds bullets whizzing by *harder* to ignore.

"They don't know that!" Arthur says.

Heller takes the microphone and presses the key on: "This is the F.B.I.!" his voice booms out.

WE CUT TO A VIEW UP AT THE HELICOPTER from the Arginians' VANTAGE POINT on the GROUND.

GRANT's AMPLIFIED VOICE, continuing:

"WE HAVE YOU SURROUNDED! *THROW DOWN YOUR WEAPONS AND SURRENDER!*"

Eduardo drops his gun, and the three of them put up their hands.

IN THE HELICOPTER, with the microphone off. "It worked!" Heller says.

FROM CARLOS'S POINT OF VIEW, LOOKING OUT the CONTROL TOWER WINDOW, he HEARS GRANT'S VOICE and SEES his brothers and sister surrendering—not to the F.B.I., but to a lone helicopter.

BACK ON THE RUNWAY, LOOKING UP.

Grant's voice: "LIE DOWN ON THE RUNWAY!"

Eduardo, Andres, and Ana lie down on the runway.

Arthur lands the helicopter and Heller jumps out, running over to grab Eduardo's gun. He holds it on the three Arginians.

Arthur cuts the helicopter engine and jumps out of the helicopter.

"Where *are* they?" Arthur asks the Arginians.

The Arginians don't say anything.

Grant waves the gun at them; but they are not about to dishonor themselves by turning in their brother.

Heller pauses a moment, still holding the gun on the Arginians, then says to Prince Arthur, "If *you* were abducting a Princess and Prince, where would *you* stash them?"

Arthur doesn't have to say anything aloud.

He looks up and sees the light on in the tower.

Arthur *runs up* the tower's staircase ...

And finds Carlos standing on a landing, blocking a door marked Battery Room.

Carlos does *not* have a gun.

"Ah, Your Royal Highness," Carlos says. "I do not think you are the F.B.I. after all."

Arthur climbs another few stairs.

"It's not 'Your Royal Highness,'" Arthur says. "The name's Bond. *James* Bond."

And Arthur climbs close enough for Carlos to aim a *kick* at him ... which Arthur *deflects*, knocking Carlos against the door.

The Battery Room door opens.

"Arthur!" Susan shouts.

"Daddy!" exclaims John.

Arthur climbs up the last step and the two men face each other on the landing as Susan and John watch.

Arthur puts his fists up in traditional boxing style.

Carlos puts his fists up, too ... and the two men begin fist-fighting at the top of the stairs.

Neither of them fights dirty; both are men of breeding and honor; they observe Marquess of Queensberry rules.

The fight goes on. Carlos hits Arthur in the face, almost knocking him down the stairs.

Arthur recovers, and knocks Carlos against the door—shoving it open.

The fight moves into the control room.

Susan and John watch as Arthur and Carlos go around each other—left jabs followed by right crosses.

Carlos catches Arthur with a left hook.

Arthur upper-cuts to Carlos's stomach.

The fight proceeds up a ladder to the roof of the Control Tower, and around an outside landing.

Arthur punches Carlos, almost knocking him off the tower—then grabs him and pulls him inside again; then a combination—jab, jab, jab, *right cross*—Carlos goes down for the count.

A Knock Out. Carlos doesn't get up again.

Susan throws herself into Arthur's arms.

They kiss. A *long* kiss.

They break, and Arthur runs his hands through John's hair.

Then Arthur says to Susan, "Shall we go *home* now, darling?"

Susan nods. "Please."

"Yay!" says John.

A few minutes later.

Susan and John following behind, Arthur pushes the now-recovered Carlos out of the tower to join his brothers and sister in front of the gun Grant is holding on them.

"What do you want to do with them?" Arthur asks Heller.

"Me?" Heller asks. "Why would *I* want them?"

"We can't fit them in the helicopter," Arthur says.

Princess Susan steps forward. "Arthur, let's let them go."

"What?" Arthur says.

"Do you want to spend the rest of our *lives* testifying in American courts?" the Princess asks.

Arthur ponders this for a second.

Then he takes the gun from Grant and says to Carlos, "I'll give you all of two minutes to climb into that airplane and fly out of here. If you're not airborne by then, I'm calling the American authorities."

Carlos smiles. "Thank you, 'Senor Bond.'"

Princess Susan, Prince John, Heller, and Carlos's brothers and sister all look at Carlos strangely, but Arthur nods in acknowledgement.

As Ana, Eduardo, and Andres climb into the Lear 35, Carlos stops for a moment and shouts back, "What about the Maltreated Islands?"

"I'll worry about *that* when I'm King," Prince Arthur shouts.

Carlos salutes and climbs aboard the Lear, which Ana already is starting up.

The Lear starts taxiing to take off position, then accelerates, rises, and disappears into the night.

AS SOON AS the plane is gone, SEVERAL F.B.I. HELICOPTERS *finally* arrive, and land. Special Agent Powers jumps out of one helicopter and runs over to the group. "Your Royal Highnesses? Where are the kidnappers?"

The Prince and Princess of Caterwaul, Grant Heller, and Prince John all look innocent. "What kidnappers?" Prince Arthur says.

Prince Arthur climbs into the Bell Helicopter's pilot's seat, with Princess Susan and Prince John in the back and Heller beside him.

As soon as Susan and John sit down, their heads start drooping, and they begin falling asleep.

Arthur lifts the helicopter off.

"You know, Heller," Arthur says, "I shall have to talk to the Queen about knighting you for this."

Heller smiles. "Sir Grant Heller," he says, trying it on for size.

Then Heller shakes his head firmly.

"I'm holding out for a title with land attached," he says. "Tell your mother I want to be a Duke."

Prince Arthur looks at Grant strangely. "A Duke!"

Then they both smile and the helicopter continues on into the night.

BRIGHT DAYLIGHT.
Heathcliff Airport, a Discorde jetliner landing.

A Royal Marching Band playing.

A Huge Banner:

WELCOME HOME!

A movable staircase is rolled up to the Discorde, a red carpet laid out, as Arthur, Susan, John, and Anne MacIntosh emerge from the plane, and the Royal Family wave to the crowds waiting for them.

Be it ever so Grand, there's no place like home.

THE END

Profile in Silver

I got the idea for "Profile in Silver" while driving to a lunch meeting with Robert Jaffe of Vista Films, the production company that was attempting to find a studio to finance *All the King's Horses*. Over lunch at Hamburger Hamlet in late 1983, I pitched Rob the idea as a feature and he loved it, but aside from sharing my notes with him, nothing concrete ever came of the pitch.

I also told the idea to my friend Alan Brennert and, two years later when Alan was on staff as executive story consulant for the revived *Twilight Zone*, and I was living in New Jersey, Alan phoned me and asked me if I could write my script for it at under an hour's length for the show. I said yes and Alan assigned me to write a story outline.

For the first time, I was officially employed as a Hollywood screenwriter. But I was still living 3,000 miles away, and that was a significant element in everything that followed.

"Profile in Silver" was controversial, inasmuch as nobody at that time had ever used the JFK assassination as a plot element in a TV show, or portrayed President Kennedy and his family in a fictional context. All previous portrayals of John F. Kennedy had stayed extremely close to real life, from *PT-109* to *The Missiles of October*.

How things have changed now! Oliver Stone's *JFK* portrayed the assassination from the point of view of New Orleans District Attorney, Jim Garrison, who believed in a conspiracy. *Quantum Leap* put us inside the body of Lee Harvey Oswald, and the series lead character, Sam Beckett, changes history by preventing Jackie Kennedy from being assassinated, also. The *X-Files* has the Cigarette Smoking Man assassinating JFK from an underground sewer and setting up Oswald as a patsy. NBC's short-lived, but excellent, series *Dark Skies* had JFK assassinated because he'd been told the truth behind the UFO landing at Roswell. I sometimes wonder whether any of these projects could have made it past industry executives if "Profile in Silver" hadn't been on CBS prime-time first.

Alan was concerned enough with the JFK element that I wrote two versions of the story, one with real names and history, and another version with what Alan and I called a "Greek Tycoon" approach, where the events and names were fictitious but close enough to reality that everyone would know what we were doing anyway. *The Greek Tycoon* had been a recent movie which had fictionalized Jackie's marriage to Aristotle Onassis using just that approach.

I wrote the outlines and Alan submitted them to Carla Singer, who was the executive at CBS Entertainment in charge of developing *The Twilight Zone* before it actually aired. Carla turned it down, on the grounds that using the JFK assassination as a plot element was in bad taste. Alan told me we would try again after the show was on the air and a different CBS executive was in charge of the show, and told me to develop a second story for the show in the meantime. I did, and it became "Colorblind."

Carla Singer turned that down, also. I was the only writer who had had any stories rejected, which caused Alan and Harlan Ellison, who was on the show as a creative consultant, to write several long memos to CBS complaining about being made to force the show into a straitjacket.

When *Twilight Zone* made it onto the CBS schedule, Carla Singer was replaced as overseer of the show by Tony Barr, who approved me to go to script on "Profile." But there were several story restrictions, the most emphatic was: the second assassin had to be removed from the story. Tony Barr's memo, which Alan read to me over the phone, said, "The CBS television network is not going to rewrite history."

Harlan wanted me to fight to keep the second assassin in, but there were other story elements I was more concerned about keeping in, most specifically, JFK's discussion of political power with Professor Fitzgerald on Air Force One. Alan fought for, and kept in, the story elements I most cared about.

I wrote two drafts of the script. I wrote the second draft after a telephone story conference with Alan, Harlan Ellison, story editor Rockne O'Bannon (who later wrote the movie *Alien Nation*), executive producer Phil DeGuere, and producer James Crocker.

Then, because of a production deadline, and my being 3,000 miles away where I couldn't meet their production needs, Alan did the final polish himself.

The main change that Alan introduced in his polish was taking the futuristic scenes from the beginning of my second draft and placing them in 1963. This was done because of the budget limitations on attempting to portray the Harvard campus 200 years in the future. I missed the parallel frame of having the story begin and end in the same future classroom, but Alan preserved a lot of that by beginning the story in a similar Harvard classroom in 1963, with Fitzgerald lecturing on inflation during the American revolution. Alan and I are both American Revolution history buffs, and Alan had pleasantly surprised me by taking a conversation the two of us had several weeks earlier and using my half of the conversation, almost verbatim, as Fitzgerald's lecture to his 1963 students.

Alan also felt that having Fitzgerald be too specific about the future in the Oval Office conversation with JFK was too distracting from the emotional content of the scene, so he cut that dialogue. It made the script less explicit about the author's political intent in writing the story, but dramatically stronger.

A word to budding writers: you have to be a top-level producer to have the control over your own screenwriting that a novelist takes for granted.

I flew to Los Angeles for the two-weeks filming of "Profile in Silver," and the experience was wonderful thanks initially both to the *Twilight Zone* production staff and director, John Hancock. John's major work has been as a stage and feature film director—*Bang the Drum Slowly*, *Weeds*, and *Prancer* among them.

John and I hit it off right away because my father is a violinist who had played ten years in the Boston Symphony, and John Hancock, a Harvard graduate himself, had been a violinist while at Harvard and had been concertmaster of the student orchestra at the Boston Symphony's summer residence, Tanglewood. I developed a warm relationship with him on the set, where he gave me a personal education in directing, with such wisdom as, "When the Director sits down, production comes to a halt."

John didn't sit down more than a couple of minutes for the entire shoot.

John invited me to stand as close to him as I wanted to during the entire shoot, and frequently consulted me about my opinion, in essence giving me authorial input into the final form of the production. John also invited me to discuss my interpretations on the scenes and characters with the actors.

I ran lines with Barbara Baxley, who had been cast as Dr. Kate Wang just 24-hours before her first scene, and hadn't yet had time to understand the time-travel elements of the story. Additionally, the character had been written for an Asian actress, but due to an error in the CBS casting memo describing the part, the talent agency representing most Asian actors had never sent over any Asian actresses in the right age-range to read for it. I improvised dialogue implying that "Wang" was a married name and Barbara added the words "a phrase my husband taught me" to cover the change in her ethnicity.

I also got a chance to discuss character elements both with Lane Smith, who played Professor Fitzgerald, and Andrew Robinson, who played JFK.

One of the first scenes filmed was the scene in Fitzgerald's office when Kate Wang materializes, and they discuss Fitzgerald's upcoming trip to Dallas. Lane was having trouble with his extensive speeches in that scene because Lane has a natural Southern accent which he was having to change to a Boston accent for the role. I suggested to him that he let his natural accent come out in the office scene, because it would be exactly like an actor coming out of a role for Fitzgerald to talk with someone from his own time. Lane took my suggestion, with John Hancock's approval.

I also got a chance to discuss my story intents with Andy Robinson before the scene between JFK and Professor Fitzgerald on Air Force One that set-up the entire emotional context of the story. Through interpretation, Andy was able to restore much of the meaning of my earlier drafts, even with JFK dialogue that was no longer explicitly in the Oval Office scene.

Many people have wondered why Andy Robinson, who had been best known as the bad guy Scorpio in the Clint Eastwood movie *Dirty Harry*, had been cast as JFK. Andy told me that he had played JFK, previously, replacing William Devane in the Broadway production of the satirical anti-war play, *MacBird.*

(Devane, who starred in *The Missiles of October* about the Cuban missile crisis, later went on to play a time-travelling historian in a TV movie who was trying to prevent the JFK assassination—but could never prevent it. That movie was based on a book written after my original 1983 outline for "Profile," and was produced after "Profile" had already been shown on CBS.)

There are several milestones in the production of "Profile in Silver" that are worth mentioning.

Profile in Silver   89

The first is that I wrote into both drafts of my script JFK delivering the speech he was scheduled to give on November 22nd, 1963 at the Dallas Trade Mart. As filmed, we hear the speech in the background on the car radio, as the secret service agent is accompanying Fitzgerald to Love Field to meet Kennedy. Andrew Robinson recorded the entire speech so that CBS sound editors could lay it in the background of that scene. To the best of my knowledge, it is the only time that the speech JFK never got to make has ever been delivered by anyone in a motion picture or theatrical production.

Also noteworthy about that speech is that CBS's broadcast standards department sent a note to the *Twilight Zone* production staff questioning the authenticity of the Dallas Trade Mart Speech. The note said the speech didn't sound like authentic JFK. How time changes our perceptions! I had gotten the Trade Mart speech from a book of JFK speeches, and it's what you would expect: a speech meant to kick off JFK's bid for re-election in 1964.

CBS broadcast standards didn't have a single question about the authenticity of the speech I have JFK give at the end of "Profile," in a Harvard classroom 200 years in the future. I made that speech up completely, but it was inspirational in tone—the way we remember JFK's speeches through the lenses of time.

I was also able to make use of a wonderful coincidence. November 22nd, 1963 was a Friday—and on the CBS schedule for that night, as usual in its 7:30 PM time slot, was the original Rod Serling *Twilight Zone*. All regularly scheduled programming for that night was pre-empted by the JFK assassination in the universe we lived through—but in the universe in which my futuristic history professor prevents the assassination, CBS decides to end its news coverage of the day's events just in time for that evening's airing of *The Twilight Zone*.

In the scene in the Treasury inspector's office where the secret service agent who found the Kennedy Half Dollar is having a fellow Treasury agent inspect the coin, we hear a special news bulletin cut back to regularly scheduled programming, and we hear the opening notes of the famous *Twilight Zone* theme just as the scene cuts to the Oval Office and JFK says he finds Fitzgerald being a Soviet spy "hard to believe."

Later, in the Dallas hospital scene after the assassination, in the filmed version, you can see a white-coated doctor looking directly into the camera for a moment. That doctor is Yours Truly, who submitted to a 1963-style short haircut just before the scene was filmed, so I could pull an Alfred Hitchcock. I was not overacting. John Hancock told me to look directly into the camera, and I was just doing what the Director told me.

As edited by John Hancock for broadcast, "Profile in Silver" came in at 26 minutes and 52 seconds. Scenes are short and cut quickly, so it plays more like a theatrical motion picture than an episode of a TV series. It took ten days to film and cost about $900,000 to produce—very expensive for a TV series in 1986. When commercials were inserted, it broke the half hour and came in at 35 minutes—which left the balance of the hour for "Button, Button," starring Mare Winningham.

USA Today ran a feature on "Profile in Silver" in its March 3, 1986 television column, and I was interviewed about the show by Gene Burns on a Boston radio talk show.

Lane Smith, who plays Professor Fitzgerald, went on to play Nixon in a TV biography, the prosecutor in *My Cousin Vinny*, and a corrupt senator in the Eddie Murphy comedy *The Distinguished Gentleman*. Lane also played Perry White on *Lois & Clark*.

Andrew Robinson, who plays JFK, can be seen (through a thick layer of theatrical appliances and makeup) as Garak, on *Star Trek: Deep Space Nine*. In an interview in *Psychotronic Video*, Andy Robinson spoke extensively about how much playing JFK in that episode meant to him, and how much he liked the script.

Alan Brennert, who bought the script and polished it, later shared an Emmy as Supervising Producer for *LA Law*, and is now writing feature film scripts and outlining a new novel.

And Carla Singer, who as the first CBS Executive in charge of the revived *Twilight Zone* turned down the story for "Profile in Silver"?

When she finally saw it, she changed her mind, and decided it was one of the best episodes.

CBS must have agreed: the hour containing "Profile in Silver" was the only one which they ran three times in prime time, before the show went into syndication, where it has run another dozen or so times in a half-hour edition.

That third airing of "Profile in Silver" was seen by the veteran TV producer who gave Rod Serling his first job in television. He thought my script was one of the few that carried the spirit of the original *Twilight Zone* series, and that's how I got the assignment for *The Mars Story*.

I have written two novels, short stories, and articles published in major magazines and newspapers. But the power of television is such that even a single episode of a series show that never got more than mediocre ratings after the first week or so has been seen by so many millions of people that it's probably the only thing of mine that most people have ever seen. The episode has been syndicated worldwide and sold on videotape overseas. I was in Paris just a few weeks before it was broadcast there.

It may only be 26 minutes and 52 seconds long, but if a writer has to be remembered for a single script, I'm delighted that the one I'm remembered for is "Profile in Silver."

Before you read the two drafts of the script that I wrote, here are the two versions of the story outline that I sent Alan Brennert.

Here's the first version with the real names used.

"Profile in Silver"

Screen Story
by J. Neil Schulman

JOSEPH K. FITZGERALD, PH.D.—a descendant of PRESIDENT JOHN FITZGERALD KENNEDY—is a 46-year-old Professor of American History teaching at Harvard University in the year 2163. Not a lot else has changed at Harvard 180 years from now but future scholars—particularly those with grants from Rand-Corporation- type think tanks—have a new means of studying their past: Time Travel. The lecture we see Dr. Fitzgerald delivering—while he nervously flips an old Kennedy Half Dollar—is before a Time Trip the Professor is about to make for his think tank to get a definitive answer to the question: Did Lee Harvey Oswald assassinate John F. Kennedy?

Dr. Fitzgerald makes preparations which involve putting on a Time Belt and donning a "homing device" disguised as a Harvard Class ring. Then, also taking along his Kennedy Half Dollar for luck, Fitzgerald de-materializes from the year 2163 and re- materializes—just seconds before the Presidential Motorcade arrives on November 22nd, 1963—in Dallas's Dealy Plaza. As soon as he is standing on the Grassy Knoll, Dr. Fitzgerald pulls out a small video camera to record everything: he zooms his focus in on the crucial window of the Texas School Book Depository Company and sees Lee Harvey Oswald inside with a rifle. The open Presidential limousine passes carrying the President, Jackie, and Governor John Connally. Fitzgerald points his camera toward the President's limousine and he sees, directly in front of him, A Second Gunman raising a pistol toward the back of Kennedy's head.

Fitzgerald forgets that he must remain only an observer and—reflexively trying to save Kennedy—rushes forward toward the Second Gunman. IN RAPID SEQUENCE: Fitzgerald shoves the Second Gunman as he fires; the bullet ricochets off the limousine harmlessly. Lee Harvey Oswald shoots from the Book Depository, wounding Texas Governor Connally. A Secret Service Agent throws himself onto the President: the assassination of John F. Kennedy has been prevented.

A second Secret Service Agent—seeing that Fitzgerald has saved Kennedy—grabs Fitzgerald and pulls him into the Presidential limousine, which then speeds off. The Agent tells President Kennedy: "This man just saved your life."

President Kennedy decides to return with Jackie to the White House immediately. Kennedy invites Fitzgerald to accompany them. Aboard Air Force One, President Kennedy and Fitzgerald find an immediate rapport when Kennedy sees that Fitzgerald is wearing a Harvard class ring; but Fitzgerald is evasive about why two Harvard men of the same age never met on campus—Fitzgerald finds himself having to invent an impromptu story for Kennedy about where he's from and what he does. As well, while Fitzgerald is enthralled by meeting Kennedy, he also knows that he interfered with History: the man he's liking so much is supposed to be dead. Troubled by conflicting emotions, Fitzgerald automatically resumes his nervous habit of flipping his Kennedy Half Dollar ... and during the landing turbulence, he misses catching the coin: it rolls away from him and he loses it, with no opportunity to look for it—the plane has landed. But as the President and Fitzgerald leave Air Force One, we see that a Secret Service Agent has found the coin, and is looking at Fitzgerald suspiciously.

Back in the Oval Office, Fitzgerald stays close to the President as an immediate crisis occurs: North Vietnam—with help from the U.S.S.R.—has launched an invasion into South Vietnam. The history professor looks on in horror as Kennedy begins making plans for War, knowing that this wasn't supposed to happen in 1963: history is on a wrong course, and it's his own fault.

But the trouble isn't only political: sudden and unexplained disasters are happening all over the world—earthquakes, volcanic eruptions, airliners crashing. It seems like the Apocalypse—the very fabric of time is ripping—and Fitzgerald knows that it's because Kennedy didn't die the way he was supposed to.

Meanwhile, the Secret Service Agent who found the Kennedy Half Dollar has done some investigating and—after diverting Fitzgerald—reports his suspicions to President Kennedy: there is no record for a "Joseph K. Fitzgerald" having attended Harvard, nor any Social Security files, tax files, draft files. Then the Agent shows Kennedy the Kennedy Half Dollar—which he reports having seen Fitzgerald lose. Kennedy looks at the Half Dollar and sees his own profile on the coin. The Agent tells Kennedy that even though it's impossible on the face of it—not only is the coin dated 1964, the next year, but it's against the law for U.S. coins to depict a living person—this half dollar meets all standards of the U.S. Government mint: it seems to be genuine.

After Kennedy and Fitzgerald are again alone together in the Oval Office, Kennedy confronts Fitzgerald with his lies and shows him the Half Dollar ... and Fitzgerald confesses the truth to Kennedy: he's a time traveler and one of Kennedy's descendants. A few lovely moments as Fitzgerald tells Kennedy a little bit about the future he helped create. Then Kennedy thinks aloud—handling the coin—and looks at the date again. "Under the law," Kennedy repeats what the Agent told him, "the living cannot be depicted on money of the United States, and this coin is dated next year ..." Suddenly, Kennedy realizes that he was supposed to die in Dallas ... and that all these worldwide disasters are happening because he's still alive.

Kennedy goes to a shelf and picks up a copy of his book, *Profiles in Courage,* stares at it thoughtfully for a few seconds, then tells Fitzgerald: "I've got to go back. Can you take me back?" Fitzgerald, practically in tears, nods.

Fitzgerald explains to Kennedy that Kennedy must put on the Time Belt—it's set to take him back to the moment of the assassination and will automatically merge him back into the proper time stream. "Then how will you get back to the future?" Kennedy asks ... and Fitzgerald explains that his Harvard Class Ring is really an emergency homing device ... if he's separated from the Time Belt for more than a few minutes, it automatically sends him back to 2163.

Kennedy nods and says grimly, "Let's get this over with." While Kennedy is putting on the Time Belt, he turns his back on Fitzgerald for a second ... and Fitzgerald slugs President Kennedy.

A replay of the Kennedy Assassination in Dallas. The time stream is repaired: Fitzgerald is no longer on the Grassy Knoll to stop the Second Gunman. This time, the assassination proceeds as we remember—the screaming, the confusion, the Presidential motorcade speeding off to Dallas's Parkland Memorial Hospital.

Then, a scene at Parkland Memorial Hospital, after President Kennedy has been declared dead. A Doctor in private conference with a high-level Government Official, as the body lies under a sheet on a nearby gurney. The Doctor: "Of course there were serious head wounds, but—"

The Government Official shakes his head. "You don't understand—the country has been traumatized by this enough without raising questions about that body. The man over there is John F. Kennedy—got it?"

The Doctor raises the sheet ... and we see that the face on the slain body is Joseph K. Fitzgerald.

We jump forward in time to the lecture hall at Harvard, in 2163, where we first saw Fitzgerald lecturing, and we pan along the students as they listen to another lecture on American history, given in a familiar voice by a man wearing a Harvard Class ring. The CAMERA PANS AROUND:

And the man giving the lecture is John F. Kennedy.

The End

And here's the second "Greek Tycooned" version I did.

DAVID K. LANCASTER PH.D.—a descendant of U.S. PRESIDENT ADAM LANCASTER KENSINGTON—is a 46-year-old Professor of American History teaching at Harvard University in the year 2163.

Profile in Silver

Not a lot else has changed at Harvard 180 years from now but future scholars—particularly those with grants from Rand-Corporation- type think tanks—have a new means of studying their past: Time Travel. The lecture we see Dr. Lancaster delivering—while he nervously flips an old Kensington Half Dollar—is before a Time Trip the Professor is about to make for his think tank to get a definitive answer to the question: On October 23, 1963, in Long Beach, California, was Oscar Lynn Harrison the lone assassin who fatally shot President Adam L. Kensington?

Dr. Lancaster makes preparations which involve putting on a Time Belt and donning a "homing device" disguised as a Harvard Class ring. Then, also taking along his Kensington Half Dollar for luck, Lancaster de-materializes from the year 2163 and re- materializes—just seconds before the Presidential Motorcade arrives on October 23rd, 1963—onto Long Beach's Ocean Boulevard. As soon as he is standing on the street, Dr. Lancaster pulls out a small video camera to record everything: he zooms his focus in on the crucial window of the General Telephone Office Building and sees Oscar Lynn Harrison inside with a rifle. The open Presidential limousine passes carrying the President, the First Lady Chantale Kensington, and California Governor Cobden. Lancaster points his camera toward the President's limousine and he sees, on the street directly in front of him, A Second Gunman raising a pistol toward the back of Kensington's head.

Lancaster forgets that he must remain only an observer and—reflexively trying to save Kensington—rushes forward toward the Second Gunman. IN RAPID SEQUENCE: Lancaster shoves the Second Gunman as he fires; the bullet ricochets off the limousine harmlessly. Oscar Lynn Harrison shoots from the Telephone Building, wounding California Governor Cobden. A Secret Service Agent throws himself onto the President: the assassination of Adam L. Kensington has been prevented.

A second Secret Service Agent—seeing that Lancaster has saved Kensington—grabs Lancaster and pulls him into the Presidential limousine, which then speeds off. The Agent tells President Kensington: "This man just saved your life."

President Kensington decides to return with Chantale to the White House immediately. Kensington invites Lancaster to accompany them. Aboard Air Force One, President Kensington and Lancaster find an immediate rapport when Kensington sees that Lancaster is wearing a Harvard class ring; but Lancaster is evasive about why two Harvard men of the same age never met on campus—Lancaster finds himself having to invent an impromptu story for Kensington about where he's from and what he does. As well, while Lancaster is enthralled by meeting Kensington, he also knows that he interfered with History: the man he's liking so much is supposed to be dead. Troubled by conflicting emotions, Lancaster automatically resumes his nervous habit of flipping his Kensington Half Dollar ... and during the landing turbulence, he misses catching the coin: it rolls away from him and he loses it, with no opportunity to look for it—the plane has landed. But as the President and Lancaster leave Air Force One, we see that a Secret Service Agent has found the coin, and is looking at Lancaster suspiciously.

Back in the Oval Office, Lancaster stays close to the President as an immediate crisis occurs: North Vietnam—with help from the U.S.S.R.—has launched an invasion into South Vietnam. The history professor looks on in horror as Kensington begins making plans for War, knowing that this wasn't supposed to happen in 1963: history is on a wrong course, and it's his own fault.

But the trouble isn't only political: sudden and unexplained disasters are happening all over the world—earthquakes, volcanic eruptions, airliners crashing. It seems like the Apocalypse—the very fabric of time is ripping—and Lancaster knows that it's because Kensington didn't die the way he was supposed to.

Meanwhile, the Secret Service Agent who found the Kensington Half Dollar has done some investigating and—after diverting Lancaster—reports his suspicions to President Kensington: there is no record for a "David K. Lancaster" having attended Harvard, nor any Social Security files, tax files, draft files. Then the Agent shows Kensington the Kensington Half Dollar—which he reports having seen Lancaster lose. Kensington looks at the Half Dollar and sees his own profile on the coin. The Agent tells Kensington that even though it's impossible on the face of it—not only is the coin dated 1964, the next year, but it's against the law for U.S. coins to depict a living person—this half dollar meets all standards of the U.S. Government mint: it seems to be genuine.

After Kensington and Lancaster are again alone together in the Oval Office, Kensington confronts Lancaster with his lies and shows him the Half Dollar ... and Lancaster confesses the truth to Kensington: he's a time traveler and one of Kensington's descendants. Then Kensington thinks aloud—handling the coin—and looks at the date again. "Under the law," Kensington repeats what the Agent told him, "the living cannot be depicted on money of the United States, and this coin is dated next year ..." Suddenly, Kensington realizes that he was supposed to die in Long Beach ... and that all these worldwide disasters are happening because he's still alive.

Kensington tells Lancaster: "I've got to go back. Can you take me back?" Lancaster, practically in tears, nods.

Lancaster explains to Kensington that Kensington must put on the Time Belt—it's set to take him back to the moment of the assassination and will automatically merge him back into the proper time stream. "Then how will you get back to the future?" Kensington asks...and Lancaster explains that his Harvard Class Ring is really an emergency homing device...if he's separated from the Time Belt for more than a few minutes, it automatically sends him back to 2163.

Kensington nods and says grimly, "Let's get this over with." While Kensington is putting on the Time Belt, he turns his back on Lancaster for a second...and Lancaster slugs President Kensington.

A replay of the Kensington Assassination in Long Beach. The time stream is repaired: Lancaster is no longer on Ocean Boulevard to stop the Second Gunman. This time, the assassination proceeds as history remembers—the screaming, the confusion, the Presidential motorcade speeding off to Long Beach Memorial Hospital.

Then, a scene at Long Beach Memorial Hospital, after President Kensington has been declared dead. A Doctor in private conference with a high-level Government Official, as the body lies under a sheet on a nearby gurney. The Doctor: "Of course there were serious head wounds, but—"

The Government Official shakes his head. "You don't understand—the country has been traumatized by this enough without raising questions about that body. The man over there is President Adam L. Kensington—got it?"

The Doctor raises the sheet ... and we see that the face on the slain body is David K. Lancaster.

We jump forward in time to the lecture hall at Harvard, in 2163, where we first saw Lancaster lecturing, and we pan along the students as they listen to another lecture on American history, given in a familiar voice by a man wearing a Harvard Class ring. The CAMERA PANS AROUND:

And the man giving the lecture is Adam L. Kensington.

The End

The Twilight Zone
Profile in Silver
by J. Neil Schulman

First Draft

FADE IN

EXT. CAMPUS - HARVARD UNIVERSITY - 2163 A.D. - DAY

SERIES OF SHOTS and SUPERIMPOSED TITLES—
"HARVARD UNIVERSITY - 2163 A.D."—
to establish. Even almost two centuries in the future, Harvard still has ivy-covered buildings and students running late to class—or taking advantage of warm, sunny weather to study outside. The only obvious indication of a future century—aside from odd clothing and hairstyles—is that after a group of students climb into a beat-up car and rev the engine, the car shoots off *vertically*.

INT. "DEPARTMENT OF HISTORY" LECTURE HALL

and this, too, has changed little. Students are seated at tablet armchairs listening to a lecture. That is, those students who aren't catching up on sleep or secretly finishing work for their next class.

Delivering the lecture is their professor, DR. JOSEPH K. FITZGERALD, a handsome man in his mid-forties, whose suit and hairstyle is obviously *professorial*, but still, somehow, futuristic. While he lectures, as a nervous habit, Fitzgerald is flipping a silver coin in his hand.

FITZGERALD
Living today in worldwide freedom, peace, and
prosperity, it's almost impossible for us to
comprehend political violence two centuries

ago. The Twentieth Century was a time of
world wars, brushfire wars—the everpresent
threat of nuclear war. Genocide, riots,
hijackings, tyranny—political terrorism. But
there was one event which encapsulates the mad
violence of that period: the assassination in
November, Nineteen-sixty-three of the American
President, John F. Kennedy.

A STUDENT wearing a LETTER SWEATER raises his hand with perhaps a touch of arrogance. Fitzgerald recognises him.

LETTERMAN
Your *ancestor*, Professor Fitzgerald?

FITZGERALD
Yes, I am proud to say. While I can hardly
expect you to approve the politics of that
insane era, John Fitzgerald Kennedy rose above
the insanities of his time by being a man of
vision and a man of courage. Most important
to *you*, John F. Kennedy was a *Harvard* man.

STUDENTS laugh appreciatively.

When they stop, Fitzgerald waves his hand in an odd way; suddenly the lights dim and WE SEE FILM PROJECTED behind him: STOCK NEWS FOOTAGE of that fateful day in Dallas—the motorcade, the shots, screams, the limousine tearing out into traffic.

FITZGERALD
(continuing over film)
There have always been unanswered questions.
Was Lee Harvey Oswald the assassin? Was there
a conspiracy? Did this relate to other
political killings of that era—Diem of
Vietnam, Robert Kennedy, Martin Luther King?
Until now, we could only speculate.

Fitzgerald pauses, then resumes flipping his coin nervously.

FITZGERALD
(continuing)
After trying for six years, my historical-research grant from the Rand Institute has come through. I leave for the past tonight. In the next lecture, I hope to bring you some firsthand answers.

As Fitzgerald continues lecturing, his VOICE FADES AND WE HEAR:

NARRATOR
Dr. Joseph Kennedy Fitzgerald, a Professor of History at Harvard ... descendant of a man who graduated Harvard and went on to make some of the history the Professor teaches. In a few hours, Dr. Fitzgerald will make a journey back in time to a fateful day in history ... November twenty-second, Nineteen-sixty three. Dr. Fitzgerald is searching for an ending to a history lesson. But the ending he finds will go beyond history ... it will go beyond politics ... it will stretch the limits of human courage. Perhaps it will stretch even the boundless dimensions of ...

CLOSE ON THE COIN

as it drops into Dr. Fitzgerald's hand. WE SEE that it is a 1964 KENNEDY HALF DOLLAR.

NARRATOR
(continuing)
... The Twilight Zone.
CUT TO:

ESTABLISHING SHOT *"RAND INSTITUTE FOR TEMPORAL*

STUDIES" - NIGHT

a formidable-looking hi-tech glass-and-steel office complex, still active at night, its sign also glowing in the darkness.

EXT. "TEMPORAL DISPLACEMENT PLATFORM" - NIGHT

which looks like a sports arena during a night game, with a floodlit riser at its center—the PLATFORM. But except for two TECHNICIANS sitting at a control console near the Platform, it is vastly empty.

We follow Dr. Fitzgerald—now styled and dressed in a suit-and-tie appropriate for 1963—as he walks toward the Platform with DR. KATE WANG, a distinguished, Chinese woman in 2163 garb.

On a table near the Platform are a MAN'S LEATHER BELT with a rectangular buckle, a SIGNET RING, A WALLET, AN ANALOG WRISTWATCH, and what looks to be a 1963 MODEL 8-MILLIMETER MOVIE CAMERA. Wang shows Fitzgerald the Belt first—it matches his 1963 suit.

> WANG
> We've imbedded the temporal displacement
> circuit inside the belt, and hidden the
> control panel in its buckle. Proper I.D. in
> the wallet. The wristwatch is your computer.

Dr. Fitzgerald puts the Wallet into his jacket, then starts putting on the Wristwatch and the Belt.

> FITZGERALD
> Will it tell time?

> WANG
> That's a very old joke.

> FITZGERALD
> Sorry. Where have you hidden the emergency
> homing circuit?

WANG
In a Harvard signet ring. If the displacement
circuit in the belt fails or is separated from
the ring it will home back here directly.
We've set it on five minutes failsafe.

Dr. Fitzgerald nods, placing the Ring on his right hand. Wang hands Fitzgerald the "Movie" Camera. He straps it over his shoulder.

WANG
An F-minus-infinity retina, auto-zoom with
three-sixty peripheral. Only a fifty gigabyte
disk, but you won't need more. Ready?

FITZGERALD
I've been ready for the last six years.

WANG
Feel lucky you're going at all. After the
Sodom and Gomorrah meltdown, our insurance
premiums tripled.

Fitzgerald's only reaction is to frown and step onto the Platform.

Dr. Wang joins the Technicians at the control console. The console starts to VIBRATE with the force of great amounts of energy being gathered; the Platform starts to PULSE in changing colors.

CHIEF TECHNICIAN
Dr. Wang, I read a few grams unexpected mass.

WANG
What is it, Joe?

FITZGERALD
A family keepsake—a good luck charm.

Fitzgerald reaches into a jacket pocket and pulls out his

KENNEDY HALF DOLLAR. Dr. Wang walks up to the platform and examines it.

WANG
It's dated one year after your destination.
Against policy.

FITZGERALD
But not strictly forbidden. No anachronisms found in any historical document. I ran a full search.

He puts the COIN back into his jacket.

WANG
(wary)
Don't get involved back there, Joe. You're an historian. Stick to your job.

FITZGERALD
(smiles)
What are you worried about, Kate? Afraid I'm a revisionist?

WANG
(seriously)
Frankly, yes. You have a very Chinese view of ancestor worship.

She steps back to console and nods to the Chief Technician.

CHIEF TECHNICIAN
(to Wang)
All circuits test positive ... Tachyon modulation positive ... Phasing five point five nominal ... Plasma bottle charged ... Displacement on command—*Ready.*

WANG

Go.

The Chief Technician nods to the Second Technician who pulls a lever.

CHIEF TECHNICIAN
Energized.

On the Platform, Dr. Fitzgerald flashes *bright red*.

CHIEF TECHNICIAN
(continuing)
... We have temporal coherence.

Suddenly, Dr. Fitzgerald *shrinks to infinity* and a super-powerful laser beam shoots up from the platform to the starlit night sky, punching a hole in Time.

FLASH CUT TO:

EXT. DEALY PLAZA - DALLAS - NOVEMBER 22, 1963 - JUST BEFORE 12:30 PM

as *Dr. Fitzgerald materializes* on the sidewalk near the Grassy Knoll, just as the Presidential motorcade is approaching.

A TEXAN does a double-take as Fitzgerald pops in next to him.

TEXAN
(to Fitzgerald)
Where in Sam Hill did *you* come from?

FITZGERALD
(off-handed)
Boston.

Before the Texan can get any further into it, Fitzgerald lifts his "movie" camera up to his eye and starts recording. The Texan goes back to watching the approaching motorcade.

FITZGERALD'S POV THROUGH RANGEFINDER

VARIOUS SHOTS as he ZOOMS IN ON the open Presidential limousine and sees (our actor) PRESIDENT JOHN F. KENNEDY.

[NOTE: for reasons that will become apparent later, the two Actors playing KENNEDY and FITZGERALD should bear strong physical resemblance.]

To the President's left—*our* actors—JACKIE KENNEDY (in her famous pink suit), on the jumpseat in front of JFK, TEXAS GOVERNOR CONNALLY. SECRET SERVICE AGENT GREER is driving the limo,

SECRET SERVICE AGENT KELLERMAN is on Kennedy's right.

SECRET SERVICE AGENT RAY KINGMAN is walking alongside the Presidential limo, on Fitzgerald's side of the street.

Additional limousines follow in the motorcade with more Secret Service, VICE PRESIDENT LYNDON JOHNSON (our actor), press and dignitaries.

Crowds line the street, waving flags, shouting greetings to the President.

A "DALLAS POLICEMAN" (our actor) steps into Fitzgerald's POV and *pauses*.

Fitzgerald ZOOMS CLOSE IN on the crucial window of the TEXAS SCHOOL BOOK DEPOSITORY COMPANY, and WE SEE (our actor) LEE HARVEY OSWALD *taking aim with a rifle on the Presidential limousine.*

FITZGERALD'S POV - *IN RAPID SEQUENCE*

THE "DALLAS POLICEMAN" *is surreptitiously—with his pistol still holstered—raising his pistol.*

Oswald FIRES his rifle, hitting Texas Governor Connally—the SOUND of the SHOT is *delayed*.

Profile in Silver: First Draft

The "Policeman" now has his still-holstered pistol *aimed directly at JFK's head.*

SMASH CUT TO:

RAPID SEQUENCE - FITZGERALD AND THE "POLICEMAN"

as Fitzgerald drops his camera onto its shoulder strap and instantly realizes—*emotionally*—that the man in front of him is *not* a Dallas policeman but a Second Assassin—and *this* assassin is about to murder John F. Kennedy.

To Fitzgerald, for the first time, this is no longer the dispassionate study of the long-dead past: this is happening *now*. He *hesitates*, realizing that he's just an observer, then the emotional pain becomes too great.

FITZGERALD
NO!

And with that bellow, Fitzgerald leaps forward onto the disguised gunman just as he FIRES.

RAPID SEQUENCE - SECRET SERVICE AGENT KINGMAN

as he HEARS Fitzgerald's shout and spins around just as the "Policeman" FIRES, to SEE Fitzgerald jump him.

RAPID SEQUENCE - FITZGERALD AND "POLICEMAN"

As Fitzgerald tackles him, the "Policeman's" GUNSHOT is redirected away from Kennedy's head and *impacts harmlessly on the limo.*

RAPID SEQUENCE — SCREAMING BYSTANDERS

At the SOUND of the two GUNSHOTS.

RAPID SEQUENCE - IN LIMO - AGENT KELLERMAN

as he *throws himself* onto JFK and Jackie.

Agent Kingman and ANOTHER AGENT arrive at the spot where Fitzgerald has tackled the "Policeman". KINGMAN *grabs* Fitzgerald and pulls him toward the President's limo; the other Agent holds the assassin.

RAPID SEQUENCE - KINGMAN AND FITZGERALD

AGENT KINGMAN
(shouting to
Fitzgerald)
Come on!

RAPID SEQUENCE - THE PRESIDENTIAL LIMO

as Kingman pulls Fitzgerald onto the Presidential limousine just as everyone realizes that Governor Connally has been shot.

KENNEDY
(to agent driving)
The Governor has been hit! Get him to a
hospital!

AGENT GREER
(driving; to radio)
I'm pulling out!

LONG ON THE LIMO

as it pulls out of the motorcade and accelerates.

BACK IN SPEEDING LIMO

as Kingman and Fitzgerald are settled in the front seat, quietly TALKING to each other in the b.g. WE SEE Fitzgerald reach into his jacket, take out the Wallet, and hand a 1963 Harvard "Faculty I.D.

Card" to Agent Kingman.

> AGENT GREER
> (continuing; to radio)
> Alert Parkland Memorial Hospital that the
> Governor will be there in four minutes.

President Kennedy nods, satisfied, then notices Agent Kingman and Fitzgerald.

> KENNEDY
> (to Kingman)
> Mr. Kingman, who is this man?

> AGENT KINGMAN
> Mr. President, this is Dr. Joseph Fitzgerald,
> one of your constituents from Harvard. He
> just saved your life.

KENNEDY AND FITZGERALD

as they *look at each other for the first time.*

> KENNEDY
> (warmly)
> Dr. Fitzgerald, Harvard, and I, are in your
> debt.

CLOSE ON FITZGERALD

as he *realizes* the full impact of what he has done.

CUT TO:

EXT. EMERGENCY ENTRANCE - PARKLAND MEMORIAL HOSPITAL - DAY

as the limousine pulls up. A stretcher crew immediately takes the wounded Governor out.

JFK gestures to Agent Kellerman that he wishes to get out of the limousine, but Jackie stops him.

JACKIE
You can't do any good in there, Jack.

The others wait expectantly for a moment while JFK decides, then Kennedy nods determinedly.

KENNEDY
(to Greer)
Mr. Greer, radio ahead to the Dallas Trade
Mart. I'll speak as scheduled.

AGENT GREER
Yes, sir.

CUT TO:

INT. THE DALLAS TRADE MART

where President John F. Kennedy is delivering the luncheon address that history had never intended him to give.

Dr. Fitzgerald stands on the sidelines, an historian still, recording it all in his "camera."

KENNEDY
We in this country, in this generation are—by
destiny rather than choice—the watchmen of
the walls of world freedom. We ask,
therefore, that we may be worthy of our power
and responsibility—that we may exercise our
strength with wisdom and restraint—and that
we may achieve it in our time, and for all
time, the ancient vision of peace on Earth,
goodwill toward men.

MASSIVE LUNCHEON AUDIENCE (FROM STOCK FOOTAGE)

There is APPLAUSE.

CLOSE ON FITZGERALD'S FACE

as he realizes that Kennedy's vision was destined to be fulfilled—but will it be, now that history has been changed?

PRESIDENT KENNEDY AGAIN

KENNEDY
(continuing)
That must always be our goal—and the righteousness of our cause must always underlie our strength. For as was written long ago: "Except the Lord keep the city, the watchman waketh but in vain."

As APPLAUSE greets the end of Kennedy's speech, we

CUT TO:

SIDE WINGS OF TRADE MART

As JFK, Jackie, Vice President Johnson, Fitzgerald, and the rest of the Presidential entourage are walking out.

AN AIDE rushes up to the Vice President and addresses Johnson *frantically*.

JOHNSON AIDE
(breathless)
Mr. Vice President, we've got more problems! Tornadoes have sprung up all around the state! One is heading *here*, another just ripped its way through downtown Austin, and another just hit your ranch!

JOHNSON
(grimly, to Aide)
Better get the choppers ready, son.

The Aide runs off.

JOHNSON
(continuing; to Kennedy)
Mr. President, if I were you, I'd hightail it back to Washington and mind the store. It looks like fate is set on spoiling our barbecue tonight.

FITZGERALD

He *knows* it's not fate that's doing this.

ALL AGAIN
KENNEDY
(tersely)
Take care of your people, Lyndon. Let me know how I can help.

JOHNSON
Yes, Mr. President.

Johnson rushes out. Kennedy turns to Fitzgerald.

KENNEDY
Dr. Fitzgerald, I can use an extra Harvard professor in my Brain Trust right now. Are you free to be my guest at the White House?

FITZGERALD
(shocked)
Uh, *yes*, sir.

KENNEDY
Then let's get going. This is turning out to

be "one of those days."

As they rush out of the Trade Mart, we

CUT TO

EXT. (LOVE) AIR FIELD - STORM - AFTERNOON

as strong rain and winds surround AIR FORCE ONE while it takes off.

STOCK FOOTAGE - TORNADOES

As they wind their way through Texan cities.

EXT. AIR FORCE ONE - BREAKING ABOVE CLOUDS - AFTERNOON

to ESTABLISH.

INT. AIR FORCE ONE - IN FLIGHT

this time, not carrying a flag-draped casket and a just-sworn-in new president, but with JFK still alive and well.

Jackie is sitting forward, being interviewed by a reporter.

Kennedy is sitting catercorner to Fitzgerald in a living room area. Both men have drinks. Agent Kingman is seated nearby, reading.

AN AIDE comes up to the President.

PRESIDENTIAL AIDE
Mr. President, news out of Texas is bad.
Parts of Dallas, San Antonio, Austin—gone.
Hundreds dead, more missing. The Lieutenant
Governor is requesting federal disaster
relief. The only *good* news is that Parkland
Memorial was untouched. Governor Connally is

out of surgery in stable condition.

KENNEDY
Thank God for that, at least. Okay, get the paperwork going. I want disaster relief on my desk before I go to bed tonight.

PRESIDENTIAL AIDE
Yes, sir. One more thing. In addition to the fake policeman Dr. Fitzgerald apprehended, Dallas police arrested a man named Lee Oswald. They've charged Oswald not only with shooting the Governor, but with murdering a Dallas police patrolman.

Kennedy nods seriously.

KENNEDY
Thank you.

The Aide leaves. The historian from the future can't resist asking.

FITZGERALD
Mr. President, do you have any idea—

KENNEDY
(interrupting)
Jack. Men who've saved my life call me "Jack."

FITZGERALD
(delighted)
"Jack."...I'm "Joe" to everyone but my students.

KENNEDY
Good name. My Dad's name. Also my late brother's.

FITZGERALD
(emotionally)
I ... know.

KENNEDY
You were asking something?

FITZGERALD
(nods)
If you have any idea who would have reason to shoot at you?

Kennedy takes a sip of his drink before answering.

KENNEDY
Considering the awesome power wielded by the President, who *wouldn't*? Two centuries ago, the Founding Fathers tried to set things up so we wouldn't have a king anymore. Now, because we're always a pushbutton away from war, the President has been stuck with more power than any king in history. It's no wonder my administration has been called "Camelot."

FITZGERALD
Like King Arthur, you had to *win* your office. It must gratify you, no?

KENNEDY
What gratified me was getting the world through the Cuban Missile Crisis in one piece. Providence was with us that time. But Scripture tells us to "put not your trust in princes." Maybe someday people will take that good advice.

FITZGERALD
(drily)
That would leave you unemployed.

KENNEDY
This job gives me few moments of great joy.
I'll tell you, Joe, after I'm out of office
what I'd best like to do is help you Harvard
professors find a way to beat nuclear bombs
into plowshares.

FITZGERALD
(with certainty)
A century from now, nuclear bombs will power
rocket ships.

KENNEDY
(nods)
We've studied that idea. But how do you
prevent enemy nations from regarding nuclear
rockets as weapons?

FITZGERALD
(offhanded)
Insurance companies. Next century, people
will replace nation-states with insurance
companies.

KENNEDY
(laughs)
You have a wicked sense of humor, Joe. I'll
have to tell that one to Senator Goldwater
when I see him.

Fitzgerald is puzzling out that remark when the Aide returns.

PRESIDENTIAL AIDE
Mr. President, there's a radiophone call for
you from Defense Secretary McNamara.

KENNEDY
(rising)
Excuse me. (still chuckling) Insurance companies.

Profile in Silver: First Draft 117

The President gets up and walks aft, leaving Dr. Fitzgerald alone with his thoughts. Without thinking, Fitzgerald sticks his hand into his jacket pocket, pulling out his *Kennedy Half Dollar*, and automatically starts to flip it in his hands.

Suddenly, the plane is hit by turbulence, and Fitzgerald *misses* catching the coin. The coin *rolls* to where Agent Kingman is sitting.

Agent Kingman *sees* the coin, and looks up to meet Fitzgerald's frantic gaze; Fitzgerald looks away quickly. Kingman picks the coin up.

CLOSE ON KINGMAN

as he *sees* what the coin is.

KINGMAN AND FITZGERALD

As Kingman—seeing Fitzgerald trying to look innocent—realizes that this *must* be Fitzgerald's property.

AFT AGAIN

as President Kennedy returns to the seat next to Fitzgerald, JFK passes his Aide and waves him over.

KENNEDY
(quiet but urgently)
Listen carefully. I've just placed our
Strategic Forces on Yellow Alert. Set up an
Emergency Cabinet meeting for tonight at ten.
Rusk is on a plane to Japan—see if you can
get him back. Tell Bundy, Taylor, Sorensen.
And Bobby! But act normally and do it
quietly—I don't want the press onboard to
know anything's wrong.

PRESIDENTIAL AIDE
Yes, sir.

As the Aide leaves, Kennedy straps himself in again and turns to Fitzgerald, likewise speaking quietly but with urgency.

KENNEDY
How familiar are you with the history of our Berlin situation?

FITZGERALD
Completely. My specialty is this era.

Fitzgerald sees Kennedy's confusion and corrects himself quickly.

FITZGERALD
I mean this *area*. Why do you ask?

KENNEDY
Soviet troops just captured West Berlin. The Russian premier is demanding we pull our forces out of the rest of Germany or they'll kill every American *in* Berlin.

FITZGERALD
(shocked)
But Khrushchev never would have *done* that!

KENNEDY
(nods with finality)
Premier Khrushchev was assassinated today.

On Fitzgerald's *startled* look, we

CUT TO

EXT. AIR FORCE ONE - ON THE GROUND - AFTERNOON

as the door opens. The Secret Service, JFK and Jackie, Fitzgerald, the Warrant Officer with the "Black Bag," and the rest of the entourage begin deplaning.

AGENT KINGMAN

as he watches Fitzgerald getting into the Presidential limousine with the Kennedys, then LOOKS DOWN again at the mysterious Kennedy Half Dollar. Kingman slips the coin into his pocket then walks up to another SECRET SERVICE AGENT.

AGENT KINGMAN
I need to do some research at Treasury before
it closes. Can you spare me?

The Agent nods.

THE PRESIDENTIAL LIMOUSINE

as it departs.

CUT TO

EXT. THE WHITE HOUSE - THE LIMOUSINE ARRIVING - AFTERNOON

as JFK and Jackie get out of the limousine first and two children run to meet them: six-year-old CAROLINE and three-year-old JOHN, JR.

CUT TO

CLOSE ON THE COIN

as we see it being held in a man's hand.

WIDER - INT. OFFICE - AFTERNOON

as Agent Kingman is sitting across a desk from another TREASURY MAN.
The T-MAN is looking at the coin through a watchmaker's loupe screwed into his eye, then removes the loupe and leans back in his chair.

TREASURY MAN
Remarkable. Utterly remarkable. I've never seen counterfeit work this faithful to Mint standards. Whoever did this is a real artist.

AGENT KINGMAN
Then it *is* a counterfeit? It's not something our Mint has in the works for next year?

TREASURY MAN
Of course not. How could it be? Other countries stamp reigning sovereigns on their coins, but it's against U.S. law to mint the image of any *living* person.

AGENT KINGMAN
Could it be a practical joke of some sort? Or a prototype of a campaign handout? Maybe one of the President's brothers ... or the Republicans ...

TREASURY MAN
I doubt it very much. They'd have to *know* it's a felony ... and possibly treason, since it implies President Kennedy is going to die by Sixty-four. This man who lost it ... you *saw* him save the President's life?

AGENT KINGMAN
Absolutely. Or I wouldn't have allowed him anywhere near the President until his credentials had been confirmed.

TREASURY MAN
And were they?

AGENT KINGMAN
(nods)

I checked during the President's speech.
Matched Fitzgerald's prints with FBI. Clean.
Checked Harvard, Internal Revenue, the Army.
All in order. But that's the really odd
thing. The *documents* are all there, but I
can't find anyone who's ever heard of
Fitzgerald. It's like somebody got into the
records and just dropped him in. And *yeah*, I
checked with CIA. They've never heard of him.

TREASURY MAN
It wouldn't be the first time the Company
didn't tell us about one of their Spooks.

AGENT KINGMAN
Maybe. Still, this Harvard professor is
Johnny-on-the-Spot to save the President's
life ... he loses a coin that shouldn't exist
... he's got three of the President's family
names ... he even *looks* like the President.
Now, with a crisis more dangerous that Cuba
coming on, the President is confiding in this
stranger like a long-lost brother. If you ask
me...

Suddenly, the office starts *shaking violently* with a rolling motion Californians are too familiar with ... but that shouldn't be happening in Washington D.C.

An earthquake. Lamps fall over, fixtures swing ...

Kingman and the T-Man both jump up, startled out of their wits.

AGENT KINGMAN
My God ... an earthquake in *Washington*?

CUT TO

INT. OVAL OFFICE - THE WHITE HOUSE - SAME TIME

as JFK sits behind his desk talking on the telephone ... and the earthquake hits *here*, too.

Kennedy drops the phone and jumps to his feet ... and by doing so saves his life again as a massive BOOKSHELF *topples onto his chair where he was sitting.*

The Presidential Aide runs into the Oval Office in a flash, as the RUMBLING DIES AWAY.

PRESIDENTIAL AIDE
Sir, are you all right?

KENNEDY
I'm fine! Find out if my kids are okay!

The Aide runs out. Kennedy pulls the phone out from under some books and picks up the receiver again.

KENNEDY
You still there, Bobby? (beat) You're damn
right we felt it here! (beat) Yeah, I'll
talk to you later.

The President hangs up just as the Aide returns.

PRESIDENTIAL AIDE
Nobody hurt, sir ... the children weren't even
really frightened. I'm afraid the First Lady
isn't doing quite as well ... we just lost
half her favorite bone china.

KENNEDY
(almost smiling)
Tell her to break out the paper plates!
(more serious)
What the Devil is going on today?

PRESIDENTIAL AIDE
I don't know, sir. But my father's a minister and I can bet you his sermon this Sunday is going to be on the Apocalypse ... if we make it to Sunday.

PRESIDENT KENNEDY

as he wearily drops his face into his hands. HOLD on him, then

CUT TO

INT. WHITE HOUSE GUEST BEDROOM - FITZGERALD

as he turns a lamp upright again then starts talking to his Wristwatch Computer, rubbing his back as if it's been injured.

FITZGERALD
Resume program ... Last parameter, three-times-ten-to-the-ninth non-parallel vectors. Compute time-line status.

WRISTWATCH
(Voice like HAL 9000)
After pressure release by tornadoes at intervention site, Stable Two was achieved by Khrushchev assassination.

FITZGERALD
Stable, my aching back! What about the earthquake just now?

WRISTWATCH
Shockwave backwash from first intervention in time line. No major effects.

FITZGERALD
All right, then. With Khrushchev assassination as Stable Two, give me worst-

and-best-case outcomes on this time-line, with
assigned probabilities.

WRISTWATCH
Worst-case scenario: Three-hundred megaton
nuclear exchange between the Superpowers
within nine days, resulting in total
annihilation of biosphere. Probability:
seventy-seven percent. Best-case scenario:
surrender of Western Europe to the Soviet
Union within six years, resulting in collapse
of Soviet economy. In desperation, Soviets
blackmail West for food, West is provoked into
agro-bacterial war between the Superpowers,
resulting in total annihilation of biosphere
within century. Probability: twelve percent.

FITZGERALD
There's only an *eleven* percent possibility of
avoiding total war on this time-line?

WRISTWATCH
Three percent. Eight percent
includes all other scenarios leading to—

FITZGERALD &
WRISTWATCH
—Total annihilation of biosphere.

GIRL'S VOICE (O.S.)
Why are you talking to your watch?

Fitzgerald looks up, startled.

IN DOORWAY - CAROLINE

as she walks into

GUEST ROOM - FITZGERALD AND CAROLINE

FITZGERALD
Because it gives me smarter answers than I get from most people.

CAROLINE
You should talk to my Daddy instead. He gives me smart answers on *everything*.

FITZGERALD
(smiling wistfully)
Yes, I'm sure he does.

JACKIE'S VOICE (O.S.)
Caroline, dear! It's time for your dinner!

CAROLINE
(answering)
I'll be right there, Mommy!
(to Fitzgerald)
I talk to my pony Macaroni, sometimes. But I never get any answers. See ya!

Caroline ducks out.

Fitzgerald checks the corridor, then resumes talking to his Wristwatch, more quietly.

FITZGERALD
Since this time-line is non-viable, give me all options for repairing *original* time-line.

WRISTWATCH
There exists only one viable option for repairing original time-line. The assassination of President John F. Kennedy must occur as history originally recorded.

ON FITZGERALD'S HORROR

as the thoughts of the little girl he just met—and the answers she gets only from her "Daddy"—hit him hard. He drops his face into his hands *exactly like JFK did.*

CUT TO

INT. THE OVAL OFFICE - NIGHT

JFK is alone, in his famous ROCKING CHAIR, puffing on a cigar and thinking. A TELEVISION next to his desk is on in the b.g., a CBS TELEVISION SPECIAL NEWS REPORT.

ANCHORMAN (ON TV)
—certainly an indication of a conspiracy by
Soviet hard-liners. However, the tornadoes in
Texas and the earthquake in the Capital would
certainly have to be put down to one of those
unbelievable coincidences that you meet so
often in the news business.

There is a knock at the office door. (TV SOUND continues UNDER.)

KENNEDY
Come in!

Agent Kingman enters.

KENNEDY
Hi, Ray. (Indicates chair) Take a load off.
Want a drink?

AGENT KINGMAN
Thank you, sir, but I'm still on duty.

KENNEDY
I won't tell on you.

Kingman remains standing and smiles...letting us know that this is a game the two of them have played before.

> AGENT KINGMAN
> Mr. President, I have some concerns about Dr. Fitzgerald. I've checked with Harvard, and even though they have him in their records as a full professor on sabbatical, nobody there has ever heard of him. It's possible that Dr. Fitzgerald is a spy.

> KENNEDY
> For who?
> (with terror)
> *Yale?*

> AGENT KINGMAN
> (used to being
> straight-man)
> I don't know for who, sir, but I wouldn't eliminate the Soviets. I can't think of a better way to get an agent close to the President than to set up an assassination and have your man save the President's life.

> KENNEDY
> (shakes head)
> I know people, and Joe Fitzgerald is no Soviet spy. Also, the Soviets are subtler than that ... if they wanted to pull something this big they'd use sleeper agents who'd been in place for twenty years.

> AGENT KINGMAN
> There's more, sir.

Kingman reaches into his pocket, pulls out the KENNEDY HALF DOLLAR, and hands it to Kennedy.

AGENT KINGMAN
(continuing)
Dr. Fitzgerald lost this on Air Force One.

CLOSE ON KENNEDY - IN PROFILE

as he LOOKS at HIS OWN FACE IN PROFILE on the half dollar.

KENNEDY
I think someone is taking this Camelot stuff a bit too far.
(beat; more seriously)
All right. You'd better get Fitzgerald in here.

STANDING IN DOORWAY - FITZGERALD

Fitzgerald has his "camera" strapped over his shoulder.

FITZGERALD
I was already on my way here, Mr. President.

OVAL OFFICE - ALL

In the b.g., WE HEAR

CBS ANNOUNCER
—This concludes this CBS News Special Report. We now return to our regularly scheduled programming.

Kennedy gestures Fitzgerald into the office.

KENNEDY
Dr. Fitzgerald, were you part of an assassination conspiracy in Dallas today?

FITZGERALD

No, sir, I was not. But I knew about the assassination before I came to Dallas.

AGENT KINGMAN
(to Kennedy)
Excuse me, sir.
(to Fitzgerald)
Where did you get that coin?

FITZGERALD
It's been in my family for almost two hundred years.

KENNEDY
You'll pardon me if I say that's a little unbelievable.

IN THE B.G.., we HEAR the original "Twilight Zone" THEME MUSIC and:

ROD SERLING'S VOICE
There is a fifth dimension beyond that which is known to man. It is a dimension as vast as space and as timeless as infinity. It is the middle ground between light and shadow— between science and superstition—

FITZGERALD
(gesturing toward TV)
People of your generation should have paid more attention to the classics.

KENNEDY
My generation? You're the same generation as me!

Fitzgerald walks over to the TV set.

ROD SERLING'S VOICE

—And it lies between the pit of man's fears and the summit of his imagination. It is an area which we call—

Fitzgerald switches off the set just *before* we hear the words "The Twilight Zone." Then he faces his ancestor directly.

FITZGERALD
No, Mr. President, I am not. I am of a generation that won't be your age for another two-hundred years. I am a time-traveler from the future ... and your direct descendant by two converging lines.

KENNEDY
(concern)
Dr. Fitzgerald, the matters we are discussing are much too serious for you to joke about them.

FITZGERALD
I'm not joking, sir.

Fitzgerald picks up his camera.

In a split-second, Agent Kingman has his gun out, pointed at Fitzgerald.

FITZGERALD
(calmly)
This isn't a weapon.

Fitzgerald points his "camera" toward the wall—*away from* both Kennedy and Kingman—and turns it on.

IN FRONT OF WALL - KENNEDY GIVING SPEECH
AT TRADE MART

in a Full-size, 3-D, Full-color and Sound Playback.

KENNEDY HOLOGRAM
We in this country, in this generation are—by
destiny rather than choice—the watchmen of
the walls of world freedom. We ask,
therefore, that we may be worthy of our power
and responsibility—

KENNEDY AND AGENT KINGMAN

as they *watch* this phenomenon, open-mouthed.

KENNEDY HOLOGRAM
—that we may exercise our strength with
wisdom and restraint—and that we may achieve
it in our time, and for all time, the ancient
vision of peace on Earth, goodwill toward men.

ALL AGAIN

Fitzgerald turns the "camera" off and the Kennedy Hologram *disappears*.

Kingman holsters his pistol again. After a pause, he speaks first.

AGENT KINGMAN
Mr. President, request permission to go off
duty, sir.

KENNEDY
Granted. For both of us, also.

Kingman immediately goes over to the liquor and pours three stiff drinks. He hands one each to Kennedy and Fitzgerald.

FITZGERALD
(to Kennedy;
automatically)
Your health.

He has time to ponder his remark as the three men drink.

Fitzgerald and Kingman draw up chairs. Kennedy breaks the tension in the room.

KENNEDY
(to Fitzgerald)
Insurance companies, huh?

FITZGERALD
(smiles)
That's only a transitional phase. By my time we've put together a social system I'm sure you'd consider much-more bizarre than that. But we *have* achieved your dreams. We've eliminated war, poverty, and tyranny. Your dream of humankind moving into space has become a reality ... I took my graduate degree out near the orbit of Jupiter.

KENNEDY
I never thought humanity would achieve that sort of Utopia.

FITZGERALD
It's not even close to being Utopia, sir. We've taken the Biblical advice about not putting our trust in princes, but we *haven't* beaten our swords into plowshares. We just finally got it through our skulls that it's safer to avoid princes with big swords.

Kennedy gets up (Kingman and Fitzgerald rise immediately) and JFK starts pacing near his desk. He is still holding the Kennedy Half Dollar and he looks at it thoughtfully.

KENNEDY
You come from the future. Did you come back

to tell me what I'm supposed to do about the
Berlin crisis today?

FITZGERALD
No, sir.
(suddenly choked up)
I ... didn't know about that.

KENNEDY
(surprised)
Didn't *know*? How could you not know?

Kennedy looks at the Coin one more time.

ZOOM IN ON THE COIN'S DATE - *1964*

WIDER AGAIN

as Kennedy sees it and *suddenly realizes what it means.*

KENNEDY
You came to Dallas to observe an
assassination. *My* assassination.
(almost swooning)
Dear God in heaven.

Kennedy looks down and sees—on his desk where the earthquake left it—a copy of his book, *Profiles in Courage*.

KENNEDY
This Berlin crisis would be the end of the
world, wouldn't it?

Fitzgerald nods.

Kennedy picks up *Profiles in Courage*, then puts in down again, firmly. When he speaks again, it's with the firm resolve of a P.T. boat commander.

KENNEDY
You're *here*, which proves that it wasn't.
You'll have to take me back. Can you take me
back? Can you make it like it was intended to
be?

Fitzgerald drops his head forward. Then he looks up again and removes his Harvard Signet Ring, extending it toward Kennedy.

FITZGERALD
You'll have to put this ring on.

KINGMAN
(alarmed)
Mr. President!

KENNEDY
Agent Kingman, stay out of this!

FITZGERALD
(beat)
If there's anyone you need to say goodbye to—

KENNEDY
(gently)
I couldn't make myself leave them if I did.
And they wouldn't remember, would they?

President Kennedy takes the ring, closes his eyes, and slips the ring onto his right hand.

KENNEDY

as he flashes, on-and-off, bright red, and
freezes in place.

WIDER AGAIN

KINGMAN
What's happening to him?

FITZGERALD
You've taken an oath to protect the life of "Lancer."

KINGMAN
Only Secret Service know that code name for President Kennedy!

FITZGERALD
Yes.

Kingman *understands*.

KINGMAN
What do we have to do?

FITZGERALD
(after pause)
We've got to go back.

After several *long beats*,

CUT TO

EXT. DEALY PLAZA - DALLAS - NOVEMBER 22, 1963 - JUST BEFORE 12:30 PM

just as the Presidential motorcade is approaching.

THE TEXAN

watching the approaching motorcade. This time Fitzgerald is nowhere around.

VARIOUS SHOTS

on the open Presidential limousine, AS BEFORE.

AGENT KINGMAN

as before, walking alongside the Presidential limo, but suddenly—momentarily—he *FLASHES BRIGHT RED.*

VARIOUS SHOTS

Additional limousines follow in the motorcade.

Crowds line the street, waving flags, shouting greetings to the President.

The "Dallas Policeman" steps forward and *pauses.*

ZOOM CLOSE IN

on the crucial window of the TEXAS SCHOOL BOOK DEPOSITORY COMPANY, and WE SEE (our actor) LEE HARVEY OSWALD *taking aim with a rifle on the Presidential limousine.*

RAPID SEQUENCE - THE "DALLAS POLICEMAN"

surreptitiously—*with his pistol still holstered—raising his pistol.*

RAPID SEQUENCE - OSWALD

as he FIRES his rifle, hitting Texas Governor Connally—the SOUND of the SHOT is *delayed.*

RAPID SEQUENCE - THE "POLICEMAN"

as he now has his still-holstered pistol *aimed directly at JFK's head.*

RAPID SEQUENCE - LONG ON THE PRESIDENTIAL LIMOUSINE

as *WE SEE a FLASH OF RED LIGHT surrounding the limousine.*

RAPID SEQUENCE - THE DISGUISED GUNMAN

just as he FIRES.

RAPID SEQUENCE - SCREAMING BYSTANDERS

At the SOUND of the two GUNSHOTS.

RAPID SEQUENCE - AGENT KINGMAN

as he jumps onto the Presidential limousine.

RAPID SEQUENCE - FRONT SEAT OF
THE PRESIDENTIAL LIMO

AGENT GREER
(driving; to radio)
The President's been hit! I'm pulling out!

RAPID SEQUENCE - LONG ON THE LIMO

as it pulls out of the motorcade and accelerates toward the hospital.

CUT TO
INT. SIDE ROOM - PARKLAND MEMORIAL HOSPITAL

as a gurney holds A SLAIN BODY COVERED BY A SHEET.

Agent Kingman is next to the gurney in conference with an EMERGENCY ROOM DOCTOR.

DOCTOR
Of course there *were* serious head wounds, but
still, that doesn't account for—

AGENT KINGMAN
Use *logic*, Doctor. It couldn't *be* anyone else

...and the country will be traumatized enough
without raising silly questions about the face
on that body. This man *is* President John F.
Kennedy—*got it?*

The Doctor pulls back the sheet on the body ... and we

ZOOM IN ON

THE SERENE FACE OF DR. JOSEPH K. FITZGERALD.

CUT TO

INT. LECTURE HALL - HARVARD - 2163 A.D. - DAY

as WE SEE THE BACK of a man dressed in 2163 garb, delivering a lecture—in a wholly distinctive voice—to the HISTORY CLASS.

LECTURER
History records many facts ... some of them
right, some of them wrong. But let the record
show that, in any age, good or bad, there are
men of high ideals ... men of courage ... men
who do more than that for which they are
called upon.

CLOSE ON THE LECTURER'S HAND

as WE SEE that on it is A HARVARD SIGNET RING.

LECTURER
(continuing)
You will not always know their names. But let
their deeds stand as a monument, so that when
the human race is called to judgment, we may
say—this, too, was humanity.

REVERSE POV

and WE SEE that the MAN delivering the lecture is JOHN F. KENNEDY.

THE STUDENTS

as they RISE TO THEIR FEET IN APPLAUSE, WE HEAR:

NARRATOR
A fitting tribute of the sort only to be found
in ... The Twilight Zone.

FADE OUT

The Twilight Zone
Profile In Silver
by J. Neil Schulman

Second Draft

FADE IN

INT. LECTURE HALL - HARVARD UNIVERSITY - 2163 A.D.

Superimposed Titles—*Harvard University - 2163 A.D."*—to establish. Not a lot has changed in almost two centuries—the only obvious differences are odd clothing and hairstyles. Students are seated at tablet armchairs listening to a lecture. That is, those students who aren't catching up on sleep or secretly finishing work for their next class. Delivering the lecture is their professor, Dr. Joseph K. Fitzgerald, a handsome man in his mid-forties, whose suit and hairstyle is obviously *professorial*, but still, somehow, futuristic. While he lectures, as a nervous habit, Fitzgerald is flipping a Silver Coin in his hand.

    FITZGERALD
It's almost impossible for me to convey to you
the sheer insanity of what I've learned living
two centuries in the past. The Twentieth
Century was a time of world wars, brushfire
wars—the everpresent threat of nuclear war.
Genocide, riots, hijackings, tyranny—
political terrorism. But the event I will
witness next encapsulates the mad violence of
that period: the assassination of the American
President, John F. Kennedy. Kennedy had risen

above the insanities of his time by being a
man of vision and a man of courage—which
shouldn't surprise any of you since John
Fitzgerald Kennedy was a *Harvard* man.

As Students laugh, Fitzgerald continues lecturing; his Voice Fades and
We Hear:

NARRATOR
Dr. Joseph Kennedy Fitzgerald, a Professor of
History at Harvard in both our distant future
and our immediate past ... descendant of a man
who graduated Harvard and went on to make some
of the history the Professor teaches.
Shortly, Dr. Fitzgerald will make one final
journey back in time to a fateful day in
history ... November twenty-second, Nineteen-
sixty-three. Dr. Fitzgerald will be searching
for an ending to a history lesson. But the
ending he finds will go beyond history ... it
will go beyond politics ... it will stretch
the limits of human courage. Perhaps it will
stretch even the boundless dimensions of ...

CLOSE ON THE COIN

as it drops into Dr. Fitzgerald's hand. We See that it is a 1964 Kennedy Half Dollar.

NARRATOR
(continuing)
... The Twilight Zone.

CUT TO:

EXT. CAMPUS - HARVARD UNIVERSITY - 2163 A.D. -
EARLY EVENING

Profile in Silver: Second Draft 143

Even almost two centuries in the future, Harvard still has ivy-covered buildings and students running late to class—or taking advantage of warm, still-sunny weather to study outside. We track Dr. Fitzgerald as he walks through campus with Dr. Kate Wang, a distinguished, older Chinese woman. Fitzgerald is obviously a campus celebrity; as they walk along, Students call out things like, "Good luck, Dr. Fitzgerald!" and "Have a good trip, Professor!"

WANG
It's always hard to leave the past behind,
Joe. Particularly hard when a field
historian such as you has spent years in a
particular age building a second life—
learning to live as they did, making friends
… perhaps even falling in love.

FITZGERALD
(shakes head)
Kate, it's not that at all. I haven't even
come near making attachments in the past. How
can you get close to people when you can never
share with them anything of what you really
think? When you can't even say that your
favorite ice cream flavor won't be concocted
for another fifty years—that the "authentic"
performance of the Brandenberg Concertos
they're raving about would have made Bach roll
on the floor laughing?

WANG
Then what *is* bothering you? It's not that
ancestor worship of yours again?

Fitzgerald's silence let's Wang know that it is.

WANG
(continuing)
I don't know how you missed being born
Chinese.

FITZGERALD
It's just so *frustrating* spending years back
there, getting myself established at Harvard,
and never having been allowed to get close to
him. I never met him alive and now I'm
supposed to go back and watch him ...

Fitzgerald's voice trails off.

WANG
You don't have to do this yourself. We can
send someone else.

FITZGERALD
(shakes head)
No. This is *my* project, Kate. I conceived
it, I got the funding for it, I'm the one who
spent years in the past getting ready for it.
I'll be the one to see it through to the end.

As Wang nods, the two of them arrive at:

EXT. BUILDING - "RAND LABORATORIES -
DEPARTMENT OF TEMPORAL STUDIES"

a formidable-looking hi-tech glass-and-steel building; the door
opens automatically as they approach.

FITZGERALD
(continuing)
I'll meet you out at the Platform as soon as
I'm finished with wardrobe and styling.

Dr. Wang nods again. As they go in, we

CUT TO

EXT. "TEMPORAL DISPLACEMENT

PLATFORM" - NIGHT

which looks like a sports arena during a night game, with a floodlit riser at its center—the Platform. Two Technicians sit at a control console near the Platform. Students are seated over to one side as observers, not unlike medical students watching surgery in a teaching hospital. We follow Dr. Fitzgerald—now styled and dressed in a suit-and-tie appropriate for 1963—as he walks toward the Platform with Dr. Wang, who is still dressed in 2163 garb.

On a table near the Platform are a Man's Leather Belt with a rectangular buckle, a Signet Ring, an Analog Wristwatch, and what looks to be a 1963 model 8-millimeter movie camera. Wang hands Fitzgerald the Belt first—it matches his 1963 suit.

WANG
(to Students)
We've imbedded the temporal displacement
circuit inside the belt, and hidden the
control panel in its buckle. The wristwatch
is Dr. Fitzgerald's computer.

Dr. Fitzgerald starts putting on the Belt and the Wristwatch.

A Student calls out,

STUDENT
Will it tell time?

Other Students laugh.

WANG
That's a very old joke.

Wang holds up the Signet Ring.

WANG
(continuing)
The emergency homing circuit is in this

Harvard signet ring. If the displacement
circuit in the belt fails or is separated from
the ring it will home back here directly.

Wang hands Dr. Fitzgerald the Ring and slips it onto his right hand.

Wang hands Fitzgerald the "Movie" Camera. He straps it over his shoulder.

WANG
(continued)
An F-minus-infinity retina, auto-zoom with
three-sixty peripheral. Only a fifty gigabyte
disk, but Dr. Fitzgerald won't need more.
(to Fitzgerald)
Doctor?

FITZGERALD
(to Students)
This trip will comprise multiple
displacements, each lasting only seconds, as I
record from every possible event-locus. By
this procedure, we will finally have a
definitive answer to the question: "Was Lee
Harvey Oswald really the assassin of President
John F. Kennedy?"

Dr. Wang looks at Fitzgerald; Fitzgerald nods and steps onto the Platform.

Dr. Wang joins the Technicians at the control console. The console starts to Vibrate with the force of great amounts of energy being gathered; the Platform starts to Pulse in changing colors.

CHIEF TECHNICIAN
Dr. Wang, I read a few grams unexpected mass.

Dr. Wang walks up close to the Platform and speaks softly so only Fitzgerald can hear her.

WANG
What is it, Joe?

FITZGERALD
(also softly)
A family keepsake—a good luck charm.

Fitzgerald reaches into a jacket pocket and pulls out his Kennedy Half Dollar. Dr. Wang examines it.

WANG
It's dated one year after your destination.
Against policy.

FITZGERALD
But not strictly forbidden. No anachronisms
found in any historical document—I checked.
And I'll only be there for a few minutes this
time.

Wang nods. Fitzgerald puts the Coin back into his jacket. Wang steps back to console and nods to the Chief Technician.

CHIEF TECHNICIAN
(to Wang)
All circuits test positive ... Tachyon
modulation positive ... Phasing five point
five nominal ... Plasma bottle charged ...
Displacement on command—*Ready.*

WANG
Go.

The Chief Technician nods to the Second Technician who pulls a lever.

CHIEF TECHNICIAN
Energized.

On the Platform, Dr. Fitzgerald flashes *bright red*.

CHIEF TECHNICIAN
(continuing)
... We have temporal coherence.

Suddenly, Dr. Fitzgerald *shrinks to infinity* and a super-powerful laser beam shoots up from the platform to the starlit night sky, punching a hole in Time.

FLASH CUT TO:

EXT. DEALY PLAZA - DALLAS - NOVEMBER 22, 1963 - JUST BEFORE 12:30 PM

as Dr. Fitzgerald materializes on the sidewalk just as the Presidential motorcade is approaching.

A Texan does a double-take as Fitzgerald pops in next to him.

TEXAN
(to Fitzgerald)
Where in Sam Hill did *you* come from?

FITZGERALD
(off-handed)
Cambridge.

Before the Texan can get any further into it, Fitzgerald lifts his "movie" camera up to his eye and starts recording. The Texan goes back to watching the approaching motorcade.

FITZGERALD'S POV THROUGH RANGEFINDER

As he Zooms in on the open Presidential limousine and sees (our actor) President John F. Kennedy. [Note: for reasons that will become apparent later, the two Actors playing Kennedy and Fitzgerald should bear strong physical resemblance.] To the President's left—

Profile in Silver: Second Draft   149

our actors—Jackie Kennedy (in her famous pink suit), on the jumpseat in front of JFK, Texas Governor Connally. A Secret Service Agent is driving the limo, another Secret Service Agent is on Kennedy's right.

Additional limousines follow in the motorcade with more Secret Service, Vice President Lyndon Johnson (our actor), press and dignitaries.

Secret Service Agent Ray Kingman is walking alongside the Second Limo (the one carrying additional Secret Service) on Fitzgerald's side of the street.

Crowds line the street, waving flags, shouting greetings to the President. A Dallas Policeman steps into Fitzgerald's POV and pauses.

Fitzgerald shifts his POV through Rangefinder, toward the Texas School Book Depository Company.

Fitzgerald Zooms Close In on the crucial window of the Book Depository, and We See (our actor) Lee Harvey Oswald taking aim with a rifle on the Presidential limousine.

FITZGERALD

as he lowers the "camera" and touches his Belt Buckle.

FLASH CUT TO

INT. BOOK TOWER

as Fitzgerald pops in behind Oswald and raises his "camera."

THROUGH RANGEFINDER - CLOSE ON TRIGGER FINGER

as Oswald's finger begins squeezing.

REVERSE ON FITZGERALD

as we Hear Two Rifle Reports close up. Fitzgerald looks *hurt*. He touches his belt.

FLASH CUT TO

EXT. GRASSY KNOLL

as, again, Fitzgerald pops in. He looks around, recording with camera. There is no one there doing anything threatening. We Hear The Two Shots in the Distance. Fitzgerald touches his belt.

FLASH CUT TO

EXT. BRIDGE - OVERLOOKING MOTORCADE

as Fitzgerald pops in here, too. Nothing happening. Again We Hear the Two Shots. He touches his belt.

FLASH CUT TO

EXT. BOULEVARD - AHEAD OF MOTORCADE

Fitzgerald popping into the crowd. Again, we Hear the Two Shots. He touches his belt.

FLASH CUT TO

EXT. DEALY PLAZA - BOULEVARD - FIRST LOCATION

as, once again, Dr. Fitzgerald materializes on the sidewalk just as the Presidential motorcade is approaching.

Exactly as before, the Texan does a double-take as Fitzgerald pops in next to him.

TEXAN
(to Fitzgerald)
Where in Sam Hill did *you* come from?

FITZGERALD
(as before)
Cambridge.

Again, before the Texan can get any further into it, Fitzgerald lifts his "movie" camera up to his eye and starts recording. The Texan goes back to watching the approaching motorcade.

FITZGERALD'S POV THROUGH RANGEFINDER

As once again he Zooms in on the open Presidential limousine.

Secret Service Agent Ray Kingman walking alongside the Second Limo (the one carrying additional Secret Service) on Fitzgerald's side of the street.

Crowds line the street, waving flags, shouting greetings to the President. The Dallas Policeman steps into Fitzgerald's POV and pauses. Fitzgerald shifts his POV through Rangefinder, once again Zooming in on Lee Harvey Oswald in the Book Depository Window.

SMASH CUT TO:

FITZGERALD

as he drops his camera onto its shoulder strap and realizes—*emotionally*—that this is no longer the dispassionate study of the long-dead past: this is happening *now*. He *hesitates*, then the emotional pain becomes too great.

FITZGERALD
No!

And with that bellow, Fitzgerald starts running forward toward the Presidential limousine just as Oswald's First Shot Rings Out.

RAPID SEQUENCE - SECRET SERVICE AGENT KINGMAN

as he Hears Fitzgerald's Shout followed by the Shot and spins around in time to See Fitzgerald running forward.

RAPID SEQUENCE - FITZGERALD

As he approaches the Presidential limousine, placing himself between the President and the Book Depository. *Oswald's Second Shot hits Fitzgerald: a flesh wound in the left shoulder.*

RAPID SEQUENCE - SCREAMING BYSTANDERS

At the Sound of the two Gunshots.

RAPID SEQUENCE - FITZGERALD AND KINGMAN

As Agent Kingman arrives just as Fitzgerald is shot. Kingman catches Fitzgerald as the impact of the shot knocks into Fitzgerald's shoulder.

AGENT KINGMAN
(to Fitzgerald)
Come on!

Kingman helps Fitzgerald into the Secret Service limo, which is now right next to them. (The Presidential limo is now ahead of them.)

LONG ON THE PRESIDENTIAL LIMO

as it pulls out of the motorcade and accelerates.

IN SECRET SERVICE LIMO

as Kingman pulls the wounded Fitzgerald in. As soon as they're in, this limo begins accelerating after the Presidential limo. As the limo speeds along, We Hear Rapid Conversation on the Car Two-Way Radio:

KENNEDY'S DRIVER
(On Radio)

The Governor has been hit! Alert Parkland
Memorial Hospital that we'll be there in four
minutes!

CONTROLLER
(On Radio)
Roger. Are the President and First Lady all
right?

KENNEDY'S DRIVER
(On Radio)
The President and First Lady are unhurt—
repeat—unhurt.

The Driver of the Secret Service Limo picks up the microphone.

AGENT DRIVING
(To Radio)
This is Treasury Two. We are bringing in a
wounded civilian. Notify Parkland.

CONTROLLER
(On Radio)
Roger.

FITZGERALD
(to Kingman)
I'll be okay.

AGENT KINGMAN
You're already okay in my book. You just
took a bullet meant for the President of the
United States.

CLOSE ON FITZGERALD

as he realizes the full impact of what he has done.

CUT TO

INT. DOCTOR'S OFFICE - HOSPITAL - DAY

as Fitzgerald (his jacket and shirt off) is sitting on an examination table while a Doctor finishes up cleaning and bandaging his left shoulder. Agent Kingman is talking softly on a nearby telephone.

DOCTOR
(to Fitzgerald)
You were very, *very* lucky. The bullet just
tore some flesh—nothing serious.

FITZGERALD
It *felt* like being hit with a crowbar.

Agent Kingman covers the telephone mouthpiece and speaks to Fitzgerald.

AGENT KINGMAN
Dr. Fitzgerald, do you have a Driver's License
on you?

Fitzgerald gestures toward his jacket, draped over a chair near Kingman.

FITZGERALD
In my wallet.

Kingman gets an ordinary wallet from Fitzgerald's jacket, takes out a Driver's License, and resumes talking softly on the telephone. The Doctor finishes bandaging Fitzgerald.

DOCTOR
(to Fitzgerald
That should do it. You can get dressed now.

Fitzgerald gets off the table and begins putting on his shirt again.

Kingman hangs up the telephone.

AGENT KINGMAN
(to MD)
Dr. Fitzgerald is being released?

DOCTOR
No reason not to.

AGENT KINGMAN
(to Fitzgerald)
Then would you come with me, sir?

Fitzgerald is putting on his tie.

FITZGERALD
Where?

AGENT KINGMAN
To the Dallas Trade Mart. After his speech,
the President would like to meet you.

CUT TO:

INT. THE DALLAS TRADE MART - DAY

where President John F. Kennedy is delivering the luncheon address that history had never intended him to give.

Dr. Fitzgerald stands on the sidelines next to Agent Kingman, an historian still, recording it all in his "camera."

KENNEDY
We in this country, in this generation are—by
destiny rather than choice—the watchmen of
the walls of world freedom. We ask,
therefore, that we may be worthy of our power
and responsibility—that we may exercise our
strength with wisdom and restraint—and that
we may achieve it in our time, and for all

time, the ancient vision of peace on Earth, goodwill toward men.

MASSIVE LUNCHEON AUDIENCE (FROM STOCK FOOTAGE)

There is Applause.

CLOSE ON FITZGERALD'S FACE

as he realizes that Kennedy's vision was destined to be fulfilled—but will it be, now that history has been changed?

PRESIDENT KENNEDY AGAIN

KENNEDY
(continuing)
That must always be our goal—and the righteousness of our cause must always underlie our strength. For as was written long ago: "Except the Lord keep the city, the watchman waketh but in vain."

As Applause greets the end of Kennedy's speech, we

CUT TO:

INT. EXECUTIVE OFFICES - TRADE MART - DAY

As Fitzgerald and Agent Kingman are standing, waiting. After a few beats, the door opens, two Secret Service Agents walk in, and they are immediately followed by President John F. Kennedy.

KENNEDY AND FITZGERALD

as they *look* at each other for the first time. The physical resemblance is clear: Fitzgerald could be another of Kennedy's brothers, and JFK's initial expression acknowledges this.

ALL AGAIN

KENNEDY
Mr. Kingman, would you do the honors?

AGENT KINGMAN
Yes, sir. Mr. President, this is Dr. Joseph Fitzgerald, one of your constituents from Harvard. He's the man who saved your life.

Kennedy extends his hand to Fitzgerald. Fitzgerald grasps the hand tentatively—as if he can't believe this is really happening—then more firmly.

KENNEDY
(warmly)
Dr. Fitzgerald, Harvard, and I, are in your debt.

FITZGERALD
(sincerely)
Hardly, sir, since this gave me a long-hoped-for chance to meet you.

KENNEDY
Nonsense. As a matter of fact, I've been wanting to meet *you*, ever since I read your article applying mathematical games theory to historical analysis.

FITZGERALD
(shocked; delighted)
You read it? But the article was never *published*.

KENNEDY
A mutual friend sent me a copy of your manuscript.
(concern)
Is your shoulder hurting much?

FITZGERALD
It's not bad, sir—nothing aspirin can't
handle for a few days.

KENNEDY
(nods)
Your Dean thinks quite well of you, Professor.
I've been informed that your lectures not only
bring history alive, but that you're also a
top expert in current foreign affairs.

Suddenly, there is a knock at the office door. One of the Secret
Service agents opens it, then lets in Vice President Johnson.

JOHNSON
Mr. President, it looks like fate is set on
spoiling our barbecue tonight. Tornadoes have
sprung up all around the state. One is heading
here, another just ripped its way through
downtown Austin, and another is heading for my
ranch. If I were you, I'd hightail it back to
Washington and mind the store.

FITZGERALD

He *knows* it's not fate that's doing this.

ALL AGAIN

KENNEDY
(tersely)
Take care of your people, Lyndon. Let me know
how I can help.

JOHNSON
Yes, Mr. President.

Johnson rushes out. Kennedy turns to Fitzgerald again.

KENNEDY
Dr. Fitzgerald, events are pressing me so I'll
be direct. I can use an extra Harvard
professor in my Brain Trust right now. Are
you free to be my guest at the White House?

FITZGERALD
(shocked)
Uh, *yes*, sir.

KENNEDY
Then let's get going. This is turning out to
be "one of those days."

As Fitzgerald follows the President out of the Trade Mart offices, we

CUT TO

EXT. (LOVE) AIR FIELD - STORM - AFTERNOON

as strong rain and winds surround Air Force One while it takes off.

STOCK FOOTAGE - TORNADOES

As they wind their way through Texan cities.
EXT. AIR FORCE ONE - BREAKING ABOVE CLOUDS - AFTERNOON

to establish.

INT. AIR FORCE ONE - IN FLIGHT

this time, not carrying a flag-draped casket and a just-sworn-in new president, but with JFK still alive and well.

Kennedy is sitting catercorner to Fitzgerald in a living room area.

Both men have drinks. Agent Kingman is seated nearby, reading.

An Aide comes up to the President.

PRESIDENTIAL AIDE
Mr. President, news out of Texas is bad.
Parts of Dallas, San Antonio, Austin—gone.
Hundreds dead, more missing. The Vice
President is requesting federal disaster
relief. The only *good* news is that Parkland
Memorial was untouched. Governor Connally is
out of surgery in stable condition.

KENNEDY
Thank God for that, at least. Okay, get the
paperwork going. I want disaster relief on my
desk before I go to bed tonight.

PRESIDENTIAL AIDE
Yes, sir. One more thing. Dallas police
arrested a man named Lee Oswald. They've
charged Oswald not only with shooting the
Governor, but with murdering a Dallas police
patrolman.

Kennedy nods seriously.

KENNEDY
Thank you.

The Aide leaves. The historian from the future can't resist asking.

FITZGERALD
Mr. President, do you have any idea—

KENNEDY
(interrupting)
Jack. Men who've saved my life call me
"Jack."

FITZGERALD
(delighted)
Jack. I'm Joe to everyone but my students.

KENNEDY
Good name. My Dad's name. Also my late brother's.

FITZGERALD
(emotionally)
I ... know.

KENNEDY
You were asking something?

FITZGERALD
(nods)
If you have any idea what reason anyone would have to shoot at you?

Kennedy takes a sip of his drink before answering.

KENNEDY
Considering the awesome power wielded by the President, who *couldn't* find some damned reason? Two centuries ago, the Founding Fathers tried to set things up so we wouldn't have a king anymore. Now, because we're always a pushbutton away from war, the President has been stuck with more power than any king in history. It's no wonder my administration has been called "Camelot."

FITZGERALD
Like King Arthur, you had to *win* your office. Weren't you asking to have that much power?

KENNEDY

Sure. My father drummed it into our heads
that you need power to get anything done.
(now contemplative)
It was fun at first, being at the center of
everything. Suddenly, people are interested
in your ideas. You ask for anything, someone
gets it. You want to speak to someone in Hong
Kong—they're on the phone five minutes later.
What changed everything for me was the Bay of
Pigs.

FITZGERALD
(fascinated)
The Bay of Pigs experience changed your
feelings about power?

KENNEDY
(nods)
Now I was responsible for men's lives. It was
like having my P.T. boat sunk again, only this
time I couldn't do anything to save them.
Then the Cuban Missile Crisis, and the whole
world was on my shoulders...
(with irony)
...and me with a bad back.
(beat)
Providence was with us that time. But
Scripture tells us to "put not your trust in
princes." Let me tell you, that's good
advice. No one man should have that much
power ... no one man should *have* to have it.

FITZGERALD
(confidently)
You're way ahead of your time. It will take
another century before people see it that way.

KENNEDY
If people see it a century from now, it will

have been worth the wait.

Fitzgerald is contemplating the wisdom of that remark when the Aide returns.

PRESIDENTIAL AIDE
Mr. President, there's a radiophone call for
you from Defense Secretary McNamara.

KENNEDY
(rising)
Excuse me.

The President gets up and walks aft, leaving Dr. Fitzgerald alone with his thoughts. Without thinking, Fitzgerald sticks his hand into his jacket pocket, pulling out his *Kennedy Half Dollar*, and automatically starts to flip it in his hands.

Suddenly, the plane is hit by turbulence, and Fitzgerald *misses* catching the coin. The coin *rolls* to where Agent Kingman is sitting.

Agent Kingman *sees* the coin, and looks up to meet Fitzgerald's frantic gaze; Fitzgerald looks away quickly. Kingman picks the coin up.

CLOSE ON KINGMAN

as he *sees* what the coin is.

KINGMAN AND FITZGERALD

As Kingman—seeing Fitzgerald trying to look innocent—realizes that this *must* be Fitzgerald's property.

AFT AGAIN

as President Kennedy returns to the seat next to Fitzgerald, JFK passes his Aide and waves him over.

KENNEDY
(quiet but urgently)
Listen carefully. I've just placed our
Strategic Forces on Yellow Alert. Set up an
Emergency Cabinet meeting for tonight at ten.
Rusk is on a plane to Japan—see if you can
get him back. Tell Bundy, Taylor, Sorensen.
And Bobby!

PRESIDENTIAL AIDE
Yes, sir.

As the Aide leaves, Kennedy straps himself in again and turns to Fitzgerald, likewise speaking quietly but with urgency.

KENNEDY
How familiar are you with our Berlin
situation?

FITZGERALD
Completely. Why do you ask?

KENNEDY
Soviet troops just captured West Berlin. The
Russian premier is demanding we pull our
forces out of the rest of Germany or they'll
kill every American *in* Berlin.

FITZGERALD
(shocked)
But Khrushchev never would have *done* that!

KENNEDY
(nods with finality)
Premier Khrushchev was assassinated today.

On Fitzgerald's *startled* look, we

CUT TO

EXT. AIR FORCE ONE - ON THE GROUND - AFTERNOON

as the door opens. The Secret Service, JFK and Jackie, Fitzgerald, the Warrant Officer with the "Black Bag," and the rest of the entourage begin deplaning.

AGENT KINGMAN

as he watches Fitzgerald getting into the Presidential limousine with the Kennedys, then looks down again at the mysterious Kennedy Half Dollar. Kingman slips the coin into his pocket then walks up to another Secret Service Agent.

AGENT KINGMAN
I need to do some research. Can you spare me?

The Agent nods.

THE PRESIDENTIAL LIMOUSINE

as it departs.

CUT TO

EXT. THE WHITE HOUSE - THE LIMOUSINE ARRIVING - AFTERNOON

to Establish.

CUT TO

INT. OVAL OFFICE - THE WHITE HOUSE - AFTERNOON

as JFK sits behind his desk when his intercom buzzes. He reaches over and turns it on.

WOMAN'S VOICE
(On Intercom)

Mr. President, I have the Chairman of the
Joint Chiefs for you. He says it's urgent.

KENNEDY
Put him through.

Kennedy reaches over and touches a control, placing the call on his Speakerphone.

CHAIRMAN
(On Speakerphone)
Mr. President?

KENNEDY
Yes, General?

CHAIRMAN
(On Speakerphone;
deadly calm)
Sir, we have our first encounter. One of our
NATO B-52's en route to Berlin over East
Germany is under attack by Soviet Migs. The
pilot is requesting permission to return fire.
What shall we tell him, sir?

Kennedy pauses, knowing that this is it: the moment he has been dreading. He tries to hold his answer back as long as possible.

CHAIRMAN
(On Speakerphone;
continuing)
Mr. President, are you still there?

KENNEDY
Yes, General.

CHAIRMAN
(On Speakerphone)
Sir, what are your orders?

Kennedy takes a deep breath before answering.

KENNEDY
General, tell the B-52 pilot that the
President gives him permission ... no, that
the President *orders* him to defend his craft.

CHAIRMAN
(On Speakerphone)
Yes, Mr. President. God bless you, sir.

KENNEDY
God bless us all, General. God bless us all.

Kennedy switches off the Speakerphone.

CLOSE ON PRESIDENT KENNEDY

as he wearily drops his face into his hands. Hold on him, then

CUT TO

CLOSE ON THE KENNEDY HALF DOLLAR

as we see it being held in a man's hand.
WIDER - INT. FAMILY ROOM - NIGHT

as Agent Kingman is sitting across a desk from a Treasury Inspector, in the Inspector's suburban home. In the b.g., the Inspector's Eight-Year-Old Son is lying prone on the floor watching television—a C.B.S. News Special Report—the T.V. under Kingman and the Inspector's conversation. (The Son isn't really paying the T.V. much attention, as if he's waiting for something else.) The Inspector is looking at the coin through a watchmaker's loupe screwed into his eye, then removes the loupe and leans back in his chair.

INSPECTOR
(to Kingman)

Remarkable. Utterly remarkable. I've never seen counterfeit work this faithful to Mint standards. Whoever did this is a real artist.

T.V. Under:

ANCHORMAN (ON TV)
—an indication of a conspiracy by Soviet hard-liners—

AGENT KINGMAN
Then it *is* a counterfeit? It's not something our Mint has in the works for next year?

INSPECTOR
Of course not. How could it be? Other countries stamp reigning sovereigns on their coins, but it's against U.S. law to mint the image of any *living* person.

T.V. continuing under:

ANCHORMAN (ON TV)
—however, the tornadoes in Texas would certainly have to be put down to one of those unbelievable coincidences that you meet so often in the news business.

AGENT KINGMAN
Could it be a practical joke of some sort? Or a prototype of a campaign handout? Maybe one of the President's brothers ... or the Republicans ...

T.V. continuing under:

CBS ANNOUNCER
—concludes this CBS News Special Report. We now return to our regularly scheduled

programming.

INSPECTOR
I doubt it very much. They'd have to *know*
it's a felony ... and possibly treason, since
it implies President Kennedy is going to die
by Sixty-four. This man who lost it ... his
story is that he *saw* the assassin in a window
hundreds of feet away and immediately thought
to place himself in the bullet's trajectory?

AGENT KINGMAN
That's what he told me.

INSPECTOR
Frankly I find that a little unbelievable.

In the b.g., we See on T.V. the Opening Sequence of *Twilight Zone*—we *hear* the original "Twilight Zone" Theme Music and:

ROD SERLING'S VOICE
There is a fifth dimension beyond that which
is known to man—

AGENT KINGMAN
Fitzgerald's credentials are rock solid—even
the President had heard of him.

ROD SERLING'S VOICE
(continuing)
—It is a dimension as vast as space and as
timeless as infinity.

INSPECTOR
Still, this Harvard professor is Johnny-on-
the-Spot to save the President's life ... he
loses a coin that shouldn't exist ... he's got
three of the President's family names—

ROD SERLING'S VOICE
(continuing)
It is the middle ground between light and shadow—between science and superstition—

INSPECTOR
(continuing)
—you say he even *looks* like the President. Now, with a crisis more dangerous than Cuba coming on, you tell me that President Kennedy is confiding in this stranger like a long-lost brother—

The Inspector's Son turns the T.V. volume higher.

ROD SERLING'S VOICE
(continuing)
—And it lies between the pit of man's fears—

INSPECTOR
(to Son; annoyed)
Alan, would you turn that damn set down?

ROD SERLING'S VOICE
(continuing)
—and the summit of his imagination. It is an area which we call—

Reluctantly, the Son turns down the T.V. Sound just *before* we would have heard the words "The Twilight Zone."

INSPECTOR
(continuing to Fitzgerald)
If you ask me, this Dr. Fitzgerald could easily be a Soviet sleeper.

CLOSE ON KINGMAN

as he considers this thought.

AGENT KINGMAN
I'd better do some double-checking.

CUT TO

INT. WHITE HOUSE GUEST BEDROOM - FITZGERALD - NIGHT

as he is talking to his Wristwatch Computer.

FITZGERALD
... Last parameter, three-times-ten-to-the-ninth non-parallel vectors. Compute time-line status.

WRISTWATCH
(Voice like HAL 9000)
After pressure release by tornadoes at intervention site, Stable Two was achieved by Khrushchev assassination.

FITZGERALD
All right, then. With Khrushchev assassination as Stable Two, give me worst- and-best-case outcomes on this time-line, with assigned probabilities.

WRISTWATCH
Worst-case scenario: Three-hundred megaton nuclear exchange between the Superpowers within nine days, resulting in total annihilation of biosphere. Probability: seventy-seven percent. Best-case scenario: surrender of Western Europe to the Soviet Union within six years, resulting in collapse of Soviet economy. In desperation, Soviets blackmail West for food, West is provoked into

agro-bacterial war between the Superpowers, resulting in total annihilation of biosphere within century. Probability: twelve percent.

FITZGERALD
There's only an *eleven* percent possibility of avoiding total war on this time-line?

WRISTWATCH
Zero percent. Eleven percent
includes all other scenarios leading to—

FITZGERALD &
WRISTWATCH
—Total annihilation of biosphere.

FITZGERALD
(alone)
Since this time-line is non-viable, give me all options for repairing *original* time-line.

WRISTWATCH
There exists only one viable option for repairing original time-line. The presidency of John F. Kennedy must end as history originally recorded.

ON FITZGERALD'S GUILT AND HORROR

FITZGERALD
(softly)
What have I *done*?

And he drops his face into his hands *exactly like JFK did*.

CUT TO

INT. THE OVAL OFFICE - NIGHT

JFK is alone, in his famous ROCKING CHAIR, puffing on a cigar and thinking. There is a knock at the office door.

KENNEDY
Come in!

Agent Kingman enters.

KENNEDY
Hi, Ray. (Indicates chair) Take a load off.
Want a drink?

AGENT KINGMAN
Thank you, sir, but I'm still on duty.

KENNEDY
I won't tell on you.

Kingman remains standing and smiles ... letting us know that this is a game the two of them have played before.

AGENT KINGMAN
Mr. President, I have some security concerns about Dr. Fitzgerald. Even though he's established at Harvard, I can't find anyone who knew him before he got there. It's not impossible that Dr. Fitzgerald is a spy.

KENNEDY
For who?
(with terror)
Yale?

AGENT KINGMAN
(used to being
straight-man)
I don't know for who, sir, but I wouldn't eliminate the Soviets. I can't think of a better way to get an agent close to the

President than to set up an assassination and
have your man save the President's life.

KENNEDY
(shakes head)
I know people, Ray, and Joe Fitzgerald is no
Soviet spy.

AGENT KINGMAN
There's more, sir.

Kingman reaches into his pocket, pulls out the Kennedy Half Dollar, and hands it to Kennedy.

AGENT KINGMAN
(continuing)
Dr. Fitzgerald lost this on Air Force One.

CLOSE ON KENNEDY - IN PROFILE

as he looks at *his own face in profile* on the half dollar.

KENNEDY
I think someone is taking this Camelot stuff a
bit too far.
(beat; more
seriously)
All right. You'd better get Fitzgerald in
here.

STANDING IN DOORWAY - FITZGERALD

Fitzgerald has his "camera" strapped over his shoulder.

FITZGERALD
I was already on my way here, Mr. President.

OVAL OFFICE - ALL

Kennedy gestures Fitzgerald into the office.

KENNEDY
Dr. Fitzgerald, were you part of an assassination conspiracy in Dallas today?

FITZGERALD
No, sir, I was not. But I knew about the assassination before I came to Dallas.

AGENT KINGMAN
(to Kennedy)
Excuse me, sir.
(to Fitzgerald)
Where did you get that coin?

FITZGERALD
It's been in my family for almost two hundred years.

KENNEDY
Dr. Fitzgerald, I'm afraid that answer strains my credulity.

FITZGERALD
Mr. President, this situation is one your worldview isn't equipped to handle. You'll only be able to understand it by looking at the facts and revising your belief system accordingly. As hard as it is for you to believe, the simple fact is I am a time-traveler from two centuries in the future ... and your direct descendant by two converging lines.

KENNEDY
(concern)
Dr. Fitzgerald, the matters we are discussing are much too serious for you to joke about

them.

FITZGERALD
I'm not joking, sir.

Fitzgerald picks up his camera.

In a split-second, Agent Kingman has his gun out, pointed at Fitzgerald.

FITZGERALD
(calmly)
This isn't a weapon.

Fitzgerald points his "camera" toward the wall—*away from* both Kennedy and Kingman—and turns it on.

IN FRONT OF WALL - KENNEDY GIVING
SPEECH AT TRADE MART

in a Full-size, 3-D, Full-color and Sound Playback.

KENNEDY HOLOGRAM
We in this country, in this generation are—by
destiny rather than choice—the watchmen of
the walls of world freedom. We ask,
therefore, that we may be worthy of our power
and responsibility—

KENNEDY AND AGENT KINGMAN

as they *watch* this phenomenon, open-mouthed.

KENNEDY HOLOGRAM
—that we may exercise our strength with
wisdom and restraint—and that we may achieve
it in our time, and for all time, the ancient
vision of peace on Earth, goodwill toward men.

Profile in Silver: Second Draft 177

ALL AGAIN

Fitzgerald turns the "camera" off and the Kennedy Hologram *disappears*.

Kingman holsters his pistol again. After a pause, he speaks first.

AGENT KINGMAN
Mr. President, request permission to go off
duty, sir.

KENNEDY
Granted. For both of us, also.

Kingman immediately goes over to the liquor and pours three stiff drinks. He hands one each to Kennedy and Fitzgerald.

FITZGERALD
(to Kennedy;
automatically)
Your health.

He has time to ponder his remark as the three men drink.

Kennedy gets up and JFK starts pacing near his desk. He is still holding the Kennedy Half Dollar and he looks at it thoughtfully.

KENNEDY
As you suggest, the facts speak for
themselves—nobody now has technology of the
sort you just demonstrated. Okay, you come
from the future. Did you come back two
centuries to tell me what I'm supposed to do
about the Berlin crisis today?

FITZGERALD
No, sir.
(suddenly choked up)
I ... didn't know about that.

KENNEDY
(surprised)
Didn't *know*? How could you not know?

Kennedy looks at the Coin one more time.

ZOOM IN ON THE COIN'S DATE - *1964*

WIDER AGAIN

as Kennedy sees it and *suddenly realizes what it means.*

KENNEDY
You came to Dallas carrying a family heirloom
to observe the assassination of one of your
ancestors. *My* assassination.
(almost swooning)
Dear God in heaven.

Kennedy looks down at books shelved on his desk and sees a copy of his own book, *Profiles in Courage*.

KENNEDY
This Berlin crisis would be the end of the
world, wouldn't it?

Fitzgerald nods.

Kennedy picks up *Profiles in Courage*, then puts in down again, firmly. When he speaks again, it's with the firm resolve of a P.T. boat commander.

KENNEDY
You're *here*, which proves that it wasn't.
You'll have to take me back to Dallas. Can
you take me *back*? Can you make it like it was
intended to be?

Fitzgerald drops his head forward. Then he looks up again, nodding.

KENNEDY
(continuing)
Then you'll do this for me. We Kennedys always solve our own problems within the family.
(beat)
Joe ... the family goes on?

FITZGERALD
(proudly)
Yes, it goes on. But more than that ... the future I come from *has* seen the fulfillment of your greatest dreams. We've eliminated war, poverty, tyranny. Your dream of humankind moving into space has become a reality ... I took my graduate degree out near the orbit of Jupiter.

KENNEDY
I often wondered whether humanity could achieve that sort of Utopia.

FITZGERALD
It's not even close to being Utopia. We've just taken the Biblical advice about not putting our trust in princes.
(beat)
If there's anyone you need to say goodbye to—

KENNEDY
(gently)
I couldn't make myself leave them if I did. And they couldn't remember, could they?

Fitzgerald removes his Harvard Signet Ring, extending it to Kennedy.

FITZGERALD
You'll have to put this ring on.

KINGMAN
(alarmed)
Mr. President!

KENNEDY
Agent Kingman ... (softer) ... Ray ... No.
This is my boat.

President Kennedy hands the Kennedy Half Dollar to Fitzgerald, takes the ring, closes his eyes, and slips the ring onto his right hand.

KENNEDY

as he disappears.

WIDER AGAIN

AGENT KINGMAN
What happens now?

FITZGERALD
You took an oath to protect the life of "Lancer."

KINGMAN
Only Secret Service know that code name for President Kennedy!

FITZGERALD
Yes. You and I still have work to do.

Kingman *understands*.

KINGMAN
What do we have to do?

FITZGERALD
(after pause)
We've got to go back.

After several *long beats*,

CUT TO

EXT. DEALY PLAZA - DALLAS - NOVEMBER 22, 1963 - JUST BEFORE 12:30 PM

At the sidewalk just as the Presidential motorcade is approaching. The Texan who had seen Fitzgerald pop in is there, but this time, instead of Fitzgerald popping in, there is just the *Sound* of a "pop." The Texan looks around and—seeing nothing—just goes back to watching the approaching motorcade.

Crowds line the street, waving flags, shouting greetings to the President.

CUT TO

INT. BOOK TOWER

as Oswald prepares to shoot.

Another "pop," but Fitzgerald isn't there this time.

CUT TO

EXT. GRASSY KNOLL

as, again, a "pop" but no Fitzgerald.

CUT TO

EXT. BRIDGE - OVERLOOKING MOTORCADE

a "pop" here, too. No Fitzgerald. Nothing happening.

CUT TO

EXT. BOULEVARD - AHEAD OF MOTORCADE

A "popping" Sound in the crowd.

CUT TO

EXT. DEALY PLAZA - BOULEVARD - FIRST LOCATION

as, once again, the Presidential motorcade is approaching.

The Texan hears the "pop" then goes back to watching the approaching motorcade.

Secret Service Agent Ray Kingman walking alongside the Second Limo, and—for an instant—there is a red *flash* around him.

SMASH CUT TO:

FITZGERALD

sitting in the Presidential motorcade—where JFK was supposed to be—waving to the crowds.

DISSOLVE TO:

INT. SIDE ROOM - PARKLAND MEMORIAL HOSPITAL

as a gurney holds a slain body covered by a sheet, with only one of the hands uncovered. Next to the gurney is Agent Kingman, who speaks softly to the covered body.

AGENT KINGMAN
Well done, Agent Fitzgerald. Well done.

CLOSE ON THE BODY'S EXPOSED HAND

Profile in Silver: Second Draft 183

as we See that in the open palm is the Kennedy Half Dollar.

CUT TO

INT. LECTURE HALL - HARVARD - 2163 A.D. - DAY

as we see the back of a man dressed in 2163 garb, delivering a lecture—in a wholly distinctive voice—to the history class.

LECTURER
History records many facts ... some of them right, some of them wrong. But let the record show that, in any age, good or bad, there are men of high ideals ... men of courage ... men who do more than that for which they are called upon.

CLOSE ON THE LECTURER'S HAND

as we see that on it is a Harvard Signet Ring.

LECTURER
(continuing)
You will not always know their names. But let their deeds stand as a monument, so that when the human race is called to judgment, we may say—this, too, was humanity.

REVERSE POV

and we see that the man delivering the lecture is John F. Kennedy.

THE STUDENTS

as they rise to their feet in applause, we hear:

NARRATOR
A fitting tribute of the sort only to be found

in ... The Twilight Zone.

FADE OUT

Colorblind

After Carla Singer at CBS initially shelved the story for "Profile in Silver," Alan Brennert asked me to write another story for *The Twilight Zone*. I initially pitched Alan on an idea for a universe where entropy ran backwards, a story titled "From Grave to Cradle," but I just couldn't make it work. So, I pitched Alan "Colorblind" and he accepted it as a substitute.

The genesis for this story came to me by contemplating Stevie Wonder, the black musical genius, whom I mistakenly believed at the time was blind from birth. I only later found out that he lost his sight as a small child. I was wondering what it must be like to be a person who might be discriminated against for the color of his skin—when he could never have any idea what color even is. What must it be like to be hated by some people for something about yourself which they could apprehend and you, yourself, couldn't?

My viewpoint character in "Colorblind" is named Steve Morris. The name that Stevie Wonder was born with is "Steveland Morris."

Carla Singer initially shelved this story also, but once the "Profile in Silver" script had been given a go-ahead for production by CBS Entertainment executive Tony Barr, Alan was able to get me a go-ahead for "Colorblind," also. After I wrote two drafts, Alan was happy with the script, and wanted to go ahead to production.

Which is where Harlan Ellison comes into the story once again.

Harlan had been a big booster of "Profile in Silver," but when Carla Singer had killed "Colorblind" also, Harlan phoned me to cheer me up, and read me a letter he had sent over to CBS defending me. What I didn't realize is that Harlan hadn't read the story of "Colorblind," and when he got around to reading the script, he hated it. He compared it in discussion with me to "Let That Be Your Last Battlefield," the third-season episode of the original *Star Trek* where you have an alien played by Frank Gorshin—black on one half of his face and white on the other—who's bigoted against another of his race whose face is shaded in mirror image. Harlan hated that episode, while I always liked it.

Harlan told me he considered "Colorblind" didactic, obvious, and "knee-jerk liberal." Which I found ironic, since I considered *Harlan* a knee-jerk liberal. *I* was a knee-jerk anarchist.

Harlan had his own anti-racist script in the works at *Twilight Zone*, a script about an anti-Santa Clause titled "Nackles."

"Nackles" was a script that Harlan was supposed to direct himself, and when CBS pulled the plug on that episode, violating the network's agreement not to censor Harlan as a condition of him coming on staff, Harlan left the show on principle.

What I'm about to suggest now is psychological speculation, which is always dangerous. Let me also preface this by saying that I consider Harlan a good guy, and I don't think he ever would have done what I'm about to suggest at a conscious level. But, I have often wondered if one reason Harlan disliked "Colorblind" so much was that he felt possessive about single- handedly taking on the demons of racism with his script ... and at some level he didn't want some damned libertarian muscling in on the crusade.

Of course, as an alternative, you are always free to agree with Harlan that my script just royally sucked.

After Harlan left the show, Alan told me that he was going to try to get "Colorblind" on the production schedule for the next round of episodes CBS ordered ... but low-ratings resulted in that order for additional episodes never coming through.

The Twilight Zone had been cancelled.

Later, when *Twilight Zone* was revived for additional episodes in syndication, I had some hope that it would be produced then, but apparently its production costs made it too high-budget to be considered.

"Profile in Silver" flowed naturally for me. "Colorblind," by contrast, was hard going.

Is "Colorblind" a decent script, as Alan Brennert thought ... or was Harlan Ellison right?

I think it's good, but then again ... I'm prejudiced.

JNS

The Twilight Zone
Colorblind
by J. Neil Schulman

FADE IN

EXT. CITY NEIGHBORHOOD - DAY

You know the sort of neighborhood. Lower-middle-class poverty, American style. Middle class WASP, Irish, Jewish, or Italian thirty years ago, but blacks and Hispanics now vastly outnumber the Anglos. Integrated: apartment houses integrated with row houses integrated with furniture warehouses. Beat-up Chevrolets parked on a littered street. Noisy: we hear an ambulance siren, a ghetto blaster blaring Rap, a car horn playing *La Cucaracha*.

SOME NINE-YEAR-OLD KIDS

three each of black and Hispanic kids, with one blond, blue-eyed boy—Billy Morris—are bouncing a handball against a brick wall.

ACROSS THE STREET FROM THE KIDS - A DOUBLE-PARKED MOVING VAN

Two Movers—both black—are just finished packing. The Movers climb into the cab of the Moving Van and drive off, revealing

A STATION WAGON

parked in front of the tiny front yard of a row house marked with a real estate sign that reads "Sold." The station wagon is out of place here: not only is it packed inside and roof rack, but it's the only thing we see that's shiny new. Sitting on the curb near it are

STEVE MORRIS AND ALEX

a couple of tough-looking fifteen-year-olds listening to Bruce Springsteen on Alex's cassette player. Steve Morris is—like his younger brother Billy—also blond and blue-eyed. His friend Alex is dark-haired but also Anglo. Both teenagers look like their style was taken from Springsteen album covers—working-class tough.

ALEX
First Tony moves away, then Pete and George—
now you. The gang is wiped out.

STEVE
My Dad finally gets offered a better job away
from here, he jumps at it. You gotta admit,
Alex, this place sucks.

ALEX
Sure. You'll be okay at your new school. I'm
gonna be on my own in Hellhole High.
(standing)
If I don't find a new gang fast, I better
start paying attention in Spanish class. Or
get a dye job on my skin.

Steve and Alex shake hands.

STEVE
You'll manage. Niggers 'n spics never gave
you problems you couldn't handle.

ALEX
Yeah. If you don't hear from me, my Mom'll
tell you where to send the flowers.

Alex walks down the street, the Springsteen music following him. Steve watches his friend walk away until—

ACROSS THE STREET - FOLLOWING THE KIDS' BALL

—the ball bounces against the brick wall, over the kids' heads, then rebounds hard onto the hood of the station wagon, leaving a minor dent. The ball sets off a loud car alarm—the sort of two-tone siren that sounds like Gestapo coming to arrest Jews. The kids laugh—they obviously are enjoying the noise. One of the black kids, Jason, runs after the ball across the street toward Steve, who the ball has bounced to. Steve stands up, takes a look at the station wagon, then picks up the ball just before Jason arrives.

JASON
Can I have my ball, Steve?

STEVE
You're sure this is *your* ball, Jason?

JASON
That what I said, ain't it?

STEVE
Then it was *your* ball that put the dent in my
Dad's new car.

EXT. ROW HOUSE - OUTSIDE FRONT DOOR -
DON MORRIS

Steve and Billy's father. A blond jock type in his early forties—heading outside, and mad.

DON
Yo! You kids! Away from my car!

THE KIDS

as they stop laughing. They've obviously had run-ins with Don Morris before and are afraid of him. Don is heading outside at full steam.

All but Jason and Billy back off toward the wall.

DON AND THE STATION WAGON

When Don gets around to the driver's side, he opens the door, hits a button, and silences the siren. He gets out again, notices the dent, and glares at the kids.

DON
Can't you kids leave anything *new*?

ALL AGAIN

The kids across the street—no longer having a ball to play with—start dispersing. Billy steps forward.

BILLY
We don't have nowhere else to *play*, Dad.

DON
You do now. We're ready to go, Billy.

STEVE
It was Jason who dented the car, Dad. You want me to get his father?

Billy glares at his brother.

DON
(smirks)
A lot of good that would do. No. Let's just get the hell out of here.
(toward house)
Jill! Let's move out!

Don slides into the car behind the driver's seat, Steve into the back seat. Billy gets the ball from Steve and tosses it to Jason.

JASON
(accusingly)
Ya didn't say nothin' 'bout a new car.

BILLY
(embarrassed)
I *tole* ya my Dad got a new job.

Don honks the horn impatiently and starts the engine.

BILLY
(continuing)
I gotta go. I'll call ya sometime.

JASON
They took out our phone.

BILLY
I'll write ya.

JASON
I don't read too good.

BILLY
Then I'll visit ya.

JASON
(looking at Don)
Yeah, sure.

Billy puts out his hand to shake just as Don Morris blasts the car horn again.

JASON
(continuing)
He ever gonna let up on that thing?

BILLY
You guys don't call us honkies for nothin'.

Jason laughs, slaps Billy five, and runs across the street to the other kids.

JILL MORRIS

as she comes out the front door of the house, heading for the station wagon. Don's wife is fortyish, also blond, and kind of pretty. She stops to lock up the front door.

INSIDE THE STATION WAGON

Jill gets into the front passenger seat next to Don. Billy get in back next to Steve. Doors slam, and—blessed silence. Don tears the wagon out.

CUT TO

EXT. STATION WAGON - DAY

driving on a two-lane highway.

INT. STATION WAGON - DAY

In the back seat, Billy is wearing headphones and flipping through a comic book while Steve is reading *The Decline and Fall of the Roman Empire*.

JILL
I can't believe we *finally* got out of that
garbage dump.

DON
The city wasn't always a dump, honey. When I
was a kid it was a great place to grow up.
Gentrification will make it great again someday.

JILL
Who can wait? I can hardly believe we got out
before it killed us.

DON
Believe it, sweetheart. We're going to where

the streets are clean and safe, where there are *lawns*—

JILL
—Supermarket aisles wide enough to drive a truck through. Back *yards*. No fire engines day and night.

DON
And—best of all—where everybody speaks *English*.

EXT. STATION WAGON - ENTERING A SMALL SUBURBAN TOWN - DAY

INT. STATION WAGON AGAIN

BILLY
(removing headphones)
Are we there yet, Mom?

JILL
We're there, Billy. There's a signpost up ahead.

FAMILY POV - A ROAD SIGN AS THEY PASS

"Welcome to Pleasant Springs, Established 1842, Pop. 12,023, 'A Decent Community.'"

EXT. ANGLE TRACKING THE STATION WAGON

as it passes the sign, entering Pleasant Springs, a suburban Eastern American town, as pleasant as its name, with some old buildings dating from the 1840's, but now also sporting McDonalds, Village Video, and David's Cookies.

CUT TO

EXT. THE STATION WAGON - A SUBURBAN
NEIGHBORHOOD - DAY

as it pulls into the driveway—next to another car, also packed up—of a split-level house with a real-estate sign on the lawn: "Sold."

INT. STATION WAGON

DON
Well boys, this is it. Welcome home.

STEVE
Boy, look at the *size* of this place!

EXT. FRONT OF HOUSE

As the Morris family gets out of their station wagon and begin stretching their legs, Steve spots a basketball hoop on the front of the garage.

STEVE
Billy, look! Our own *basketball* hoop!

BILLY
Wow!

Billy runs around the house to see the back yard. A man and a woman—looking like Ozzie and Harriet—exit the front door of the house, the man carrying a box.

DON
Mr. and Mrs. Tucker—

MR. TUCKER
Mr. Morris ... hi. I guess we got the last of
our belongings out just in time.

While Mr. Tucker trudges to his car, Jill Morris turns to Mrs. Tucker.

JILL
Pleasant Springs is so *lovely*, this house is
so *lovely*. I don't blame you for wanting to
stay until the last minute.

Mrs. Tucker looks at Jill strangely, then shrugs with an obvious "What the hell—we've already got their money" look.

MRS. TUCKER
To tell you the honest truth, dearie, I don't
think we could've stood another day in this
damn town.

Don and Jill are both taken aback. Mr. Tucker starts the car engine as Mrs. Tucker gets into their car's passenger seat. Don walks forward to Mr. Tucker's side of the car.

DON
But you told me that Pleasant Springs is a
decent town—like the sign says.

MR. TUCKER
(smirking)
Oh, it's decent enough. If Pleasant Springs
is anything, it's *decent.* If I were you I'd
watch myself—they don't like Reds here.

And with that, Tucker starts backing out of the driveway.

DON
(shouting after)
Reds? I voted for *Reagan*!

The Tuckers just laugh and drive off, just as a Moving Van passes the Tuckers car on its way in, and parks in front of the Morris's new house.

As the two Black Movers exit the cab, the front door of the Morris's new next-door neighbors opens up, and a Teenage Boy—about Steve

Morris's age—pops his head out to get a look at the new arrivals. Steve Morris waves to the boy, but as soon as the Boy has gotten a good look at the Morrises, he scowls, pops back inside again, and slams his front door. Steve is completely bewildered. Don and Jill look *concerned*.

> DON
> Great. I wonder what *his* problem is—

Don is too busy to worry about it for long—the Movers start to unload a dining room set.

> DON
> (to movers)
> —Be careful with that!

> MOVER
> Chill out, we done this hundreds
> of times.

> DON
> (to Jill, softly)
> What can you expect—?

> JILL
> (softly)
> —from one of *them*?

Don and Jill then lead the movers toward the house, Don pulling the "sold" sign out of the lawn along the way.

Billy runs around the house and sees Steve, still staring next door.

> BILLY
> Steve, wait'll you see what's in the back
> yard! There's a *forest*!

> STEVE
> (amused)

Yeah? C'mon, show it to me.

As Billy drags Steve around the house we

CUT TO

EXT. FRONT PLEASANT SPRINGS HIGH SCHOOL - MORNING

as Steve Morris arrives for his first day at his new school—which is, by the looks of it—not at all new. Other students also arriving—mostly WASPS like Steve, but also a few blacks, Hispanics, and Asians.

Prominently situated in front of the high school is a large, ornate drinking fountain, of the sort found in public parks eighty years ago. Steve starts the water flowing and is about to take a drink before he goes in, when he notices a brass plaque in front of the fountain which reads: "If thine enemy be thirsty...give him water to drink. Proverbs 25:21." Something about the plaque makes Steve uneasy, but he takes a drink...and immediately regrets it, spitting out the water and trying to forget the bitter taste. He heads inside.

CUT TO

INT. HIGH SCHOOL CORRIDOR - MORNING

As Steve walks out of the Adminstrative Office, looking down at a piece of paper with the number of his homeroom. As he walks, looking at room numbers but not looking where he's going, a couple of tough-looking students speed past him.

FIRST STUDENT
Watch it, Red!

Steve looks around, failing to see anyone with red hair. He doesn't realize the student was talking to him.

STEVE
Hey, do you know where—?

But the Student walks on, ignoring Steve. A blonde Girl walks by.

Steve tries her next.

STEVE
Excuse me, but do you know where Room one-oh-three—

The Girl glares at Steve then likewise walks on as if she can't be bothered giving him the time of day.

A Black Student (Andrew Sowelle) comes by next, whistling cheerfully, but this time Steve does the ignoring, turning around without even considering asking him for directions...and Steve practically walks right into a fluorescent light bulb being carried by the elderly, black school custodian, Mr. Cleary.

STEVE
You nearly chopped off my head with that thing!

MR. CLEARY
Not me! I never kill students on school property. I hate mopping up blood.

The response is so unexpectedly bizarre that Steve isn't quite sure how to answer.

STEVE
Well, just be more careful next time.

Steve turns away quickly and begins walking.

MR. CLEARY
If you're looking for Room One-oh-three, it's the other way—next-to-last room on the right.

The custodian has surprised Steve again. Steve turns back and nods briefly—without saying thanks aloud—then walks past Cleary in the opposite direction.

CUT TO

INT. MORRIS HOUSE - MORNING

as Jill—dressed in jeans, a tied-off work shirt, and a bandana—is unpacking boxes in the living room when the doorbell rings. Jill goes to a window.

JILL'S POV THROUGH WINDOW

a well-dressed Woman at the front door, and parked in front of the house an expensive car.

JILL AT DOOR

as she pulls off the bandana, drops it into a box, and goes to the front door...but city habits die hard—she talks through the door.

JILL
Who is it?

WOMAN'S VOICE
The Welcome Wives!

Jill opens the front door to the Welcome Wife, who's looking at a piece of paper. They talk through the screen door.

WELCOME WIFE
(not looking up)
Mrs. Morris?

JILL
Yes, that's right.

WELCOME WIFE
Hi, I'm one of your neighbors, Ruth—

The Welcome Wife looks up, seeing Jill for the first time, and stops.

JILL
How do you do, Ruth. I'm Jill. Won't you come in?

Jill opens the screen door. The woman doesn't move.

JILL
(continuing)
I'm sure you're used to seeing houses in a mess.

WELCOME WIFE
(suddenly chilly)
I'm terribly sorry, there seems to have been a mistake. I'm at the wrong house.

JILL
(confused)
You said "Morris." This *is* the Morris house.

WELCOME WIFE
(obviously lying)
Yes, well I'm afraid I was supposed to call on the house of *another* family named Morris—
(inspired)
—the *William* Morris house. Sorry to have bothered you.

She starts to walk back to her car—fast. Jill steps out after her.

OUTSIDE FRONT OF HOUSE

JILL
But *we* just moved in.

WELCOME WIFE
(barely turning)

Sorry—I just go where the real-estate office
sends me!

The Welcome Wife jumps into her car, revs the engine, and tears
out.

JILL

Bewildered and hurt at being treated as if her skin was the wrong
color for the neighborhood, Jill heads back into the house.

CUT TO

EXT. HIGH RISE OFFICE BUILDING - ESTABLISHING - DAY

INT. OFFICE CORRIDOR - TRACKING DON MORRIS - DAY

As Don—in a smart business suit—is walking with another well-dressed executive, Ed Anderson.

ANDERSON
To be honest, Don, I'm a little surprised you
decided to leave DeClare for a small outfit
like us.

DON
We won't be small for long, Ed. I have a few
ideas—

ANDERSON
(interrupting)
—You've already sold me, Don—save it for the
regional managers. Especially Sam Armstrong.
Sam's tripled our revenue in the Southwest
since he took it over last year.

DON
Sounds like he knows his territory.

ANDERSON
He knows the business, period. You want to
take on DeClare, pay attention to Sam. If
Sam Armstrong says he can't move a product,
then nobody else can, either. ... Speak of
the devil.

Anderson sees two executives approaching, one white and one black.

ANDERSON
Don, Sam Armstrong and Lou Coleman. Our new
Vice President in development, Don Morris.

Ad libbing "How do you do?"s and "Welcome aboards," Don shakes the white executive's hand heartily, and the black's very briefly.

ANDERSON
(continuing)
Don comes over from DeClare. He's got ideas
for a new line of top-end machines to beat
DeClare at their own game.

BLACK EXECUTIVE
'Bout time, if you ask me. Control the top
end, you control the whole market.

DON
(brushing him off)
Not in *my* experience.

Don doesn't pick up on it, but Anderson is beginning a slow burn. Don turns to the White Executive, ingratiatingly.

DON
(continuing)
I'm anxious to discuss marketing requirements
of the new line with you.

WHITE EXECUTIVE
(confused)
I can't see why you would.

DON
Don't be so modest. Ed tells me you're the
top expert on marketing here.

WHITE EXECUTIVE
Not me—I run Accounting. (Hooks thumb toward
Black Exec.) Sam here, he's your marketing
expert.

Don is taken aback. And three of the company's top men have Don's number.

SAM
(coldly)
I hope you can eyeball machines better than
you eyeball people. (To Anderson) If you'll
excuse us, Ed.

Armstrong and Coleman walk down the hall together. Anderson looks at Don, disgusted.

ANDERSON
Sam could be your best friend at this company,
Don. It's a bad mistake to antagonize him.

DON
(nods)
Maybe. But somebody should tell him that it's
a worse mistake to antagonize me.

They walk O.S. through an office door.

CUT TO

INT. HIGH SCHOOL BIOLOGY CLASSROOM - AFTERNOON

With large lab tables—students seated at them—facing an animal cage in the front of the room with two white rabbits in it. Also up front is an fairly young biology teacher, Ms. Garrison, who is already lecturing as Steve enters the classroom.

MS. GARRISON
—before categorization, it is essential that we are able to distinguish between defining characteristics and "accidents" that are true only in a particular case.
(noticing Steve)
Who are you?

STEVE
Steve Morris. I just started today. Sixth period biology with Miss Garrison?

MS. GARRISON
Ms. And you're *late*, Morris.

STEVE
Asking directions to class around here is like asking a probation officer where you can score a gun.

MS. GARRISON
I'm not interested in your excuses. You're holding up my class. Find yourself a seat.

Ms. Garrison creates deliberate tension in the room by waiting for him to be seated. Steve walks behind the tables looking for an empty seat while students deliberately ignore him. Steve sees a seat with books on it and—not wanting to make a scene—passes it by. He goes to the next row back and spots an empty seat then sees a boy taking his books off the lab table and placing them on the chair.

Steve has had enough: he goes to that chair, picks up the books, drops the stack on the floor loudly, and takes the seat.

Ms. Garrison glares at Steve. He glares back.

STEVE
You were saying?

MS. GARRISON
I had finished "saying," Mr. Morris. I was about to *ask*. Perhaps you can tell us. What are the two most important things that these rabbits have in common?

Steve looks at the cages before replying confidently.

STEVE
Well, since they're caged together and there's only two, they're probably the same sex.

Two Students laugh, then shut up when other students glare at them.

MS. GARRISON
A good deduction, Mr. Morris: they are both male. But this is not one of the most *important* things they have in common.

STEVE
It looks like they have the same ears, and they're both pure white. Are they twins?

Ms. Garrison shakes her head.

STEVE
(continuing)
You said something about "accidents." Do they both have two broken legs or something?

MS. GARRISON
No.
(to class)
In science, it is imperative to avoid an error in reasoning called "The Fallacy of the Accident." When any question is asked, one must first know how to separate the essential elements from the nonessentials, which are called "accidents." Mr. Morris has failed to do this.

STEVE
(belligerent)
Yeah? Well if it's something I can't see—

MS. GARRISON
(shakes head)
What you're not seeing is the *obvious*, Mr. Morris. The two most *important* things these two rabbits have in common ... are that they are both *alive*, and that they're both *rabbits*.

As a few students laugh and Steve tries to disappear, we

CUT TO:

EXT. FRONT HIGH SCHOOL - AFTERNOON

at the end of the school day, as Steve and other students leave. On the way out, Steve sees other of the students stopping at the ornate water fountain and drinking. Obviously there's nothing wrong with the fountain so Steve goes over and warily, he takes another drink. At his first sip, Steve makes the expression one would make having ordered cola and being served root beer by mistake—it's not *bad* like it was the first time—its just *unexpected*. He pauses for another second, not sure he likes it, then takes a longer drink.

CUT TO

INT. KITCHEN - MORRIS HOME - EVENING

as the Morris family is sitting down to dinner. There's still some evidence of a house not-yet-fully-moved-into: half-empty boxes, closets open—in fact, the family is eating sandwiches on paper plates, which Jill is preparing.

JILL
There's something *creepy* about this town, Don ... I don't know what it is.

She takes a plate of sandwiches and joins her family at the table. Everybody digs in, and talks while eating—Walton style.

DON
Look, honey, there are creeps and losers everywhere. You can't get away from them. One of the regional managers at the new job—

JILL
—It wasn't just the woman from the Welcome Wives. I couldn't find a clerk to help me at the hardware store. A teller at the bank closed his window just before I got to him. And at the supermarket ... it was as if everyone thought I had AIDS. They'd take one look at me then turn away.

DON
C'mon, honey, you're overreacting.

STEVE
No, Dad, I got the exact same thing at school. I sat at a table in the lunchroom, everyone moved to another table. And the only teacher who called on me at all was my new biology teacher—and *she* went out of her way to make me look stupid.

DON
We're the *new family* in a small town. You
have to expect a little resistance at first.
I'm sure by next week everybody in town will
have sniffed us—like a dog does to someone
new—then will warm up a bit. How 'bout it,
Billy? Did you make any friends at school
today?

BILLY
(nods while
swallowing)
Two of them.

Don looks up at his wife and older son, with the expression, "See?"

DON
What are their names?

BILLY
Raul and Mohammed.

Don and Jill's exchanged expressions clearly say that things aren't going as they'd planned.

JILL
Well, that's good for a start, honey, but be
sure you make *lots* of new friends, okay? We
moved here so you could have some friends of
your own kind.

Billy shrugs, not getting it.

BILLY
I guess so.

On Don and Jill's discomfort, we

CUT TO

INT. STEVE'S BEDROOM - MORNING

Obviously a teenager's room—a Bruce Springsteen poster is already up over a desk, Steve's clothes draped over a chair. Steve is asleep, under the covers, when his radio Alarm Clock goes off, tuned to a rock station. We see the covers rumble around and a hand reaches out to shut off the radio.

STEVE

as he throws off covers, swings pajama-clad legs off the bed. He yawns, gets out of bed, and heads o.s. to

THE BATHROOM

as Steve looks at himself in the bathroom mirror. *In his reflection, Steve is surrounded by a Red Glow.* Not a nice glow, but something harsh and menacing. Steve is startled.

STEVE
Jeez ...

Thinking that it might be a trick of lighting from being in a new house, Steve pulls the curtains open, letting sunlight flood in ... but it only makes the glow around him in the mirror clearer.

THE KITCHEN - STEVE RUNNING IN

in his pajamas, and he sees his parents already in the kitchen—Don dressed for work, Jill in a bathrobe.

STEVE
Mom, Dad! Look at me!

Don and Jill look up at Steve, expectantly, but they don't react.

STEVE
What *is* it?

JILL
What is what, honey?

STEVE
Don't you see it? There's some sort of, I dunno, red *glow* around me.

DON
The healthy glow of breathing fresh air.

STEVE
No, I *mean* it, Dad. There's some sort of creepy red *light* around me.

ON DON AND JILL ONLY

as they both look closely.

JILL
There's nothing *I* can see, Steve. You're not kidding around? Maybe you need to see an eye doctor.

ON STEVE

Steve looks at his hands—pulls up his pajamas to check his legs. He doesn't see anything unusual. There's a mirror—unpacked but not yet hung up—on a chair against the wall. Steve looks into it.

IN MIRROR

as Steve sees that he looks perfectly normal.

STEVE
Boy, that was so *real*. I've never had a dream that lasted after I got *up*.

Billy comes in, also in pajamas. Steve looks at him for a moment, catching Billy's eye. It's obvious that Billy doesn't see anything wrong, either. Steve shakes his head slowly, tousles Billy's hair, then exits o.s.

CUT TO

EXT. FRONT HIGH SCHOOL AT FOUNTAIN - MORNING

as just before school Steve takes another drink from the fountain before going in. Whatever the taste of the water is, he really seems to like it, now that he's used to it.

CUT TO

CLOSE ON A CHALKBOARD - MORNING

with the chalked words: "Johann Christoph Friedrich Von Schiller, 1759-1805...Ludwig Van Beethoven, 1770-1827"

as we Hear a recording of the final choral movement of Beethoven's Ninth Symphony sung in Theodore Spencer's English translation:

RECORDING
Joy, thou spark from Heav'n immortal,
Daughter of Elysium!
Drunk with fire, toward Heaven advancing
Goddess to thy shrine we come.

CLOSE ON STEVE IN BACK OF CLASSROOM

sitting at a tablet armchair in the last row, next to the window, his eyes looking down while he takes notes on a notepad. In Steve's reflection in the window, We can See that he's *glowing red* again, but Steve isn't yet aware of it. He lifts his hand to his face to scratch his nose and Sees (which we see in reflection) that his hand glowing red again. He gasps involuntarily.

ENCOMPASSING VIEW OF MUSIC TEACHER AND
OTHER STUDENTS

the Music Teacher sitting in front of the classroom next to a tape player, following the music with a score. And, as we See them, we see that the Teacher and the Other Students are glowing a Bright Blue.

The Teacher—hearing Steve's gasp—pauses, looking up from his book to glare at Steve—but at Steve's interruption, not at his glow. The other Students (including the black student, Andrew Sowelle) also look at Steve briefly, then look away quickly, obviously seeing nothing odd. The Teacher resumes following from his book.

RECORDING
Thy sweet magic brings together
What stern custom spreads afar
All mankind know men as brothers
Where thy happy wing-beats are!

CLOSE ON STEVE

as he's really shaken by this phenomenon. Steve and we hear Beethoven's music while Steve wonders what the devil is going on around here.

CUT TO

INT. HIGH SCHOOL CAFETERIA - STUDENTS AT LUNCH - DAY

As Steve—carrying his lunchtray and looking for a empty table—sees that everybody in the cafeteria is Glowing Bright Blue, except for one long table where only male and female Students—each with a Red Glow like Steve's own—are sitting together. Two of them are the Students from Steve's biology class who laughed at his rabbit joke. Steve walks over to the Red table.

STEVE
Anybody mind if I sit here?

FIRST RED BOY
We were wondering when you'd see it. Sure.
Sit down.

Excited, Steve puts down his tray and grabs a seat. The other Red Students continue eating while the two Red Boys from Steve's class, and one Red Girl, do the talking for the group. Steve tries to be friendly.

STEVE
I'm Steve Morris.

FIRST RED BOY
Yeah, we know who you are. You're in my Biology class.

STEVE
Sorry—I didn't remember. I'm new here.

SECOND RED BOY
Real new. You probably didn't get enough of the fountain water in you to even *see* the aura until today.

STEVE
(excited)
You mean you all see it, too?

RED GIRL
Everyone around here *sees* it. You can't *help* seeing it.

STEVE
I'm glad to run into you guys. Everyone's been treating me like a nigger.

FIRST RED BOY
You got it *backwards*. They're like niggers, treating us like the only *whites* in town.

They *know* we're smarter than they are and they
hate us for it. This fountain stuff gets
right to the heart of the matter—it lets
everyone know who the *real* whites are—
(points to his head)
—the ones who are "white" where it counts.

SECOND RED BOY
Which *you* proved by the way you talked back to
that dyke *Ms.* Garrison. Showed some spunk.

STEVE
Then how come you didn't say anything then?

SECOND RED BOY
Why should I've stuck my neck out for you?
You'll find out—it doesn't pay to make waves
around here.

There's the Sound of Loud Laughter from another table.

RED GIRL
(gestures at blue
tables)
Look at them all. They're all so smug. They
think they're better than everybody just
because people outside the town can't see the
auras—you'd think they *invented* water instead
of just drinking it.

Steve misses the irony of the pot calling the kettle black.

FIRST RED BOY
They won't be smug for long, though. Every
once in a while they need to be taken down a
couple of pegs. You interested?

STEVE
(excited)

Yeah, sure I'm interested. Just tell me who
we're fighting, and when.

The Red Girl looks at Steve as if he's crazy, but before she can say anything, the Second Red Boy waves her into silence.

SECOND RED BOY
(conspiratorially)
We handle things *differently* here, Morris. We
work *quietly*. Slash their tires. Slip a dog
turd in the punch at the prom. Paint
swastikas on their houses. That sort of
thing.

STEVE
(horrified)
But, that's the sort of stuff *cowards* do.
Where's your guts? Where's your sense of
honor?

FIRST RED BOY
You're being taken in by blue propaganda.
These are *scum* we're talking about, not
people. You don't think they actually *believe*
that stuff they spout at us, do you?

Realization time. Steve looks at the Blue students in the cafeteria, eating, talking happily, laughing. Then he looks at the Red Students at his table. He gets up slowly.

STEVE
Excuse me.

Steve runs out of the cafeteria.

CUT TO

INT. THE SCHOOL BASEMENT - CUSTODIAN'S ROOM

No windows, so we don't know what time it is. The school custodian, Mr. Cleary—blue aura—goes to a closet to get a rolling bucket and mop—he's just about to start the floors.

INT. CLOSET - LIGHT FLOODING IN FROM OUTSIDE

As Cleary takes the bucket out, there's a sound of something being knocked over, and Cleary sees Steve Morris over to one side of the closet, sitting up.

CLEARY
Dark enough for you?

STEVE
What?

CLEARY
If you like, I can stuff some rags under the door so the light doesn't leak in. I wouldn't want you to miss any sleep.

STEVE
What time is it?

CLEARY
Three-thirty. What did you want to hide down here for?

STEVE
I couldn't stand the idea of anyone seeing me.

CLEARY
Oh.

STEVE
You can't see it in the dark. The aura, I mean. Do you know how come?

CLEARY
You don't "see" the aura—you just think you
do. You don't expect to see things in the
dark, so you don't.

STEVE
Can you take pictures of it?

CLEARY
Uh-uh. If you could, this town would've been
swamped with psychics and UFO nuts years ago.

STEVE
What causes it? What's in the fountain?

CLEARY
The fountain's built on the first well to be
sunk in Pleasant Springs, when the town was a
station on the Underground Railway before the
Civil War. Maybe it's something natural—like
the fluoride they found in some town that was
preventing cavities there.

STEVE
No kidding?

CLEARY
Or maybe some abolitionist chemist figured out
a way to identify the bounty-hunters sent
after escaping slaves.

STEVE
Yeah?

CLEARY
Or, maybe it's a secret voodoo, carried from
Africa by a captured witch doctor, and handed
down through generations.

STEVE
Well which *is* it?

CLEARY
How should I know? Who do you think I am—Yoda?

STEVE
(laughs)
You haven't told me who you are yet.

CLEARY
Cleary. *Obi-Wan* Cleary.

Steve laughs again. Then he stands up and Cleary turns on the closet light. We now see that there's a broken mirror in the closet and We See in the mirror that Steve's aura is now Bright Blue—the same color as Cleary's. Steve squints and lifts his hand to block his eyes against the light, then he sees, too, that his aura has changed.

STEVE
Mr. Cleary, it's turned *blue*.

Cleary nods.

STEVE
(continuing)
Why *me*? How come the fountain doesn't turn *everybody* blue?

CLEARY
All the fountain can do is to allow you to see someone's essence—starting with your own—to see whether a person glows with rage or compassion. If your inside glow changes so will your outside glow.

Steve nods, understanding, then follows Cleary out of the closet
O.S.

CUT TO

EXT. PLEASANT SPRINGS - VARIOUS SHOTS TRACKING
STEVE - AFTERNOON

as Steve is walking home. As he passes other people—both adults and students his own age with Blue Auras—he sees a complete reversal of their attitude towards him.

A MAN (BLUE AURA) MOWING HIS LAWN

as he smiles at Steve. Steve smiles back.

TWO TEENAGE GIRLS (BOTH BLUE AURAS)

as they smile as Steve. Steve smiles back, they giggle, and continue walking. Then

EXT. FRONT SUBURBAN HOUSE - A TALL BLACK
TEENAGER - DAY

also with a Blue Aura, shooting baskets at a hoop—never missing—in the driveway of a suburban house a lot like Steve's, as Steve stops to watch. The Teenager sees Steve, catches the ball, and walks toward him.

SOWELLE
Hi.

STEVE
Uh, hi.
(beat)
You're in my music class, right?

SOWELLE
Right. Andrew Sowelle.

STEVE
Steve Morris. We just moved here, over on

Spooner Lane.

Steve hesitates just one beat before sticking his hand out. Sowelle transfers the ball to his left hand and they shake hands. (No "heavy-handed" close ups, please.)

STEVE
(continuing)
You're pretty good with that basketball.

SOWELLE
Thanks. It runs in the blood.

Steve looks almost shocked.

SOWELLE
(continuing)
I mean my uncle played with the Celtics. He taught me. You play?

STEVE
Well, yeah, but I'll never make pro. I don't have the height.

SOWELLE
My uncle is *your* height. You want to shoot a few?

STEVE
(dropping his books)
Sure. But only for a few minutes. My mom'll have dinner waiting.

SOWELLE
You want to put some blood into it? Penny a basket?

STEVE
Well ... why not?

Sowelle tosses Steve the ball. Steve *shoots* from the street end of the driveway.

CLOSE ON THE BASKETBALL

as it sails long over Sowelle's head and right through the hoop.

STEVE AND SOWELLE

as Sowelle looks at Steve, amazed, then laughs.

SOWELLE
Now who's hustlin' *who* here?

On Steve's wide grin, the boys start playing again and we

CUT TO

EXT. STREET OF MORRIS HOUSE - DAY

as the next-door Boy who shunned Steve before now smiles and waves to Steve as Steve walks up the Morris driveway. Steve waves back—it's obvious they'll take the time to meet later.

INT. MORRIS KITCHEN - DAY

as Steve arrives home. Steve's parents and Billy are already in there. Steve sees that both his parents have Red Auras, but that Billy has a Blue Aura.

JILL
Oh, *there* you are. Kept after school, already?

STEVE
No...I just made some new friends.

DON
I told you you would. In your class?

STEVE
One of them is. The other's ... the other's a teacher.

JILL
Well you should invite them over for dinner some time.

STEVE
(smiling secretly)
I just might. How's the new job, Dad?

DON
Fine, just fine. The only problem's a black—one of the regional managers—who thinks he knows it all. I'm going to have to take him down a couple of pegs.

Steve reacts to the phrase.

DON
(continuing)
I thought by moving here we could get away from these low-lifes—but they're *everywhere*. If it isn't a lazy Hispanic, it's a pain-in-the-butt black.

BILLY
(lightly; as a joke)
You mean a spic and a spook?

Steve is horrified, not only because of what Billy has said, but because just as Billy says it, Billy's Aura changes—for a few seconds—from Blue to Red, before settling on Blue again.

Jill carries dinner over to the table.

JILL
You're not supposed to call them that, Billy.

It's not polite. We're *supposed* to call them
"blacks" and "Hispanics."

DON
That's right, Billy. But you got my meaning.

CLOSE ON STEVE

as we see him thinking as he sits down to dinner.

CUT TO

EXT. MORRIS DRIVEWAY - DAY

as Steve and Billy are outside, shooting baskets.

BILLY
Well, why do you have to show it to me, *now*?

STEVE
I *told* you—it's a secret. I'll tell you
what. I'll give you a quarter.

BILLY
Nah.

STEVE
Fifty cents.

BILLY
A buck.

STEVE
Sold.

Steve drops the basketball through the hoop one more time.

CUT TO

EXT. PLEASANT SPRINGS HIGH SCHOOL - THE FOUNTAIN - DAY

as Steve and Billy ride up on bicycles. They park their bikes by the fountain.

BILLY
This is what you want to show me?

STEVE
Yep. You've got to taste it.

BILLY
Is it icky or something?

STEVE
It's fine. Look, I'll drink first.

Steve takes a drink first, then licks his lips.

STEVE
See? Your turn.

Billy hesitates. Steve takes out a dollar in change and jingles it. Billy takes the money from Steve and shoves it into a pocket.

BILLY
This better be *good.*

Billy takes a tentative sip from the fountain.

BILLY
(continuing)
It tastes funny. Not *bad,* just funny.

Billy takes another—longer—drink. Steve watches his brother drinking.

STEVE

It doesn't taste all that funny once you get
used to it.

As we Pull Back from Steve and Billy drinking from the Fountain, we

FADE OUT

Timeshare

After I'd sold two scripts to *Twilight Zone*, I had a pretty good "in" there to submit to them. I was already developing one story for them (which never got finished because the long-distance telephone story conferences with staffers bantering back-and-forth were too diffuse for me to figure out what they wanted) so Kate and I decided to work up a spec script and just submit it.

Alan Brennert liked this script. I think if *Twilight Zone* had lasted another season, it might have gotten made.

While Kate and I were writing this, we imagined Myron and Etta Stein as Darrin and Samantha's annoying neighbors, the Kravitzes, from *Bewitched*.

Seeing this one made just would have been sheer fun.

JNS

Timeshare
by Kate O'Neal & J. Neil Schulman

FADE IN

EXT. VACATION HOME - DAY

Picture postcard perfect. A two-storey wood-and-stone house set on a spacious lawn with nearby lake and forest, blue sky and sunshine overhead.

SALESMAN (O.S.)
—the ideal vacation get-away. All the
rustic elegance of country living
combined with all the modern conveniences
of your own home.

ANGLE WIDENS TO REVEAL:

that the vacation home is a brochure photo.

INT. APARTMENT - NIGHT

The apartment is middle-income and predictable—the sort of place with plastic on the furniture. The brochure is open on a coffee table in front of Myron and Etta Stein, who are being pitched to by smooth salesman Roger Palmer. The Steins are in that awkward age after the kids have grown up and moved out, but before retirement. Super-salesman Palmer, wearing a loud green jacket with the pocket-patch-logo of "Timeshare Vacation Living," smells their sales-vulnerability.

PALMER
(continuing)
—You'd have boating, swimming, fishing,
fresh air, gentle breezes, whirlpool and
all modern appliances—all for only a

tenth of the price you'd expect to pay
for such luxury.

ETTA
But what if we don't *like* the other
people we're sharing the house with?

PALMER
You don't *have* to—that's the beauty of
timeshare living. You're sharing *time*
with the other house owners, but not
space. Your yearly two-week holidays are
scheduled so you'll never even meet any
of the other owners.

MYRON
I don't know ... Mr. Palmer, how can your
company make a profit selling us a
lifetime of two-week vacations for *eight
hundred dollars*?

PALMER
(delighted)
Too good to be true, right?

MYRON
Not that I'm saying you're a crook, but—

PALMER
—But you can't take chances with your
hard earned money. Mr. Stein, my company
bought this property many, many years
ago, when real estate prices were—to
coin a phrase—dirt cheap. Now, we're
able to pass the savings on to *you*.

MYRON
I guess that makes sense.
(to his wife)

Whadd'ya think, Etta?

ETTA
It sounds good to me if it sounds good to
you, Myron.

Palmer places a contract in front of Myron Stein and extends him a pen. Myron takes the pen.

MYRON
(hesitates)
Well ...

PALMER
(going in for kill)
If you don't take it today, someone else
will tomorrow.

MYRON
You only live once, I guess.

Myron signs the contract and Palmer takes it.

PALMER
Congratulations! You're in for the time
of your lives!

Palmer opens his attache case and drops the contract on a thick stack of identical contracts. Myron extends the pen back to Palmer.

PALMER
(smiles artificially)
Hey, keep the pen. A special gift from
Timeshare Vacation Living.

CUT TO

INT. AUTOMOBILE - DAY

tracking the Steins' Buick as it rumbles up a wooded drive toward their new vacation home. And, to tell the truth, it looks almost as good as the brochure picture.

ETTA
Look, Myron, it's *beautiful*!

EXT. VACATION HOME

as they park alongside the lakeside cottage and get out. There is a nearby pier belonging to the cottage, and nobody else around.

MYRON
Well, it looks good on the *outside*.

Myron starts toward the trunk to get their luggage.

ETTA
Don't you want to look through the house
first?

MYRON
(opening trunk)
That Palmer salesman already got our
money, Etta. We're stuck with it,
whatever it's like.

ETTA
Myron!!

Resignedly, Myron slams the trunk without getting the luggage and follows his wife toward the house.

INT. HOUSE

as the Steins enter and they see an absolutely *marvelous* luxury cottage: modern kitchen, a living room in early American. A touchtone phone near the entrance. Staircase to upstairs.

ETTA
Myron, it's *beautiful*! So rustic ... yet
so *modern*!

MYRON
(still suspicious)
Well, it *looks* good on the inside.

ETTA
Would you stop worrying? For *once* we got
what we paid for.

MYRON
Don't be so sure. Let's see what the
upstairs looks like.

The Steins start up the stairs. As they do, there's a *rumbling* sound and everything becomes hazy and out-of-focus for a second—but only for a second. They pause on the stairs, both disoriented.

ETTA
Myron, are you all right?

MYRON
I felt dizzy for a second.

ETTA
So did I.

Myron is triumphant at having found something wrong with the house.

MYRON
You see? I bet these *stairs* aren't
level.

They continue up.

INT. UPSTAIRS BEDROOM

as the Steins enter. The bedroom is beautiful with a king-size bed. But it looks lived in—bedspreads, make up on a dressing table, clothes hanging in a closet.

MYRON
Looks like whoever was here last left
some of their stuff behind.

INT. BATHROOM

as Etta looks it. There are personal belongings all around the sink—shaving kit, toothpaste, brushes.

ETTA
They didn't even clean up the *bathroom.*

INT. BEDROOM

as Etta returns. Myron is looking out the window.

MYRON
Etta, take a look at this.

Etta joins her husband at the window.

WINDOW - STEINS' POV OF THE LAKE

where another couple is fishing off a pier with a station wagon parked nearby. The Steins' Buick is visible below.

ETTA
The *nerve* of some people, fishing off our
pier! Myron, you'll have to make them
leave!

Myron sighs at the inevitability of the situation, then nods.

EXT. PIER - DAY

as the Steins walk toward the other couple, also middle-aged. The two couples regard each other suspiciously. The other woman speaks first.

JENNY DOVER
Hello.

MYRON
Hi. I'm Myron Stein, this is my wife,
Etta. You folks live around here?

HARV DOVER
Uh-huh. Jenny and Harv Dover. We spend
two weeks every spring at our timeshare.

Harv points to the cottage the Steins just came from.

ETTA
Oh, Myron, no!

MYRON
Would you let *me* handle this, Etta?

Myron pulls folded papers out of his pocket and extends it to Harv.

MYRON
(continuing)
I hate to be the one to tell you, Harv,
but you've got your date wrong. *Our* two
weeks start today. Here's my contract.

Harv Dover looks at the contract then laughs with relief. He hands the contract to his wife, who also smiles.

JENNY
I'm afraid *you're* the ones who've made
the mistake. This says your vacation
starts on the first Saturday in June.

MYRON
That's right.

HARV
Well, this was still May, last time I
looked. May eleventh, to be exact. You
folks are a month early.

ETTA
What are you talking? Today's June
seventh.

MYRON
Would you let me handle this, Etta?
(to Harv)
She's right. Look, I'm sorry if you
missed your time, but you can't just take
over our vacation.

Jenny takes a newspaper off the pier, where a fish has been wrapped in it, and extends it to the Steins, who back off at the smell.

JENNY
I bought this paper this morning. See?
May *eleventh*.

INSERT - NEWSPAPER FRONT PAGE

and it's dated May 11th.

ALL AGAIN

MYRON
You wrap fish in old newspaper. So what?

JENNY
Oh, for heaven's sake! Look at the *date*
on my watch!

INSERT - JENNY'S WATCH

Dated: May 11.

ALL AGAIN AT PIER

ETTA
You're a month slow, dear.

Etta extends her own wrist.

INSERT - ETTA'S WATCH

Dated: *June 7th.*

ALL AGAIN AT PIER

HARV
Look, this whole thing is silly. We'll
go up to the house, pick up the phone,
and ask the operator what date it is.
Okay?

ETTA
And whoever's wrong *leaves*.

HARV
Just what I had in mind.

Myron nods.

EXT. PATH TO HOUSE - STEINS AND DOVERS - DAY

The four of them all start walking toward the house when there's another *rumble* and everything becomes wavy, but this time the effect lasts longer than the first time, and:

EXT. HOUSE CHANGED - STEINS AND DOVERS - DAY

Harv Dover recovers first, and looks around, startled.

HARV
What the—!

Etta, Myron, and Jenny also look around, shocked.

It is now Autumn, leaves turning color and falling.

JENNY
Harv, why are the leaves down already?

HARV
Well, we're up north. The seasons change
earlier here ... I guess.

The four continue walking toward the house. In the yard there is now a decorative installation that looks like a futuristic laser cannon.

MYRON
I don't remember that being here before.

Etta looks at the side of the installation and reads aloud:

ETTA
Nuke-o-Matic Home Missile Defense System
... Myron, what's going on?

MYRON
I don't know ... but get a loada that!

Myron points toward the house where a White Van without wheels floats a few feet off the ground not far from the Steins' Buick.

ETTA
(scared)
Myron—

MYRON
Now take it easy, Etta. I'm sure there's
a simple explanation.
(to Harv)
You're one of them guys who hypnotize
people in a nightclub, right?

JENNY
(nervously)
Uh-uh. Harv manages a chain of dry
cleaners.

MYRON
That's some delivery van you got.

HARV
(uneasily)
That's not my ... van.
(taking charge)
C'mon, we'd better get to a phone.

They all walk to the house more quickly.

INT. HOUSE - DAY

as the Steins and Dovers enter. The living room decor is the same, but the kitchen appliances are different ... futuristic. In the living room, where the touchtone phone was before, is now a sophisticated video-computer phone. Harv looks at it, confused.

Suddenly, there's an imperious female voice O.S. from the top of the stairs:

WOMAN'S VOICE
All of you down there! Freeze and get
your hands up!

TOP OF STAIRS - A UNIFORMED WOMAN

The uniform is shiny and tight-fitted, though obviously military. She's holding some sort of weapon pointed downstairs at the Steins and Dovers.

ETTA
Don't shoot! Don't shoot!

WOMAN
I said hands up—*now*!

HARV
Take it easy and do as she says!

The uniformed woman comes down the stairs slowly, keeping her weapon trained on the other four.

LIVING ROOM AGAIN

WOMAN
I'm Major Scott of the Hundred Eighty Second Militia Command. Who are you people and how did you get onto a government reservation?

MYRON
Government reservation? But we bought this house on timeshare! Mr. Palmer didn't say anything about—

MAJOR SCOTT
Palmer! You can put your hands down but keep them where I can see them. All right, what does Quartermaster Palmer have to do with this?

JENNY
Quartermaster Palmer? Youngish guy with dark hair, real fast talker?

ETTA
You bought the timeshare from Palmer too?

Jenny nods.

MAJOR SCOTT
What do you mean "bought"? You know very well that since the War—

MYRON
—the "War"?

HARV
I hope you don't mind my asking, Major, but what's today's date?

MAJOR SCOTT
The date? Sixteen October.

HARV
Er ... what *year*?

MAJOR SCOTT
Are you all brain-dead? Sixteen October 2149, of course.

JENNY
Time sure flies when you're having fun.

HARV
Uh, Jenny honey. I don't think she's kidding. Look, Major, I don't know what's going on here, but it's easy to figure that Palmer is at the bottom of it somehow.

MYRON
He's a crook, I knew it all along!

MAJOR SCOTT
That doesn't explain what you people are
doing here dressed up in those costumes.

ETTA
Costume? You should talk, huh!

Suddenly, another rumble and more waving around. This time, all the furniture disappears completely. Then:

TWO COLORED SPHERES MATERIALIZING

Like Glinda in the Wizard of Oz, two colored spheres appear, and two androgynous humanoids, dressed even more oddly than Major Scott, materialize. As the spheres disappear, the humanoids look at all the others wonderously.

MAJOR SCOTT

as she raises her weapon toward the newcomers.

ALL AGAIN

The First Humanoid, named Grickzorp, waves his arm and the Major's weapon disappears.

The Second Humanoid, Mrs. Grickzorp, looks at her mate anxiously.

MRS. GRICKZORP
Grickzorp?

GRICKZORP
(to Myron, sternly)
T'zala kneft ulltip?!

MYRON
What? What did you say?

Grickzorp points his arm at Myron for a moment, then speaks in English.

GRICKZORP
I interrogated what you all are doing in my vacation house!

MYRON
Well, it all started when this salesman named Roger Palmer—

GRICKZORP
Palmer!

HARV
I see you know him, too.

MRS. GRICKZORP
Sentient Palmer *was* the person who gave us this house, for a time.

HARV
Gave, huh? What did you have to "give" him in return?

MRS. GRICKZORP
Palmer required nothing in return. But we did give him the customary love offering.

HARV
Uh-huh, I get it.

GRICKZORP
We register surprise, though. Palmer did not inform us there would be, concurrently, other sentients in residence.

MAJOR SCOTT
(recovering wits)
All of us seem to have been given the
same impression.

MRS. GRICKZORP
(sadly)
This was to have been our second
honeylune.

GRICKZORP
I think we had better summon Sentient
Palmer to resolve this small difficulty.

GRICKZORP

as he takes a small, polished disk out of a pouchlike pocket.

CLOSE ON THE DISK

as the image of Palmer appears.

WIDE AGAIN

as Palmer materializes as the Grickzorps did, dressed as we saw him before, carrying his attache case.

Palmer looks around, takes in the scene, and looks very nervous.

PALMER
Uh-oh.

Everyone tries talking at once:

MYRON
—What are you trying to pull here—

MAJOR SCOTT
—What's going on here, Quartermaster—

JENNY
—Palmer, if you think you can—

Palmer tries backing away—and backs into Grickzorp.

PALMER
It's not my fault!

Mrs. Grickzorp holds up her palm for silence.

MRS. GRICKZORP
(to others)
I am an Advocate credited to address the
Grand Tribunal. If you will allow me to
speak for us all?

ETTA
(to Myron)
What did she say?

MYRON
It's a lawyer, Etta.

Everyone except Palmer nods approval for Mrs. Grickzorp to proceed.

MRS. GRICKZORP
Sentient Roger Palmer, what is your
explanation for this?

PALMER
C'mon, I'm just a small guy trying to
make an honest—

Palmer looks at Major's Scott's murderous expression, then sighs.

PALMER
(continuing)
I guess there's been a timequake.

(looking around)
Or two. (looks again) Or three.

HARV
What the hell is a "timequake"?

PALMER
Well, it's like an earthquake, only the faultline isn't in the earth, it's in the fabric of time. You people just tumbled forward in time a bit.

MAJOR SCOTT
How much is a "bit"?

PALMER
(looks at humanoids,
sighs)
About thirty thousand years.

MYRON
Thirty thousand years!

HARV
Jeez, my money market must be worth a fortune!

MYRON
This was supposed to be for two weeks! I want my money back!

PALMER
Check your contracts! Timeshare Vacation Living is not responsible for natural disasters!

MRS. GRICKZORP
(accusingly)
It is "natural" that you constructed

recreational property in a temporally
unstable sector?

PALMER
We had all the right permits for every
era, signed by all the right officials—

MRS. GRICKZORP
(moving closer)
And if we were to inquire deeply in this
current era, no doubt we would discover
which such officials had received illicit
remuneration ...

PALMER
(quickly)
Of course I don't want anyone here to
feel cheated. Suppose we keep this whole
thing quiet and I give back your ...

HARV & MYRON
Money.

MAJOR SCOTT
Ration credits.

GRICKZORP
Love energy.

Palmer sighs. He opens his attache case, removes contracts and stacks of money, hands them to Myron and Harv, then hands Major Scott a contract and ration tickets. Then he faces Grickzorp, who hands Palmer the shiny disk. Palmer holds it to his forehead and the disk glows for a second.

PALMER
(grabbing attache
case)
Now if you folks would excuse me—

PALMER

as he waves his hands. A sphere appears around him, then both he and the sphere dematerialize.

ALL AGAIN

MRS. GRICKZORP
Equity has been restored.

MYRON
Yeah? How are we supposed to get home?

GRICKZORP
It is within our capabilities to return each of you to your own time and place of residence.

ETTA
(sarcastically)
Great, I just love spending my vacation at home watching baseball on TV.

GRICKZORP
In your home-time they still play baseball?

Etta nods.

MRS. GRICKZORP
How romantic!

JENNY
(getting an idea)
Maybe we don't have to go home ... right away?

Grickzorp shakes his head.

JENNY
(continuing)
Harv, you remember that wild party at the
Gordons when everyone threw their car
keys in a hat?

CUT TO

INT. MYRON AND ETTA STEINS' APARTMENT - DAY

as the Grickzorps materialize, smile broadly, turn on the television to a baseball game, and make themselves comfortable, with their arms around each other, on the couch.

CUT TO

INT. FUTURISTIC DWELLING UNIT - DAY

as Major Scott, Jenny and Harv Dover, and Myron and Etta Stein materialize in a Dali-esque room with a thrilling view of a far-future city. They all gaze happily at the exotic skyline.

MAJOR SCOTT
(to others)
Okay, we all rendezvous back here with
the Grickzorps in two weeks, right?

HARV
Right.

Major Scott and the others nod, then Major Scott, the Dovers, and the Steins each head out.

CUT TO

EXT. BUSY FUTURISTIC STREET - MYRON AND ETTA - DAY

as we watch them walk off, surrounded by future humanoids.

MYRON
Etta, this is going to be better than
last year in San Francisco!

ETTA
That was thirty *thousand* years ago,
Myron.

MYRON
Don't start up with me, Etta.

As the two of them walk away on their adventure, we

FADE OUT

No Strings Attached

Let me start out by saying that I have been obsessed with classical violin since I was around four or five years old, and gained enough sentience to realize that my father, Julius Schulman, who plays violin, could do something that other daddies couldn't do.

Interestingly, I don't think it was seeing my father play the violin that brought on this realization. I remember it as some rainy day at my grandmother's house in Forest Hills, New York, when to amuse me, my grandmother put on her Victrola some radio transcriptions of my father playing the fast movement of the Mendelssohn Violin Concerto with the WOR Mutual Network Symphony Orchestra.

I'm not sure how my life would have turned out if I had somehow communicated to my parents how I felt at that moment of "grokking." I'm not even sure if what I was feeling was worship of the violin or worship of my father—the memory doesn't differentiate it for me. But I wonder what would have happened if I had convinced my parents to start me on violin lessons at that moment. For all I know, I may have even tried; I don't remember. But I know that my father, whose career had not yet recovered from the WOR strike that had caused the Mutual Network to replace its live orchestra with canned music (thus eliminating my father's position as the orchestra's concertmaster and putting him out of work for a year) would not have been particularly anxious for his son to get into "this lousy business."

Child development pioneer Jean Piaget theorized that there are certain developmental windows for cognitive development in children. If an ability isn't developed in time, the child will never develop that ability. I believe the developmental window for becoming a virtuoso violinist is between the ages of three and five. While plenty of professional violinists have learned to play violin later than that, I am not aware of any of the top- ranking virtuosos who did. Jascha Heifetz, for example, began playing at four and performed the Beethoven Violin Concerto at age seven.

My father began violin lessons at five. At eight he performed the Mendelssohn Violin Concerto at Carnegie Hall.

I didn't convince my parents to start me on violin lessons for another three or four years, when my father was a member of the Boston Symphony Orchestra, and I was eight or nine. My violin teacher was Gerry Gelbloom, another violinist in the Boston Symphony. My parents tell me that I played in tune right from the beginning, but all I remember is that I got frustrated by my difficulties in learning to read music, and particularly frustrated by listening to the horrible sounds that came out of the violin when I played it, as compared to the sounds that came out of it when my father played it. I think my father noticed the discrepancy also; I remember one day when I was practicing for a lesson in my bedroom and my father was practicing repertoire in the bedroom he used as a studio, that he told me to practice later because my practicing was making it impossible for him to concentrate. I don't think it was more than a few months later that I quit practicing entirely and stopped taking violin lessons.

Some people may assume from this that it was the "emotional bruise" from this incident that caused me to quit the violin. I think they would be wrong. Some people would also assume that there was some Oedipal conflict between myself and my father, with the violin taking the place of Oedipus's mother. This is more amusing and can lead me to giving a detailed description of the violin as a symbol for the female body (I'll leave it to your imagination what the bow is supposed to be)—but I think it's also wrong.

My assessment is that by the time I started violin lessons, the window of opportunity had already closed for me. Whether there is an age when learning to read music is as easy as learning to read words, or an age when the associative imprints from practicing are made quickly enough that one doesn't get frustrated and quit, is more than I know for sure.

Alternatively, maybe my father's dexterity is genetic, and I was simply missing the gene.

In any case, destiny did not intend Julius Schulman's son to be a violinist like his father. Instead, he found another business, just as insecure and rotten as being a professional musician, to go into.

But he can still listen to his father playing the violin and be mesmerized.

The genesis of *No Strings Attached* comes, I believe, from three additional moments of realization.

The first moment was when a rock band called The New York Rock and Roll Ensemble performed with the Boston Pops Orchestra (that's the same thing as the Boston Symphony during their off-season) in 1969.

I was sixteen that year, played rock guitar a little, was heavily into photography, and was an usher for Symphony Hall. The New York Rock and Roll Ensemble came onstage with the Pops orchestra. First the Boston Pops played Bach's Brandenburg Concerto Number Five. Then the New York Rock and Roll Ensemble, all of whom were classically trained musicians, performed a piece of their own called "Brandenburg," which started with the Bach piece, then spun off into a rock number.

I have the band's album containing "Brandenburg," and the energy level in the recording makes it sound like sixties folk rock, but in Symphony Hall that day, it was *electric*.

I used my backstage privileges to meet the band, talk them into letting me do an album photo shoot for them on spec, and spent some time hanging around Boston that week with the band's leader, Michael Kamen, who's now a successful film composer (*Brazil, Lethal Weapon, Mr. Holland's Opus*). They even let me jam with them late at night at The Jazz Workshop. It made an impression. (Michael Kamen was one of the first people I sent this screenplay to. We had a couple of nice phone conversations about it but don't know if he ever found time to read it.)

The second "moment of realization" came when I was driving a rental car on Ventura Boulevard in Studio City, during the 1985 filming of my *Twilight Zone* episode, "Profile in Silver." The director of my episode was John Hancock, a well-respected feature film director, with whom I'd been hanging out during free moments during the shoot. John had told me that in his Harvard days, he'd been a violinist in the student orchestra at Tanglewood, the summer headquarters of the Boston Symphony, and had also directed stage productions early in his career, and while I was driving along, suddenly I had the image of a battle field with a symphony orchestra on one side and a rock band on the other. My thought was that this was an idea it would be interesting to approach John with if I could figure out a way to develop it.

The final "moment" came months later. My (now ex-)wife, Kate

O'Neal, had begun composing songs using a computer and MIDI keyboard. For family reasons, we were spending the Christmas, 1986 holidays apart—she with her mother and sister in Chicago, me with my parents in San Antonio; we would be flying back to our apartment in Jersey City so we could be together for New Years Eve.

While I was at the airport in San Antonio, just before my flight to Newark, I got into a discussion with my father in which I was arguing that the loss of work which acoustic musicians were experiencing because of synthesizers—a big issue in my father's musician's union journals I'd been reading during the visit—was counterbalanced by the increased power which synthesizers were giving to composers. You can imagine that my father, who (as you'll recall) had lost one of the best jobs he'd ever had because live musicians were replaced by "canned" music, was not entirely open to my point. On the other hand, I had seen my wife—whose professional musical training is in voice, and who plays no instrument—become a sophisticated composer in a matter of months using a Commodore 64 computer (primitive enough that I referred to it disparagingly as a "Comedy 64") and a MIDI sequencer program called Dr. T.

As you can imagine, my loyalties were divided. I asked my father, "How would you feel if the only way you could play violin was to use a synthesizer?" I don't recall his answer, but the question stayed with me.

The morning after I flew home, I woke up with the idea for *No Strings Attached*, fully blown. I am not exaggerating. The story was completely laid out in my head, beat by beat. It took me only an hour or so to have the outline for the screenplay done. It took me three weeks to complete the first draft.

There is one scene near the end of the screenplay (you'll know it when you get there) that I read to my parents over the phone, as soon as I finished writing it. My father told me that it made him want to cry. And, when I sent him the finished screenplay to critique, he thought it was the best thing I'd ever written.

Okay. Maybe there are other things I could do instead of play the violin.

I got a lot of good feedback on this screenplay. It got good coverage at the major agencies. Werner Klemperer (Colonel Klink on *Hogan's Heroes*) agreed to play the role of Smith-Kensington. Tracy

Ullman's agent recommended it to her. But I could not get it produced or even optioned. It seemed to fall between the cracks too many ways. The central conflict in it seems to be restricted to the American music industry; British readers found it hard to understand how classical musicians could be so opposed to rock music or synthesizers.

There are also production challenges. For a high budget film, it would need a young male film star to play the lead role—but unless the star is miraculously a violinist already (and I looked *hard* for one without finding any), you are looking at several million dollars of special effects to carry off the two opening extended sequences of violin playing. You'd probably need a computer-controlled camera with the actor braced into position to match a violinist double, or stop-motion animation with a live actor for minutes at a time, for the audition scene and the club scene.

Or you need an actor who is willing to spend months learning to play violin well enough to be able to mime technically difficult fingerings and bowings for thirty or forty seconds at a time. (This does not need to match up with actual fingerings and bowings later on in the film, for reasons that will become obvious).

It was the production hurdles inherent in "faking the violin" well enough to pull off the film that caused John Hancock originally to take a pass on it. (John is now ready to direct it, if financing becomes available.)

The low budget approach is to be willing to release a film without a known star in the lead role of Igor—and to find a young, male virtuoso violinist ... who can also act.

I found one, and spent a year and a half busting my butt trying to produce this movie, after I couldn't find anyone else who wanted to try. (What the hell—it was during the longest Writers Guild strike in recent memory, and I had nothing else to work on at the time anyway.)

His name was Dmitry Sitkovetsky, one of the finest violinists in the world today. He has a perfect memory and can memorize dialogue at a glance. Aside from a Russian accent that would have needed to be reduced somewhat (and I provided him with Jack Catran's accent reduction tape course to do that), he would have been wonderful—spontaneous and expressive.

And, I had the rock band all set up, too. The Soviet rock band,

Avtograf. The lead guitarist of which was Sasha Sitkovetsky—Dmitry's first cousin and boyhood chum.

I had wonderful young actress/rock singer to play Cambridge—Meri D. Her mother was the co-manager for Avtograf.

I had a composer to write the "Concerto Grosso for Violin, Rock Band and Orchestra": William Ross, an award-winning modern classical composer and film composer.

And, I even had a budget that said the movie could be made for two million dollars by the simple expediency of doing some of the filming in Moscow with a mixed American-Soviet crew, which would have enabled the purchase of two million dollars of production services for around $400,000. And I had firm interest from the Soviet Ministry of Culture in doing it.

I could not get a known director to commit to the project.

I could not get a negative pick up, even for two million dollars.

I could not get anyone I knew, or anyone who knew anyone I knew, or anyone who knew anyone who KNEW anyone I knew, to invest.

I went for broke trying to produce this movie. And I made it. I went broke.

So here is *No Strings Attached*, which my-father-the- violinist thinks is the best thing I've ever written.

Maybe Industrial Light and Magic or Pixar will come up with a miraculous low-budget solution for faking violin playing one of these days, and you'll see this on the silver screen in THX sound 6-track Dolby.

As for me, it would be the next-best-thing to playing the violin, myself.

—JNS

No Strings Attached
A Screenplay
by J. Neil Schulman

FADE IN

INT. A CONCERT AUDITORIUM - NIGHT

The stage is lighted, but empty except for a large movable screen—the sort you'd find as an acoustic reflector for an orchestra—stretching from one wing to center stage. Only a grand piano is partly visible.

And before we notice anything else, we hear a solo violin playing classical music with the piano accompanying it. The violin playing is professional enough, but this is no virtuoso we're hearing. As the violin continues, we

REVERSE ON AUDITORIUM SEATS

and the only people seated in the hall are a dozen men and women—mostly men, dressed in casual jacket and tie—clustered near the center about ten rows back. This is the Orchestra String Audition Committee. Each of them has a lap-held clipboard with a sheaf of standard, Xeroxed forms on it.

CLOSE PAN FROM CLIPBOARD TO CLIPBOARD

In a space marked *Candidate* each form has written in: #53 — and there are ratings labelled Intonation, Accuracy, Interpretation, Feeling, etc. This particular violinist is getting ratings between 4's and 6's.

We stop on one particular clipboard.

REVERSE ON THE MUSIC DIRECTOR, INCLUDING

COMMITTEE

seated dead center tenth row. This is the distinguished ERIC SMITH-KENSINGTON, wearing a turtleneck and jacket. He catches the eyes of the other committee members.

> SMITH-KENSINGTON
> (quietly, to others)
> Have we heard enough of this one?

They all nod.

> SMITH-KENSINGTON

> SMITH-KENSINGTON
> (loudly, to stage)
> Thank you very much—
> (glances down)
> —Number fifty-three. Number fifty-four, please.

STAGE AGAIN

Violin and piano come to an abrupt halt, violin strings being strummed halfheartedly. Hard shoes walk off across the hardwood stage, then another set walk on. But we can't see the new performer at all.

THE COMMITTEE

as they yawn, stretch, light cigarettes, and flip to the next form.

> SMITH-KENSINGTON
> (continuing loudly to stage)
> The Sibelius, please.

We hear a few seconds of tuning up, a few beats of silence, then the dramatic introduction of a violin playing the Sibelius Concerto.

Immediately we can tell—by the sudden alertness of the Committee, if nothing else—that we're hearing a violinist of virtuoso caliber. *Now* we're really hearing first-rate playing, something wonderfully special. After a few seconds of this, we see pens go into motion.

CLOSE PAN FROM CLIPBOARD TO CLIPBOARD AGAIN

only this time we're seeing 8's and 9's. Again we stop on the center clipboard with 9's in most categories and a big *10* next to *Feeling*.

REVERSE ON SMITH-KENSINGTON

nodding appreciatively to the CONCERTMASTER, seated next to him.

Abruptly, the violin stops playing—the piano stopping a second later—and the silence is jarring. The Music Director calls out:

SMITH-KENSINGTON
Why did you stop? I didn't ask you to stop.

STAGE

VIOLINIST (O.S.)
(assertive)
I like to know who I'm *playin'* for.

ACCOMPANIST (O.S.)
Hey, you're not allowed to—

THE AUDITION SCREEN

as it rolls out of the way, to reveal the bewildered ACCOMPANIST and IGOR DAVIDSON, a strikingly attractive Russian-looking young man in his twenties, dark hair and penetrating eyes. An open-collar white shirt with rolled up sleeves display powerful arms. With one hand he's holding his violin and bow while his other hand is shoving the audition screen out of his way. There's the slightest trace of a Russian accent.

THE COMMITTEE

as the shock of their procedures being flouted registers on them.

DAVIDSON

—the screen pushed most of the way off—returns to center stage.

DAVIDSON
Now, maybe, we can communicate.

He readies his violin and bow to start playing again.

AUDITORIUM, VARIOUS VIEWS

as from the eleventh row the Principal Second Violinist—SYLVIA—leans forward to the Music Director.

SYLVIA
You'll have to disqualify him.

Other committee members mumble agreement.

DAVIDSON
Disqualify me? For what?

SMITH-KENSINGTON
(resignedly)
The audition screen is designed to ensure
that the Committee doesn't discriminate
on the basis of race or sex or age. We
will, I'm afraid, have to disqualify you.
I'm sorry.

DAVIDSON
What, you don't trust yourself to play fair?

SMITH-KENSINGTON
Not at all a question of trust. The symphony must do this for its own legal protection. Otherwise one of the candidates might bankrupt us with a discrimination lawsuit.

DAVIDSON

DAVIDSON
(getting angry)
Okay, I get it. Perfect. Sure.

He starts walking off stage, then whips around again.

DAVIDSON
You want something to disqualify?

He raises the violin again, and starts playing unaccompanied. This time, he rips full-force into perhaps the most technically difficult violin piece ever written, the Paganini Twenty-fourth Caprice ...and he is *cooking*. This isn't about trying out for a *job* anymore. He's defying a system that cares more about rules than about ability.

THE COMMITTEE

as Sylvia leans forward to the Music Director again and Smith-Kensington gestures her away to let him listen.

DAVIDSON

Davidson plays until he reaches the end of a particularly treacherous passage ...stops ... and smiles sharply at the Committee.

DAVIDSON
Disqualify *that*.

He starts to walk off.

SMITH-KENSINGTON

SMITH-KENSINGTON
Wait a moment, please.

DAVIDSON

as he stops, takes a deep breath, and waits.

THE COMMITTEE

SMITH-KENSINGTON
(continuing softly, to
Committee)
I think we can safely use ratings made
before secrecy was broken. Yes?
(hearing no argument)
Very well.
(to Davidson)
You're still in the running. Please be
sure the Personnel Manager knows where to
reach you.

DAVIDSON

DAVIDSON
Thanks. (1/2 beat) Thanks a lot.

Smith-Kensington waves acknowledgement. Davidson raises his violin in parting, then walks off.

BACKSTAGE SYMPHONY HALL

as Davidson—just finished putting his violin in its case—is met by the Symphony's Personnel Manager, EVERETT WINSTON, who is holding a clipboard.

WINSTON
You're at the Hyatt, Mr. Davidson?

DAVIDSON
(nods)
Room 2116. Uh, who would I ask whether a phone call came for me?

WINSTON
(smiles)
Me. You play another audition today?

DAVIDSON
(smiles back)
Uh-uh. I'm in town with my brother.

Winston hands Davidson a note

DAVIDSON
Thanks.

Davidson looks at the note, then heads out.
CUT TO

EXT. SYMPHONY HALL - NIGHT

as Davidson, with violin case, walks out into warm evening air. He pauses a moment, alone, in front of a bill showing the orchestra's fall season, and finally allows his cool to dissolve. He looks at the poster for a moment, longingly, then speaks softly, as if he's talking to a lover ... or praying.

DAVIDSON
C'mon, c'mon, *I'm* the one you want.

Then he realizes he's being corny, and laughs it off with some shtick.

DAVIDSON
(continuing)
We can make some beautiful music together. See ya, sweetheart.

He heads out into the night.

CUT TO

EXT. DR. KATO'S NUCLEAR CHILI - NIGHT

A high-tech hangout. Lots of neon, chrome, and a big color photo of DR. KATO, a muscular Japanese man in a lab coat, holding up a beaker of dangerous-looking chili. The place is jumping—and the loud rock music inside can be heard from half a block away.

Davidson is waiting outside, looking uncomfortable, when a rental car pulls up to valet parking and a bearded man in his thirties, Igor's brother ALEX DAVIDSON, gets out, tossing car keys to the valet.

>   ALEX
>   (to valet)
>   Crash this for me, willya? They're
>   charging me twelve bucks a day for the
>   insurance.
>   (to Igor)
>   You get it?

>   DAVIDSON
>   I'll know tomorrow. Alex, you know how I
>   feel about this volume level. Why do you
>   always do this to me?

>   ALEX
>   'Cause I want your opinion—this is a
>   band I'm thinking about representing.

>   DAVIDSON
>   They should turn down their amplifiers—
>   *that's* my opinion.

Alex grabs Igor's arm and drags him inside.

INT. DR. KATO'S - NIGHT

as Alex and Igor approach the desk. The interior shows real style, super high tech. There are radiation warning signs everywhere—a purple trefoil with the words: *Warning: Nuclear Chili Zone.* All the waiters and waitresses wear white radiation suits. Signs advertise a house drink called *The Nuclear Freeze.*

VIEWS INCLUDING LIVE BAND

a very tight rock band called DEARSMOKE is putting out some really basic hard rock. The female vocalist—CAMBRIDGE, early twenties, terrific looking with a knock-out figure and a great rock voice—is singing this one. But the first thing Davidson notices is the club's huge P.A. speakers—anathema to a classical musician.

> CAMBRIDGE
> (singing rock ballad)
> You ask me why I'm leavin'
> That's you alright, you never listen.
> You think you're the only one
> Who needs to be told how good you are
> Well, genius, that's what I been missin'.

DR. KATO AND THE BROTHERS

There are already several couples in line behind Igor and Alex. Dr. Kato, wearing a white lab coat, steps up to the desk and looks over to Alex.

> ALEX
> Got a table for two away from those
> speakers?

> DR. KATO
> Sure. If you don't mind waiting a half
> hour. Or there's a table just being
> cleared up front.

Alex looks over to his brother. Davidson doesn't look thrilled but shrugs.

ALEX
We'll take the one up front.

They head forward. As they pass the bar Davidson grabs a cocktail napkin and starts ripping makeshift ear plugs. A waitress cuts in front holding a tray with chili and a blue-and-red warning flasher. Davidson has the earplugs in well before they get to their table.

ANGLE INCLUDING BAND AND THE BROTHERS

as Cambridge is belting out, hard and sad. She checks Igor and Alex out, and doesn't miss that Davidson's carrying a violin.

CAMBRIDGE
(singing next verse)
You ask me if you'll make it
And I go, it's there for the makin'.
But I got dreams of my own
I need to hear I can make it too
Just dreamin', you're real good at
takin'.

A busboy finishes clearing. Davidson tucks his violin under the table before sitting. Dr. Kato hands them menus and signals the busboy to bring water.

DR. KATO
Enjoy your dinner.

A radiation-suited WAITER—looking like a tight end playing for Chernobyl State—shows up. He leans in close so he can be heard above the music.

ON DAVIDSON TABLE

WAITER
(almost shouting)
What'll it be?

DAVIDSON
(shouting)
Number eight with fries, diet cola.

ALEX
(also shouting)
Cheeseburger, rare. Side of chili.
Coffee to drink.

WAITER
How hot you want the chili? Containment, Weapon's Grade, or Meltdown?

ALEX
Meltdown.

WAITER
I need to see some picture I.D.

ALEX
For what? Coffee?

WAITER
We're not allowed to serve chili above Weapon's Grade to anyone under twenty-one.

ALEX AND WAITER

Alex gives the waiter a look. The waiter doesn't crack a smile. He just waits. Not knowing if this is for real or an advertising ploy, Alex laughs, gets out his wallet, and shows the I.D. The Waiter nods and leaves.

ANGLE INCLUDING CAMBRIDGE AND DAVIDSON

Meanwhile, Davidson has been noticing Cambridge. He checks her out. Thoroughly. Whether or not the music's his type, she definitely is.

Cambridge senses his look, and they both play, I know you're looking but I'm not going to let you know that I know. But it doesn't quite work...their eyes meet...and Cambridge decides to sing the final reprise direct to Davidson:

CAMBRIDGE
Whenever you're low I'm there for you
I'm always around to care for you
But what you never seem to see
Is nothin' in life comes free
And you're never there for me.

DAVIDSON

Contact.

ANGLE ON STAGE AGAIN

The band finishes the song and gets enthusiastic applause, from both the audience and the two brothers. Davidson isn't knocking himself out applauding, but he manages to let Cambridge know that he liked *her*. She makes sure he knows who she is with a standard band intro.

CAMBRIDGE
Thank you. That's Leo on keyboards,
Sasha and Art on guitar and vocals, Lenny
on bass guitar, Vic on drums, I'm
Cambridge, our band is Dearsmoke.

As the band makes in-between-numbers noises, Cambridge gets inspired.

CAMBRIDGE
(continuing)

Okay. It's open mike time here at Dr. Kato's—

ON DR. KATO

seating a couple, as his reaction lets us know this is news to *him*—

UP FRONT AGAIN

CAMBRIDGE
(continuing)
—your big chance to come up here and do some chops with the band.

THE BAND

Two other band members—LEO on keyboards and SASHA on lead guitar—are looking back and forth at each other, shrugging. This is news to them, too. They're wondering what Cambridge is getting them into.

ON CLUB

Several hands shoot up at the tables.

UP FRONT AGAIN

Cambridge catches Davidson's eye and gives him a look.

ALEX
(to Igor)
If you're interested, here's your chance.

INCLUDING CAMBRIDGE AND DAVIDSON'S TABLE

as Davidson figures, what the hell, and goes for it. He puts up his hand too, then immediately starts getting out his violin.

CAMBRIDGE
(continuing)

Looks like we got us a victim. And this
is a first. We don't see a whole lot of
fiddle players here at open mike.

DAVIDSON
(to Alex)
I'll just bet.

Cambridge overhears. Now it's her turn to wonder what she's letting herself in for.

CAMBRIDGE
(continuing; cool)
C'mon, guys, gimme some hand action to
get this dude up here.

ON STAGE

As the audience applauds, Davidson joins Cambridge on stage. He knows he's in for some needling, but is cool about it.

CAMBRIDGE
(continuing)
Well you're not one of the homeboys, are
you? What's your name?

DAVIDSON
Davidson. Igor Davidson.

CAMBRIDGE
Igor?

ANGLE ON TABLES

Cambridge gets the laugh she was expecting, then chides the audience.

CAMBRIDGE
(continuing)

Like the Russian composer, Igor
Stravinsky, right?

ANGLE ON DAVIDSON

DAVIDSON
(doing Lugosi)
Igor, like Dr. Frankenstein's assistant.

VIEWS INCLUDING CLUB AND STAGE

as the audience laughs and Vic gives Davidson a rim shot. Davidson does a quick hunchback impression and gets *another* laugh.

CAMBRIDGE
I'll bet you're fun at weddings.

DAVIDSON
(quickly)
And funerals.

Another laugh and rim shot. Cambridge knows she's got a professional.

CAMBRIDGE
Okay, Quasimodo, whadd'ya wanna play?

DAVIDSON
You guys know the Bach Toccata and Fugue?

Davidson plays the opening notes of the famous horror-movie theme.

CAMBRIDGE
(waits out laugh)
Sorry, we just did that in the last set.

DAVIDSON
Something by Handel? Or Vivaldi?

CAMBRIDGE
Know the tunes ... don't know the words.

DAVIDSON
Hmmm ... Then how 'bout *The Devil Went Down to Georgia?*

There's enthusiastic hooting and applause from the tables. Cambridge looks impressed. She looks over to the other band members, who nod.

CAMBRIDGE
You got it. Sasha, lemme take the guitar
on this one.

Cambridge grabs a spare guitar, moving over to a stand-up mike.

DAVIDSON AND BAND

which launch into the famous Charlie Daniels talking ballad. After the intro of country fiddle playing, Davidson starts the vocal:

DAVIDSON
(talking it)
The Devil went down to Georgia
He was lookin' for a soul to steal .....

REACTIONS ON TABLES

The audience is getting into it.

DAVIDSON AND BAND

DAVIDSON
(continuing)
... the Devil jumped up on a hickory stump

And said, "Boy let me tell you what.
I guess you didn't know it but
I'm a fiddle player, too ...."

Davidson changes the lyrics around a bit—

DAVIDSON
(continuing)
The boy said, "My name's *Igor*
You can call me Mr. David*sin*—
—And I'll take your bet
You're gonna regret
Cause I'm the best that's ever been."

ANGLE ON CAMBRIDGE

as she leads the band in the backup chorus, altering the lyrics to match Davidson's improv.

DAVIDSON

as he sticks his violin under his chin and gives the Charlie Daniels Band a run for its money in hot country fiddle playing. The guy's as good with country as he is with Paganini.

CAMBRIDGE

watching him, impressed as hell, and more interested than ever.

ON TABLES

and they're really into it now. This song sells 'em every time if the fiddle player is good enough ... and Davidson is good enough.

ON CAMBRIDGE AND DAVIDSON

as Cambridge does the Devil's work on guitar, soon joined by Davidson on fiddle—and Davidson and Cambridge are almost *dueling*. The energy flowing between them, as each realizes how good the other is, almost causes as many sparks as a Tesla coil.

WHOLE BAND AGAIN

Near the end of the section, Davidson shouts out to the band—

DAVIDSON
Skip the chorus and stick with me—

Cambridge and the others nod.

ANGLE ON DAVIDSON AND VIOLIN

And he launches directly into a red hot fiddle riff ... only he goes way beyond the licks of a country fiddle player and works into a musical potpourrie—bringing in classical, mixing it with Cajun and bluegrass—signaling the band to follow him whatever he does as he zips into style after style ...

THE AUDIENCE

as Davidson is knocking their socks off. They start clapping in rhythm with the music—

ALEX

in the audience, really enjoying this.

DAVIDSON AND BAND

as he stretches it out, until he finally signals the band he's going into the home stretch ...

DAVIDSON
(continuing)
Take the chorus!

CAMBRIDGE AND BAND

as they sing the final square-dance type chorus—

DAVIDSON

as he sticks the violin under his chin again, lays down a few bars more of pyrotechnics ... and they finish *together*.

AT TABLES

and the audience is on its feet, hooting and hollering. Davidson has wowed 'em.

ALEX

as he flashes his brother an okay sign.

DAVIDSON AND CAMBRIDGE

while the audience—and the band—applauds. Davidson looks at her directly with a clear message. She grins: Okay, you win here, too.

CUT TO

EXT. DR. KATO'S - NIGHT

while Igor and Cambridge are talking in the b.g., Alex is talking to Sasha. The valet pulls Alex's rental car up.

ALEX
(to Sasha)
—So you'll send me the new demo when it's done and I'll see what I can do.

SASHA
Great.

Alex and Sasha shake hands, then Alex slips money to the valet.

ALEX
(shouts to Igor)
You wanna lift to the hotel on my way to the airport?

DAVIDSON
I'll walk, thanks. Have a safe flight home.

ALEX
You too. Call me as soon as you hear from the orchestra.

As Davidson waves, Alex drives off.

CUT TO

EXT. STREETS - NIGHT

as Davidson and Cambridge are walking together later. They're already chatting like old friends. Davidson is in the middle of a story that Cambridge finds hysterically funny.

DAVIDSON
Okay ... try and picture this. I'm four, and my grandfather—this eighty-year-old Russian virtuoso—is trying to give me my first violin lesson. Only thing is, I hardly speak English and *he* says—
(imitating, heavy Russian accent)
I *American* now, I speak only American.

Cambridge laughs, really into the story.

DAVIDSON
(continuing)

I'm standin' there like a dummy, cryin'
cause I can't understand him. And *he's*
getting p.o'd at me 'cause I don't
understand English.

CAMBRIDGE
(still laughing)
So he taught you in Russian?

DAVIDSON
The hell he did. First year of lessons,
my mother is in there *translating*
Grandpa's English into *Russian*.

Both of them really crack up at this.

DAVIDSON
(trying to get serious)
And it's a good thing. That old man
could *play*. He was from the old school
... St. Petersberg ... where half the
greats came from ... Zimbalist, Elman,
Heifetz. Grandpa was right up there.
Performed the Beethoven concerto at seven
... composed his own first concerto at
ten. I was a retard compared to him.

CAMBRIDGE
Right ... I bet you didn't compose your
concerto until the ripe age of *twelve*.

EXT. DAVIDSON'S HOTEL - NIGHT

as Davidson and Cambridge pause on the street in front. Davidson notices where they are.

DAVIDSON
Nah. I really screwed the pooch on that
one. Didn't have it done till nineteen.

(beat)
Want to come up to my room and I'll play
it for you?

Cambridge gives him an expression that means, "Right, sure you will."

CUT TO

TIGHT ON A VIOLIN

as we see hands playing it and hear a very traditional, very beautiful violin concerto, sounding as if it was composed about the time of Brahms or Tchaikovsky.

INT. DAVIDSON'S HOTEL ROOM - NIGHT

as we see Cambridge sitting cross-legged on the bed, wearing only Davidson's shirt.

BACK VIEW ON DAVIDSON, INCLUDING CAMBRIDGE

as we see him standing playing his concerto for her ... wearing only men's bikini underpants.

Davidson accelerates to top speed as he goes into what is obviously the last few bars of the last movement ... and ends with a final flourish. Cambridge applauds and Davidson acknowledges it with a full bow, mooning the camera.

ANGLE ON BOTH—DAVIDSON'S UPPER TORSO ONLY

CAMBRIDGE
(enthusiastically)
Davidson, that was *fantastic*. Have you
recorded it?

DAVIDSON
(laughs)

I couldn't even get a passing *grade* on it
in composition class at Juilliard. You
compose a violin concerto today, it has
to sound like an alley cat fighting it
out with a garbage truck ... and the
truck *losing*.

FAVORING CAMBRIDGE

Cambridge laughs merrily.

DAVIDSON
Okay, *this* is the composition that got me
an *A*.

BOTH AGAIN

He lifts the violin under his chin again and begins playing. It sounds *exactly* like an alley cat fighting it out with a garbage truck... and the truck *losing*.

Cambridge makes a face. This is really awful.

Davidson stops playing and smiles. He puts his violin and bow into the case. Then he throws himself on top of her. She squeals as she slides under him. They begin making passionate love for the second time that night. Davidson reaches over and turns out the light.

IN BLACK OUT

CAMBRIDGE
Kiss me on the Vivaldi.

CUT TO

INT. DAVIDSON'S ROOM - MORNING

Davidson and Cambridge are asleep in each others arms, as the phone rings.

After a few rings, Davidson untangles himself enough to slip a hand onto the phone and bring the receiver to his ear.

> DAVIDSON
> Yeah? ... Speaking ...
> (really awake now)
> Yeah, sure I can ... my flight isn't
> till four. ... Okay, Mr. Winston ...
> eleven-thirty. *Great.* And listen,
> thanks a lot!

He hangs up the phone and looks over, seeing Cambridge still dead asleep. For a few seconds he considers waking her, then decides against it.

He untangles himself from the sleeping girl, gets out of bed—still nude—and pads into the bathroom, closing the door. From behind the door we hear at full volume:

> DAVIDSON (O.S.)
> *Yah-hooo!*

CLOSE ON CAMBRIDGE

as this wakes her up with a jolt anyway.

CUT TO

EXT. SYMPHONY HALL - DAY

as Davidson returns, fiddle case in hand, but this time with Cambridge holding his other hand. Near the stage door, he puts down his violin and kisses her long and hard. They break for air.

> CAMBRIDGE
> When you coming back?

DAVIDSON
Let me know when you're off from the band
... and that's when I'll apartment hunt.

One more passionate kiss, then Cambridge walks away, turning once to wave.

Davidson waits till she's around a corner. Then, triumphantly, he salutes the Symphony Poster he soliloquized to before, picks up his violin, and heads in.

INT. SYMPHONY OFFICES - DAY

as Davidson is sitting facing Winston's desk.

WINSTON
Now ... your orchestra contract. This is
for one full season, fifty-two weeks
starting this fall, at the yearly base
salary of sixty-three thousand—

Winston slides the orchestra contracts to Davidson, who flips to the last page and begins signing.

WINSTON
(continuing)
—plus recordings and incidentals ...
travel per diem, medical, dental,
pension, full dress allowance, instrument
insurance—

DAVIDSON
The Symphony pays the insurance on my
violin?

Winston nods.

DAVIDSON
Fantastic. The premiums have been

bankrupting me.

WINSTON
What do you have in that case—a del Gesu Guarnerius?

DAVIDSON
(shakes head)
A Stradivarius.

WINSTON
(impressed)
Same thing in my book. How does a kid your age get hold of a Strad?

DAVIDSON
It was left to me by my grandfather. Mischa Rudlensky.

WINSTON
Rudlensky!

Davidson nods. Winston looks even more impressed.

CLOSE ON ORCHESTRA CONTRACT

as Davidson signs it, then slides it over to Winston.

BACK TO SCENE

Winston signs the contract for the orchestra.

WINSTON
(continuing)
At the end of the first year, you go before the String Audition Committee again. If they're satisfied, you get tenure ... and probably moved forward, since we'll likely be having a few more

players retiring by then.
(beat)
The way *you* play fiddle, you'll make
concertmaster someday.

Winston slides one signed copy across the desk to Davidson.

Davidson lifts his violin case onto his lap and opens the case, slides his copy of the contract into a pocket inside the case, then zips the case shut.

Winston stands up ... and Davidson stands also.

WINSTON
You report for first rehearsal nine a.m.,
September fourth. That gives you all
summer to make sure you know the fall
season's programs.

DAVIDSON
I sure will, Mr. Winston.

Winston extends his hand and Davidson shakes it.

WINSTON
Welcome to the Symphony.

CUT TO

EXT. AIRPORT TERMINAL - DAY

as Davidson arrives by hotel shuttle bus for his flight home. He's carrying only one small duffle over his shoulder and his violin case.

INT. TERMINAL SECURITY CHECK POINT - DAY

as Davidson checks through security, sending his duffle through X-ray. But he hands his violin case directly to the INSPECTOR.

DAVIDSON
Hand inspection for this, please.

Davidson walks through the metal detector without incident then joins the inspector on the other side.

INSPECTOR
Please open the case for me, sir.

Davidson unzips the violin case, and the Inspector sees that there is, in fact, a violin inside. He starts to reach for it but Davidson reaches it first and takes it out for him.

DAVIDSON
(nervously)
Please let me. That's an irreplaceable
instrument ... an antique.

INSPECTOR
I must examine it, sir, antique or not.

DAVIDSON
Look, I'll hold it for you so you can see
inside clearly. Okay?

Davidson turns it up so the Inspector can look into it.

DAVIDSON
(continuing)
See?

INSPECTOR
(hesitating)
Well ... I still need to hold it. Just
for a second. To feel how heavy it is.

Davidson sighs, then shows the Inspector how to hold it properly from the neck and end pin.

DAVIDSON
Okay ... hold it *here* and *here* ... that
way you won't damage the varnish.

The Inspector feels the violin for only a few seconds, then carefully hands it back to Davidson, nodding.

CUT TO

INT. "TRANS NATIONAL AIRLINES" PASSENGER GATE - DAY

as Davidson checks in. The counter is labelled *TNA Flight 451 to Newark*. Passengers are already boarding.

Davidson hands his ticket to the AIRLINE GATE AGENT, a smartly uniformed woman. Then the Agent notices the violin case and points.

AGENT
I'm afraid you'll have to check through
that case, sir.

DAVIDSON
I hand carried it on your flight *here*.

AGENT
Well they shouldn't have allowed it. It
doesn't meet FAA standards for carry-on.

Davidson is starting to be overwhelmed by all these regulations.

DAVIDSON
Look, I'm a professional, flying on
business. This is an irreplaceable
instrument ... and I'm not about to have
it crushed between two pieces of
Samsonite.

A blue-suited male PASSENGER in line right behind Davidson is watching the argument carefully.

The Agent pauses for a long moment, then hands Davidson his boarding pass.

    DAVIDSON
    Thanks.

Davidson grabs his violin and immediately boards, disappearing into the Jetway.

The Male Passenger in line behind Davidson hands his ticket to the Gate Agent.

GATE AGENT'S POV ON TICKET ENVELOPE

as the Gate Agent sees the I.D. of a Trans National Airline SECURITY CHIEF.

GATE AGENT AND SECURITY CHIEF

    SECURITY CHIEF
    Got a seat somewhere near that one?

The Gate Agent nods.

INT. TRANS NATIONAL JET CABIN - DAY

as Davidson straps into a coach-class aisle seat, next to an exit. His violin case fits most of the way under the seat in front of him, but sticks out a little between his feet.

The Security Chief takes a seat a few rows behind Davidson.

Davidson grabs a magazine out of the seat pocket and begins reading. A few seconds pass, then a female FLIGHT ATTENDANT comes by and sees the violin case extending between Davidson's feet.

    FLIGHT ATTENDANT
    (to Davidson)

Sir, you'll have to check through that
case. It doesn't fit under your seat.

DAVIDSON
(sighs)
I've already been through this with your
agent at the check-in counter. *She* said
I could carry it on. Okay?

FLIGHT ATTENDANT
No, sir, that's beyond the Gate Agent's
authority. F.A.A. regulations require—

DAVIDSON
(making a joke)
Okay ... I admit everything. You got me.
I've got a *weapon's grade* violin in here.
Runs off plutonium batteries.
(conspiratorially)
This violin could *blow up an entire
orchestra*.

The Flight Attendant, hearing a foreign accent, is now worried.

ANGLE INCLUDING SECURITY CHIEF

as he stands up and sees the Flight Attendant's worried expression. The Security Chief moves into the aisle next to Davidson.

SECURITY CHIEF
(to Attendant)
Let me take care of this.
(to Davidson)
I work for Trans National. Sir, you'll
have to get off this plane.

DAVIDSON
(not moving)
Look, I told the Gate Agent before she

checked through my bag—

SECURITY CHIEF
I don't care what you told the Gate
Agent. You're getting off this plane.
Now.

Davidson is outraged, but doesn't argue.

DAVIDSON
You want me off the plane? You got it.

Davidson gets out to the aisle and lifts his violin case with his right hand.

THE SECURITY CHIEF

as he reaches to grab the case out of Davidson's right hand.

SECURITY CHIEF
I'll take that case.

DAVIDSON AND SECURITY CHIEF

Davidson brushes the Security Chief's hand away with his left hand.

DAVIDSON
Like hell you will.

THE SECURITY CHIEF

Like lightning, as he grabs Davidson's left elbow with both of his hands.

CLOSE ON DAVIDSON'S LEFT ELBOW

as the Security Chief *twists* and Davidson's elbow cracks sickeningly.

THE SECURITY CHIEF AND DAVIDSON

as the Security Chief wrests the violin case out of Davidson's right hand.

DAVIDSON

in a moment frozen in time, as the pain registers on his face ... and a second later as we see his agony of knowing what has just happened. He tries to move his left fingers ... and realizes that his ring finger and pinkie won't move.

DAVIDSON
(low panic)
I can't move my fingers.

FOLLOWING DAVIDSON AND SECURITY CHIEF

SECURITY CHIEF
Come along.

Davidson just stands there, dumbfounded for a second, then the Security Chief begins pushing him forward.

Davidson is too overwhelmed to resist and lets himself be pushed forward. As they move forward:

DAVIDSON
You stupid son of a bitch, don't you
realize what you've done? *I can't move
my fingers!*

CUT TO

INT. ORTHOPEDIC OFFICE - DAY

as Davidson is sitting opposite the desk of DR. SEYMOUR POLLOCK. Davidson's left elbow is wrapped, but not in a cast.

DR. POLLOCK
—and when he twisted your elbow, the
ulnar groove narrowed, pinching into the
nerve which controls your fourth and
fifth digits—your ring finger and
pinkie.

Davidson takes this in gravely.

DAVIDSON
So my bones are okay—it's the nerve
itself that's been hurt.

DR. POLLOCK
That's right.

DAVIDSON
Well, how long before the nerve heals?

DR. POLLOCK
(delicately)
That's something, I'm afraid, that even
state-of-the-art orthopedics can't answer
very well. It's possible ... now that
pressure on the ulnar nerve has been
relieved ... that feeling and movement
could return in a few days or weeks.

Davidson understands the unspoken implication.

DAVIDSON
You're telling me it's possible that it
won't return for months or years. Or
ever. That I might not be able to play
violin by the fall ... or ever.

DR. POLLOCK
(gently)
I'd rather not speculate about that, this

early on. Particularly because of your teenage injury to the arm, it's very difficult to predict what will happen.

DAVIDSON
But it's possible I might not play again.

Dr. Pollock nods gravely.

DR. POLLOCK
In a case like this, it's always a good idea to get a second opinion ... and even a third and fourth. I recommend you consult a neurosurgeon and neural physiologist as well as an orthopedic surgeon.

This is really getting to Davidson.

DR. POLLOCK
(continuing)
Since you're living in New York City, there are fine teams at Columbia Presbyterian. Or you might prefer Peter Bent Brigham in Boston ... or Temple University in Philadelphia.

Davidson nods, emotionally drained.

CUT TO

EXT. VIEW - A JET AIRLINER LANDING - NIGHT

at Newark Airport, showing any airline logo *but* Trans National.

CUT TO

EXT. HIGH RISE APARTMENTS, NEW YORK CITY - NIGHT

as a taxi pulls up in front and a doorman opens the door for Davidson.

DAVIDSON
Thanks, Michel.

Davidson pays the taxi, gets out, then heads toward the entrance.

INT. DAVIDSON'S STUDIO APARTMENT - NIGHT

as Davidson enters and turns on the light to a typical musician's single—a convertible couch, walls lined with records and books, an elaborate stereo, coffee table cluttered with music and a music stand also with music on it. The apartment is stifling from being closed up with the air conditioning off.

Davidson puts down his violin case, slides his flight bag off and drops it in his foyer, takes some letters out from between his teeth and drops them on a table—all using only his right hand.

He is finally home, but completely drained, performing everything out of habit. First thing, he opens the sliding door to his terrace and lets some air—and city noise—in.

KITCHENETTE

as Davidson searches through his freezer for something edible, finds it, and shoves it into his microwave oven. He gets out a bottle of beer and opens it, one-handed, on the refrigerator handle.

DAVIDSON

as he returns to the living area and notices the message light on his answering machine blinking. Still standing, he sets down the bottle, rewinds, and picks up the bottle again, swigging while it plays back.

DAVIDSON'S AGENT (FILTER)
Beep!

(Hollywood-ish voice)
Hi, kiddo. No go on the commercial.
DiPasquali says they changed their mind
and are using synthesizer. Sorry ...
(pause)

SARA (FILTER)
Beep!
(Sexy voice)
Davidson? This is Sara. Listen, we've
moved the rehearsal to Wednesday at
three. Paul had to change his dentist's
appointment. Oh ... Can you bring the
second violin part for the Brahms
Quartet? Carl Fischer's not going to
have it in until next week. Bye!
(pause)

RECORDED OPERATOR (FILTER)
Beep! If you'd like to make a call,
please hang up and dial again. This is a
recording.
(pause)

DAVIDSON

The messages continue, as Davidson begins experiencing his grief fully for the first time.

DAVIDSON'S MOTHER (FILTERED)
Beep!
(Russian accent,
hates machines)
This is your *mother* calling. I guess
you're not back yet ... or are are you
out celebrating? ... I was shopping when
you called. ... Your father gave me the
wonderful news about the audition, and
we're both *thrilled* to death ...

Davidson walks out to his terrace with his beer.

EXT. TERRACE - NIGHT

as Davidson walks out, the message continuing in the background. The terrace is about ten stories above a park of landscaped concrete with an occasional caged tree. Nobody below. Davidson looks down, considering that it would be easy as hell just to end it all now.

DAVIDSON'S MOTHER (FILTERED)
(continuing)
... Of course I'd like to make a small
dinner party to celebrate. Is next
Saturday all right? Do you want to bring
a date, or should I invite Anne Bronster
... you know, Elaine and Nat's daughter?

The message continues in the background ...

DAVIDSON

as it's all become too much for him. But he doesn't jump off. Instead, using a windup that would work in the major leagues, he throws his beer bottle off the terrace.

THE BOTTLE

as it sails out then drops the ten stories, smashing to smithereens on the empty concrete below.

DAVIDSON

as he takes a deep breath, then heads inside again, in time to hear the *ready* jingle from his microwave oven.

INSIDE AGAIN

as Davidson heads back to the phone, shuts off the machine, then immediately picks up the cordless receiver and punches in a number. A few seconds pass while Davidson heads into the kitchen, cradles the phone in the crook of his neck, and gets his food.

DAVIDSON
Hi, Nance? ... Yeah, I know it's
late—I just got back ... So she told you
already ... Thanks. Listen, is my
brother still up? ... Thanks ...

Busying himself while he's waiting, then:

DAVIDSON
(continuing)
... Hi, buddy ... Yeah, Nance told me
Mom called ... Thanks, but never mind
that now, I need your help. ... Uh-huh,
professionally. ... No, I plan to *make*
trouble.

DISSOLVE TO

EXT. CENTRAL PARK - DAY

as Davidson is jogging through the Park with Alex.

ANGLE ON DAVIDSON

as we see that his left elbow is no longer bandaged.

TRACKING THEM AS THEY JOG

DAVIDSON
I want that airline gestapo agent to rot
in prison. I want his kids to starve.
If he has a dog, I want his *dog* to
starve. And I'm gonna *own* that damn
airline.

ALEX
Look, Iggie, it'll be at least three
years before we even *see* the inside of a
courtroom. Another five years for
appeals. And you'll be spending that
time in doctors' offices—not only *your*
doctors, but *their* doctors.

DAVIDSON
But I'll *beat* em, right?

ALEX
Probably. Maybe. If they don't pay off
some passenger to swear you started it.

DAVIDSON
They do, I'll kill the lying bastard.

ALEX
Get serious, huh?

DAVIDSON
I *am* serious.

ALEX
Sure. In junior high you couldn't even
pith a *frog* without puking your guts out.

DAVIDSON
So I'll puke afterwards. I'll still kill
the bastard.

Davidson slows down a little, Alex pacing him.

ALEX
Drop the suit and take their offer,
Iggie. David got you a *wonderful*
settlement. Take it from me, you don't
wanna spend the rest of your life in

court.

DAVIDSON
Why not? I don't *have* a life anymore.
The bastard took that away from me.

ALEX
Well you ain't gettin' it back in a
courtroom, believe me. All you'll end up
with is money ... and they're offering to
settle for more than you'll ever need
right now.

NEAR THE BASEBALL DIAMOND

as they jog past an informal baseball game. Davidson puts on a burst of speed... then slows down to a walk, Alex slowing also.

ALEX
Save yourself the heartache, buddy. I'm
talkin' not only as a lawyer ... but as
your brother.

Davidson thinks about it, slowly, then comes to a decision and nods.

DAVIDSON
(slightly breathless)
Okay. I'll settle. I'll drop the damn
suit. Okay.

ALEX
Good boy.

They walk on in silence for a few seconds, then:

ALEX
(continuing)
Does the Symphony know yet?

DAVIDSON
Called their personnel manager, Everett
Winston. Their policy is, if I can start
working any time before the contract
expires, I still have the job.

He holds up his left hand and flexes, his two fingers still dead.

DAVIDSON
(continuing)
Taking off therapeutic and practice time,
I've got a year for these to start
working again. If they're gonna.
Mean time, I've been learning what I can
do with my two good fingers.

ALEX
(surprised)
You can still play?

DAVIDSON
Not a whole lot. A little slow Bach is
about it. Been practicing just so my bow
arm doesn't dry up, too.

ALEX
What are you going to do if—
(checks himself)
—now?

They walk a little further, noticing the Park's activity ... roller skaters, bicycles, stunt dancers.

DAVIDSON
You know, Alex, when we were kids, I was
always jealous of you. You were always
skateboarding, playin' football—

ALEX
—while you were stuck inside practicing
... yeah, I know the tune by now.

DAVIDSON
(cracks a smile)
I couldn't even toss a football around
with you 'n Dad ...ball'd hit a finger
the wrong way, couldn't practice for a
week.

ALEX
... Or that time fishing on Lake George.
You caught the hook under a fingernail.

DAVIDSON
(nods)
Couldn't play right for *two* weeks.
(beat)
My entire life's been inside—even when
I was touring. 'Cause I was spending
days practicing and nights performing ...
or 'cause I couldn't risk hurting my
hands.

DAVIDSON

DAVIDSON
(continuing)
I think I'm gonna take some time seeing
what outside looks like.

ON BOTH AGAIN

as Alex nods, and the two brothers resume jogging.

CUT TO

INT. DAVIDSON'S APARTMENT - NIGHT

as Davidson takes an old 78 record out.

CLOSE ON THE RECORD BOX - PHOTOGRAPH OF MISCHA RUDLENSKY

a black & white photograph of a distinguished dark-haired and very Russian-looking man playing violin, and the title *Mischa Rudlensky: Unaccompanied Bach.*

BACK TO SCENE

Davidson places the record on his stereo, and listens. A few seconds of scratching, then some definitely not high fidelity—but definitely high quality violin—playing the Bach.

Davidson listens for a while, emotionally very overcome by the experience. It obviously evokes deep memories for him of what his life used to be about ... and can't be right now.

Finally, Davidson gets up and lifts the tone arm off.

DAVIDSON

as he goes to a closet, and gets out his violin case. He sets the case on a table, takes out his violin and bow, then tunes for a few seconds.

Then he begins to play the Bach piece his grandfather was playing.

CLOSE ON HIS HANDS

as we see that the left-hand third and fourth fingers—the ones that were injured—are motionless, and it is the pointer and middle finger that are doing all the work alone.

BACK TO SCENE

The Bach sounds pretty good ... Davidson is doing all right. His expression shows satisfaction that he can still play a little.

He stops playing the Bach ... pauses a moment ... then begins the Paganini 24th Caprice we heard him playing at the audition.

DAVIDSON'S LEFT HAND

A few seconds into it, as his left fingers reach fast notes they just can't handle ... and the piece comes to an abrupt halt.

BACK TO SCENE

He pauses, takes a breath, and strums the violin strings once. Then he places the violin and bow back into their case.

ON DAVIDSON

as he heads right toward the telephone, punching in a number from memory, then taking the cordless receiver out to his terrace.

EXT. DAVIDSON'S TERRACE - NIGHT

as Davidson gets an answer.

DAVIDSON
Cambridge? Hi, it's Davidson. ... No
change ... Otherwise, surviving, I guess
... No, I decided to settle the lawsuit, so I
can't say when I'll be back your way.
But look ... how much time between gigs
does Dearsmoke leave you? ...

DISSOLVE TO

EXT. OPEN MOUNTAIN COUNTRYSIDE - DAY

A quiet, sunlit day, far from civilization. It could be in a little used section of Alaskan parkland ... or in the mountains of Mexico or Central America, for all we know.

We're facing a hill. Suddenly,

BREAKING OVER HILL - TWO ALL TERRAIN VEHICLES

rushing toward us with a roar, Davidson on one, Cambridge on the other.

REVERSE POV

The ATV's continue roaring away, disappearing into the distance.

CUT TO

EXT. CAMPSITE - DUSK

Not the sort that a thousand campers have used before, but a virgin site...a natural clearing with woods on all sides.

A handmade campfire with steaks cooking over it is being tended by Cambridge, a tent set up in the clearing. The ATV's are parked nearby.

And it's just a bit too overcast and windy.

Davidson and Cambridge are chatting while the steaks are cooking.

DAVIDSON
—So here I am in eighth grade, the new geek in town. Not bad enough I'm stuck with a Russian accent and the name *Igor* ... but I lug a *violin* back and forth to lessons.

CAMBRIDGE
So you became the class cut-up.

DAVIDSON
(nods)

But all the way through school, there's always some asshole on my back ... always when Alex wasn't around to help out.

CAMBRIDGE
Definitely not too great.

DAVIDSON
Junior year high school I was in a fight, wrecked up my left hand for a year. Missed all the big competitions for scholarships and tours. I nearly snuffed it, I was so depressed.

Cambridge listens gravely.

DAVIDSON
(continuing)
Anyways ... no scholarships, no backers ... that's how come I learned country fiddle ... starting up a band at Juilliard to play gigs for tuition.

CAMBRIDGE
(laughs)
A real shit-kicking band at Juilliard?

Davidson nods, smiling.

CAMBRIDGE
(still laughing)
What'd you call it?

DAVIDSON
(shakes head)
It's too lame.

CAMBRIDGE
C'mon, I won't tell.

DAVIDSON
(embarrassed)
A Boy Named Igor.

Cambridge makes gagging sounds.

DAVIDSON
(laughing)
Thanks for not rubbing it in.

CAMBRIDGE
But it's not as lame as the name I came
up with for a sixties nostalgia band I
was in. Geriatric and the Pacemakers.

DAVIDSON
(laughing)
That your first group?

CAMBRIDGE
Third. My brother Leo and me got our
first band goin' when he was fourteen and
I was twelve. We use to listen to
Creedence Clearwater albums and get the
licks off 'em. Leo started me on guitar,
then piano—

DAVIDSON
When he's fourteen, your brother was
giving you *piano* lessons?

CAMBRIDGE
When he was *eleven* and I was nine. He
used to come home from lessons, show me
what he'd picked up. Then while our
folks are listenin' to *me* practice, he's
all over town with his friends.

Davidson laughs, just as in

THE SKY

thunder and lightning crackle.

CAMPSITE

as the heavens open up and they're hit by a downpour. The fire is sizzling out already.

CAMBRIDGE
(shouting)
Forget the steaks—make for the tent!

DAVIDSON
Christ, that's *cold*!

They both run for the tent—

INT. TENT

as they make it inside, Cambridge immediately lighting a Coleman lantern.

The two of them are completely drenched to the bone—whooping from cold and wetness—but laughing, still in good spirits. They sit down on their double sleeping bag, peeling wet clothes off down to their underwear.

Cambridge shivers.

CAMBRIDGE
(laughing)
Next time you see him, you have my permission to kill him on sight.

Davidson rubs Cambridge's shoulders briskly to warm her up.

DAVIDSON
Kill who?

CAMBRIDGE
The weatherman who reported clear skies
tonight.

DAVIDSON
(innocently)
Weather report? I was supposed to listen to a *weather* report?

Cambridge laughs again, then throws a wet sock into Davidson's face. He peels it off then grabs Cambridge and starts tickling her. She resists and he wrestles her down, kissing her.

Suddenly, a gust of wind comes up.

THE TENT

as the wind lifts it, pulling up stakes and letting the rain in, drenching them even more.

They both shout with the shock, jump up, and run outside in their underwear.

EXT. CAMPSITE

as they both grab onto the tent, and Cambridge begins pounding the stakes into the ground again.

CAMBRIDGE
(shouting over wind)
I thought you said you knew how to set up
a tent!

DAVIDSON
(over wind)
I do! I read the instruction booklet
twice!

CAMBRIDGE
You *read* the *instruction book*?

Davidson nods. Cambridge stands there, being soaked, not believing the situation. Then the sheer ridiculousness of it gets to her.

CAMBRIDGE
(laughing)
You dork!

AT MOUTH OF TENT

as they head in again:

DAVIDSON
So *this* is the great outdoors I've been missing.

INT. TENT

as they climb into their sleeping bag, break into sustained laughter, then begin making love again.

CUT TO

INT. CAMPING LODGE - DAY

as a completely ratty looking Davidson and Cambridge walk in, the ATV's visible parked just outside.

RENTAL COUNTER

as Davidson and Cambridge walk up to it. An old-as-the-hills Indian is behind the counter. Davidson and Cambridge throw the ATV keys down on the counter.

DAVIDSON
We've decided we're interested in a *different* sort of vacation.

Cambridge nods intensely.

CUT TO

EXT. JETLINER IN FLIGHT - DAY

flying through clear blues skies.

CUT TO

EXT. OCEAN - LONG ON A CABIN CRUISER - DAY

the cruiser at anchor in deep waters on a beautiful, sunny day ... the only sounds coming from the ocean itself.

STERN OF THE CRUISER

Two fishing rods are mounted side-by-side off the stern of the boat, two empty deck-mounted fishing seats behind them.

We hear two *intense* sets of animal-like vocalizations, getting faster and faster ...

Suddenly, one of the lines has caught something ... line begins unreeling rapidly then the pole is yanked off its mount and splashes into the water, a *big* one breaking water in front of it.

FORWARD ON CRUISER - DAVIDSON AND CAMBRIDGE

on the forward deck making love, their rhythm now slowing down.

CAMBRIDGE
There goes your deposit.

Davidson looks as if he's already aware of it.

CUT TO

EXT. MARINA - ON CRUISER - DAY

late afternoon, as Davidson takes the cruiser in.

An employee of the boat rental agency throws Cambridge a line, and she ties up to the dock.

EXT. MARINA PARKING LOT - DAY

as Davidson and Cambridge get into a snazzy rented convertible, its top locked. Davidson takes the wheel, lowers the top, and pulls out into wide, resort-town boulevards.

INT. CONVERTIBLE - DAY

as the car drives past resort apartments and shopping.

CAMBRIDGE
—So after we shower up, why don't we
head out, get a bite, and find some
dancing?

DAVIDSON
Actually, I had in mind something a
little different. Order room service up
and spend the night in.

Cambridge is delighted and leans over, grabbing him playfully.

CAMBRIDGE
That's not *different*. I'm just surprised
you still can.

DAVIDSON
(too charming)
Guess I'm full of surprises.

Cambridge kisses his cheek, then leans back. A few seconds later she leans forward again and turns on the car radio.

She flips around for a few seconds, then settles on a rock station.

After a few seconds:

> DAVIDSON
> If you don't mind, honey, I can do
> without that.

He turns off the radio.

> CAMBRIDGE
> (smiles)
> Okay ... I'll find *your* kind of music.

She reaches for the radio with her left hand ...

ANGLE ON HER HAND

as Davidson grabs her hand with his right...and doesn't let go.

ON BOTH AGAIN

He's still holding her hand tightly. She's hurt...then more worried than hurt.

> CAMBRIDGE

> CAMBRIDGE
> (continuing; calmly)
> Davidson, you're hurting my fret hand.

> DAVIDSON

He lets go, realizing that he grabbed harder than he meant to.

> DAVIDSON
> Sorry. I ... just want peace and quiet.

ON BOTH

as Cambridge rubs her hand—which isn't damaged—and quickly

figures this out.

> CAMBRIDGE
> That's why you want to stay in tonight.

> DAVIDSON
> What're you—

> CAMBRIDGE
> Don't give me that crap, Davidson.

> DAVIDSON

as he realizes she knows what he's thinking.

> ON BOTH

> CAMBRIDGE
> (continuing)
> Camping in the middle of nowhere? Deep sea fishing? Not even a day on the beach... somebody might be playing a radio.
> (beat)
> You can't avoid it all your life. It's *everywhere*. Elevators. Movies. TV commercials. You gonna run away to a desert island next?

> DAVIDSON

as he doesn't answer for a long moment, then:

> DAVIDSON
> (slowly)
> I needed to know what the world sounds like...without music.

> CAMBRIDGE

as she looks at him, with new understanding ... but now even more worried.

CUT TO

EXT. RESORT HOTEL - DAY

as Davidson and Cambridge pull up in the convertible and are met by the parking valet.

INT. HOTEL SUITE - DAY

as they enter. Davidson drops down flat on the bed, while Cambridge notices that the phone is flashing.

CAMBRIDGE
Message for one of us.

DAVIDSON
Maybe it's my orthopedist, calling to
notify me I can move my fingers.

DAVIDSON

as he smiles, lifts his left hand, and flexes it stiffly...the ring finger and pinkie still don't work.

BOTH AGAIN

CAMBRIDGE
(not cruelly)
If you think your hand is lame,
Quasimodo, try your jokes.

She lifts up the phone and punches for the hotel operator.

CAMBRIDGE
(into phone)
Messages for 416? ... Thanks, I'll hold.

There's a long pause.

DAVIDSON

as he picks up a travel guide and flips through it.

ON CAMBRIDGE

CAMBRIDGE
(continuing)
Okay, thanks.

She hangs up.

BOTH AGAIN

Davidson can't tell what it is from her expression.

DAVIDSON
Your doctor. We're going to have a baby.

CAMBRIDGE
(flatly)
It's from my brother. Your brother got Dearsmoke a contract to do an album. We leave for London next week to start recording.

Davidson sits up, and smiles.

DAVIDSON
Honey, that's *fantastic*. But why'd you say it like you were reading an obituary?

CAMBRIDGE
(uncertain)
Because, isn't it ... for us? If you can't take listening to the radio, how could you stand *me* ... if it's ever *me* on

the radio?

DAVIDSON

as it hits him that his self-destructive pity might destroy more than he bargained for.

He pulls himself together, then gets up.

ON BOTH

as Davidson walks over to Cambridge and puts his arms around her. They hug tightly, both of them near tears.

CLOSE ON THEM

DAVIDSON
(softly)
Look, sweetheart, I'll make it through
this in one piece. I promise. Your not
living your life isn't gonna help me live
mine. I'm not sayin' it won't be hard on
me at times ... but it's *my* job to handle
it. Not yours. Okay?

Cambridge nods.

DAVIDSON
(continuing)
And I goddam *well* don't want you feelin'
guilty about your highs because I might
be jealous.
(beat)
You wanted to spend tonight dancing?
That's what we'll do. Spend the night
out celebrating.

Cambridge smiles, kisses Davidson firmly...then pushes him onto the bed, falling on top of him.

CAMBRIDGE
If it comes to celebrating ... I think I
like your original idea better.

As they begin making love one more time, we

CUT TO

INT. THEIR HOTEL SUITE - NIGHT

Davidson is asleep. Dressed only in a night shirt, Cambridge gets out of bed, carefully not waking him, and pads over to the desk, turning on a small desk lamp.

Quietly, she searches in the top drawer, finds a piece of hotel stationery and a pen, and begins writing.

CLOSE ON PAPER

as we see what Cambridge is writing:

Look, sweetheart,
I'll make it through this in one piece.
Your not living your life
Ain't gonna help me live mine.
I'm not sayin' it won't be hard on me at times ...
But it's *my* job to handle it, not yours.

CAMBRIDGE

as she finishes writing, folds up the paper, gets up, and drops it into her purse.

Then she turns off the desk lamp and crawls back into bed.

CUT TO

EXT. RESORT BEACH - DAY

Another beautiful one. Davidson and Cambridge are side by side on a blanket, soaking up rays. Neither one is moving a muscle. A radio a few blankets over is playing rock, Mick Jagger singing.

MICK JAGGER
You *can't* al-ways *get* what you *wa-ant* ...

CAMBRIDGE
Davidson.

He still doesn't move a muscle.

DAVIDSON
Yeah.

MICK JAGGER
You *can't* al-ways *get* what you *wa-ant* ...

She doesn't move either. The song continues. Davidson doesn't seem to notice.

CAMBRIDGE
Come to London with me.

JAGGER
But if you try some-*times*... you might *find* ...you c'n get what you *need*.

A long pause. Neither one of them moves.

DAVIDSON
Okay.

Jagger singing the main verses continuing over, we

CUT TO

EXT. CONCORDE JETLINER - DAY

as it reaches supersonic speed and *breaks* the sound barrier.

INT. CONCORDE PASSENGER CABIN - DAY

as Davidson and Cambridge join the other passengers—including Alex Davidson and the rest of the band—in whooping and applauding.

EXT. HEATHROW AIRPORT - DAY

as the Concorde comes in for landing in London.

CUT TO

INT. AIRPORT CUSTOMS

as Cambridge and Davidson pass through the Nothing-to-Declare tables without stopping.

As they begin walking out together, the Jagger song fades and we

CUT TO

EXT. LONDON - DAY

morning, as Cambridge and Davidson are walking together in Central London—the area between Charing Cross and Piccadilly Circus. Cambridge has her pocket book slung over her shoulder and is carrying a guitar case; Davidson, for once, is the empty-handed one.

CAMBRIDGE
—So we'll be rehearsing ... probably
until six or so.

DAVIDSON
You free for lunch?

CAMBRIDGE
Wouldn't count on it. Better make it
dinner.
(beat)
Got plans for the day?

Davidson shakes his head.

CAMBRIDGE
Then can you do me a big favor?

DAVIDSON AND CAMBRIDGE

DAVIDSON
Sure. What?

CAMBRIDGE
The band is short one song for the album.
Write it for us.

DAVIDSON
(laughs)
What gave you the idea I'm a song-writer?

CAMBRIDGE
If you can write a violin concerto, a
song should be easy.

Davidson gets a little suspicious.

DAVIDSON
What's this ... my brother's idea of
occupational therapy? The musical
equivalent of basket-weaving?

CAMBRIDGE
(comes back hard)
Don't flatter yourself, Davidson. This
album's *important* to us, and if you write

us a song that sucks, we ain't usin' it.

Davidson looks relieved.

DAVIDSON
Well ... Guess I might come up with a half-decent melody. But you have to write lyrics—I wouldn't know where to start.

Cambridge pulls out of her pocket book the piece of paper she wrote in the hotel room.

CAMBRIDGE
Start here.

She hands it to Davidson. He looks at it...not recognizing it at first.

DAVIDSON
What's this?

CAMBRIDGE
It'll come to you.

It dawns on him slowly.

DAVIDSON
This is what I said to you, the night—

CAMBRIDGE
I got it down on paper while you were asleep.

DAVIDSON
But it looks like song lyrics.

CAMBRIDGE
(laughs)

That's why I wrote it down, you jerk!
Just fix it so it scans and you got half
a song already.

EXT. RECORDING STUDIOS

as Cambridge pauses in front of a door leading to a flight of stairs, and kisses Davidson.

CAMBRIDGE
See you back here at six.

She opens the door and starts running up the stairs.

INT. STAIRCASE

as Davidson calls after her.

DAVIDSON
Hey! What instrument am I supposed to
work out the harmony on? My fiddle's
back in the States!

CAMBRIDGE

at top of stairs, calling down.

CAMBRIDGE
Get yourself one of those toy electronic
keyboards! A three-year-old can play 'em
with one hand tied!

Cambridge disappears through another door.

DAVIDSON

as he considers this, then heads out to the streets again.

CUT TO

EXT. "FARRER'S ELECTRONIC MUSIC" STORE - DAY

as Davidson looks into a display window showing a variety of both amateur and professional electronic keyboards and synthesizers of all types, brands, and sizes...Yamahas, Casios, Rolands, custom jobs...the works. He goes in.

INT. STORE - PROFESSIONAL DEPARTMENT

The sights and sounds of musicians at work, trying out instruments. Davidson looks around, seeing a part of the music world which has been completely reshaped since he was in a country music band at Juilliard.

DAVIDSON

as he passes music computers with displays of new software, books on programming, a big diagram on one wall showing waveform characteristics.

Then he sees something that really catches his eye.

A DISPLAY CASE

which is filled with electronic and synthesized violins.

DAVIDSON

as if a magnet is drawing him in to look at the violins.

He's staring openly when one of the store's young partners, BRIAN FARRER, notices Davidson's interest and walks up to him. Brian speaks with a bit of a Scottish accent.

DAVIDSON AND BRIAN

BRIAN
Let me guess. Your instrument's violin.

Davidson holds up his left hand, flexing it to show that only two fingers still work.

> DAVIDSON
> Used to be. Can't do much anymore.
> Guess I'm in the wrong section of the
> store now.

Brian doesn't react with the automatic sympathy we might expect, but acts like he's a doctor and Davidson's his patient.

> BRIAN
> How much movement you still got?

Davidson looks surprised, then answers.

> DAVIDSON
> Left first and second fingers are still
> good ... which isn't very.

> BRIAN
> You can still bow?

> DAVIDSON
> Right's as good as ever.

> BRIAN
> I think I can fix you up with something.

Brian goes to a display case. He picks out an obviously electronic violin—there are electronic pick-up lines instead of real strings—and a bow. Then Brian motions Davidson to follow him.

Davidson hesitates, worried and skeptical.

> BRIAN
> Come along, then.

Brian leads Davidson into the back.

IN BACK OF STORE

which looks like a cross between a nuclear physics laboratory and launch control at Cape Canaveral.

Still walking, Brian extends a free right hand to Davidson.

BRIAN
Brian Farrer.

DAVIDSON
Igor Davidson.

They shake. Brian leads Davidson over to a computer terminal, pulls out a cord, and plugs the violin in.

BRIAN AND DAVIDSON

as Brian hands Davidson the violin and bow, then takes a seat behind a computer terminal.

Brian brings up a pre-set program on the computer.

BRIAN
Right, then. Let's see what you can do.
Just treat the pick-up lines like real
strings.

Davidson begins playing the Bach Air—the music coming out from the tiny computer speaker with a rich, natural violin tone—while Brian looks at information coming up on his terminal.

After maybe ten seconds, Brian stands up and looks directly at Davidson's left hand and what it's doing. He hits a key on his terminal and motions Davidson to stop playing.

BRIAN
(continuing)
That should do, for a start. Your first

finger's doing most of the work. Right?

Davidson nods.

BRIAN
(continuing)
Right. Now try something you can't play
anymore.

Davidson goes into a later section of the Paganini 24th Caprice... but very slowly. He's able to handle it until he gets to a chord he has to play...and can't with only two fingers.

Brian watches his computer terminal.

BRIAN
(continuing)
Don't have the speed and can't cluster
the notes at all ... that about it?

DAVIDSON
That's about it.

He starts to put the violin down. Brian shakes his head.

BRIAN
Not finished yet. Now let's try the bow
arm, eh? The violin you're on has got
three separate pick-up zones for the bow.
Each one's a separate channel. See the
marks?

DAVIDSON'S POV - CLOSE ON THE VIOLIN

as he sees that on the bow side of where the bridge would be there are lines painted across, as if they're guitar frets.

BACK TO SCENE

as Davidson tries playing again, drawing the bow across in each zone. He's in three separate keys, depending where he bows.

DAVIDSON
(still playing)
It's like I've got three differently
tuned violins.

BRIAN
Or as if you're on three different
instruments. (hits key) Try the
different zones again.

Davidson continues playing. In the first zone it sounds like violin ...then he bows in the second zone and it sounds like saxophone ...and it sounds as if he's playing a flute when he bows across the third.

BRIAN
It just as easily could have been oboe,
tuba, and trumpet. Whatever you want.

Davidson stops playing, realizing this isn't getting him anywhere.

DAVIDSON
I can't get what I *want* ... which is to
play classical violin in a symphony. Not
with two fingers. Not on an electronic
instrument.

BRIAN
(almost to himself)
Playing in a symphony with two fingers
... in real time. Now that'd be a job
and a half, wouldn't it?

Brian turns back to his terminal and begins programming.

BRIAN
Left hand. We'll double your normal
seven positions to compensate for loss of
speed ... giving us fourteen left-hand
zones. Net forty percent of max normal
finger-seconds, optimax closer to thirty,
weighting roughly sixty-six point six
percent on one.

DAVIDSON

as he puts down the violin and bow, and begins paying *very* close attention.

ON BOTH

BRIAN
(continuing)
Let's see ... we'll work in an expert
system circuit to handle real-time note-
clustering.
Right hand, four strings, three zones,
normal input mechanism rated at one
hundred percent, for a max rating of
three-hundred percent.

DAVIDSON
Are you telling me you can *do* it?

BRIAN
(not looking up)
You Yanks are used to bleedin' miracles,
aren't you?

Brian looks carefully at his terminal, then spins around on his chair.

BRIAN
You'll have to learn new fingerings, of

course. And, I've got some new sampling chips in that sound like a Guarnerius to the fifth decimal.

Davidson is practically in tears.

DAVIDSON
It'd have to be my Stradivarius.

BRIAN
Then bring it in and we'll sample it. But I've gotta tell you right off. It'll cost plenty.

Davidson laughs.

DAVIDSON
I can afford it.

BRIAN
Thank God for rich Americans.

CUT TO

EXT. W.E. HILL & SONS - DAY

the most famous and distinguished violin dealership in London... the world, for that matter.

INT. HILL & SONS

as Davidson enters. On display is a selection of violins, bows, mutes, and other musical paraphernelia. Davidson approaches a very upper class Englishman in his fifties, typically overdressed by American standards.

CLERK
Good day. How may I help you, sir?

DAVIDSON
I currently own a Stradivarius, and need
a less-expensive second violin that can
be used for outdoor concerts.

CLERK
Very good. Do you have anything in
particular in mind?

DAVIDSON
Yes. I'd like an exact duplicate of my
violin—at least as far as measurements
and appearance.

CLERK
If you could show me your violin, perhaps
we have one that might fit your needs.

DAVIDSON
(shakes head)
It's back in the States.

The Clerk takes a large book and opens it for Davidson.

CLERK
Then let's see if it's in our catalog.
If it's a Stradivarius, the chances are
excellent we sold it at one time or
another.

Davidson flips through a book showing photographs and history of various classic violins, and finds his own. He points.

DAVIDSON
This one.

The Clerk looks at the catalog.

CLERK
One moment, please.

The Clerk disappears into a back room for a moment, then returns with two violin cases, and sets them down on a counter. He opens the first case and takes out a violin.

CLERK
This is a Villaume, made in France, from
1872. If you'd care to try it?

The Clerk hands Davidson the violin and a bow. Davidson adjusts the bow, tunes the violin, then plays the Bach Air. After a few seconds, he hands the violin back and shakes his head.

DAVIDSON
This is much too fine a violin for my
purposes. How much are you selling it
for?

CLERK
Forty-two thousand pounds, sir.

DAVIDSON
That's what I thought.

The Clerk gets the other violin.

CLERK
This might be more suitable. A Klotz,
German made, from 1889.

He hands Davidson the second violin. Davidson takes it, plays a little of the same Bach, and nods.

DAVIDSON
That's more like it. How much is this
one?

CLERK
Nine thousand, six hundred pounds, sir.

Davidson looks at the violin.

DAVIDSON
The tail piece, bridge, and chinrest
would need to be replaced to match my
violin more closely.

CLERK
We could do that in one week.

DAVIDSON
Fine. I'll take it.

Davidson takes an American Express Gold Card and plunks it onto the counter.

DAVIDSON
Oh ... one more thing. I need to have it
fitted with some electronics. Can you
give it to me disassembled then have it
glued back together for me?

THE CLERK

as he reacts as if Davidson had asked him to deliver it to a whorehouse. He gives Davidson a *very* disdainful look.

CLERK
If you insist, sir.

CUT TO

INT. HOTEL LOBBY - DAY

as Davidson is making a PhoneCard telephone call at a British Telecom kiosk.

DAVIDSON
Mr. Winston? This is Igor Davidson ...
Fine, thanks ... as a matter of fact
that's what I'm calling about—I'll be
able to start the orchestra season after
all ... Well, all I can say is it's a
miracle ...

CUT TO

EXT. RECORDING STUDIO - DAY

where Davidson left Cambridge off earlier. He heads in and up the stairs.

INT. CORRIDORS

as Davidson looks at doors. Music can be heard from several sources, but none of it very loud. He doesn't know which studio Dearsmoke is in. Davidson sees one door marked "Rehearsal Studio A" and goes in without knocking.

INT. STUDIO A FOYER

Wrong studio—Davidson can see and hear through the glass—instead of Dearsmoke a great looking lady is rehearsing a bizarre song to synthesized accompaniment.

WOMAN IN STUDIO

SINGER
(belting out)
If you have mice, you won't have roaches
Mice ... eat ... roaches.
If you have dogs you won't have burglars
Dogs ... eat ... burglars.
If you have television you won't have books.
Television ... eats ... books.

DAVIDSON

as he heads out to look for Dearsmoke.

INT. STUDIO B FOYER

Davidson sees Dearsmoke performing in the studio through a glass window. His brother, Alex, is in there, watching them. There's a connecting door with a sign that reads, "Please Close Outer Door Before Opening This One."

THROUGH WINDOW

Art is doing lead vocals on a song. Cambridge is singing backup. Then she sees Davidson through the window and waves him inside. Davidson makes sure the outer door is closed then goes into the studio.

INT. STUDIO

as Davidson enters. We hear Art singing:

ART
I like things way they used to be
You wanna play it fast and loose
The old time's good enough for me
But you kept askin'—What's the use?
(next verse)
We ended goin' separate ways
Not like you gave me a real choice
Left me back in the good old days
Was that your words, or just your voice?

THE BAND AND DAVIDSON

as Dearsmoke finishes the song with a reprise of the chorus:

ART
You said you wanted *no* strings attached

And now you want another rematch
Now it's my turn to say
I guess that it's okay
But ... no *strings* attached.

Immediately the band members begin between-number noodling on their instruments. Cambridge smiles at Davidson, Alex waves to him.

ALEX
Hey, Igor. Cami says you're doin' a song
for the band. When do I get a look at it?

Davidson laughs.
DAVIDSON
(to Cambridge)
Not taking any chances, huh?

Cambridge shrugs, innocently, as she unstraps her guitar and begins putting it in its case.

Davidson takes a few sheets of music out of a pocket and—making sure he'll get an objective view—hands them not to Cambridge or Alex, but to Sasha.

CAMBRIDGE
What ... already?

ANGLE ON DAVIDSON

It's his turn to shrug.

DAVIDSON
(to Cambridge)
I had a couple spare hours in a music
store.
(beat)
Sasha ... I—uh—took the liberty of
writing in a violin part ... if it works

for you.

SASHA
Okay ... I'll let ya know.

CAMBRIDGE AND ALEX

as the possible meaning registers on them.

CUT TO

INT. EAST INDIAN RESTAURANT - NIGHT

as Davidson, Alex, and Cambridge are having dinner.

ALEX
—And how long you think you can get away with it?

DAVIDSON
About fifteen seconds after somebody who knows gets a good look at my left hand fingering ... which might be a while since I'll be sitting last stand, second violins ... and Winston says I won't have a stand mate.

ALEX
Then you *do* know you'll be caught. I don't get it ... unless you're gonna use this to get publicity for a solo career—

DAVIDSON
(shakes head)
All that'd do is turn me into a sideshow attraction ... *Igor and his Frankenstein Violin* ... no thanks. But I figure if I can play in the symphony three or four weeks before they catch me out, I have

No Strings Attached   335

better than track odds on convincing them
to let me stay.

Cambridge thinks of a gentle way to bring up a touchy subject, then decides to try it head on.

CAMBRIDGE
Look ... why knock yourself out like
this? With your talent—and what you
say this magic fiddle can do—you could
write your own ticket in pop music.
Matter of fact, you could be in
Dearsmoke, starting now. Right, Alex?

Alex nods. Davidson has obviously been expecting this offer for a long time.

DAVIDSON
Cambridge ... your side of the street is
a lot of fun for me. I like the violent
energy in the music ... the hard metallic
rhythms of a pneumatic hammer going full
blast. I like the waves of energy you get
back from the audience. Classical is a
museum compared to that.
(a beat)
It *is* a museum. It's two-
century-old music played on instruments
that haven't changed much in two hundred
years ... often played on the actual
museum pieces.

Cambridge takes note of what Davidson's just admitted ...

DAVIDSON
(continuing)
... You even have to dress up in clothes
that've been out of style for a hundred
years. But I was *raised* in that museum.

I know it like my tongue knows the roof
of my mouth ... And more than that, there
are pieces in that museum that you can't
find anywhere outside museums anymore.
Rock is World War Three ... classical is
pistols at dawn. Rock is simple and
hard-driving ... classical is mysterious
and logical. Rock hits between the legs
... classical in the mind and heart.

CLOSE ON DAVIDSON

DAVIDSON
(continuing)
They're not from the same century ... the
same world. Your time—your world—
is a place I can visit ... but I can't
survive living in it all the time.

CAMBRIDGE

as she tries to show him what he's just said.

CAMBRIDGE
Davidson ... what happens if your people
don't want a device from my century ...
invading the museum?

THE THREE OF THEM

as the question registers on Davidson and hangs in the air.

CUT TO

INT. FARRER'S RESEARCH & DEVELOPMENT LAB - DAY

as Davidson and Brian Farrer are working together. Davidson's using the same electronic violin we first saw him try, and Brian's at the same computer console. A music stand is set up in front of Davidson.

BRIAN
Scales once again, please.

Davidson begins playing—reading the music in front of him—but what *we* hear is not musical scales but a repeating sequence of notes in a completely arbitrary pattern. Farrer is programming at the console while Davidson plays.

BRIAN
(continuing)
That should do it.

Davidson continues to play. Brian hits a key and the pattern of the notes become sequential—in the correct *order* of a major scale—but some of the notes are completely missing, for example—going from *A* to *C* while missing *B*.

CLOSE ON DAVIDSON'S LEFT HAND

as we see him fingering.

BRIAN (O.S.)
(continuing)
You're overshooting again. Remember, Davidson—your positions are precisely *half* what you're used to.

BACK TO SCENE

DAVIDSON
(tense)
Sorry.

Davidson continues playing, and we're now hearing a normal violin playing a correct, major scale.

BRIAN
Very good. Now the major triads.

Fingering exactly the same ... but *bowing* second zone.

CLOSE ON VIOLIN

showing Davidson fingering single notes...but we're not hearing the proper scales of chords but sequences of three out-of-sequence notes.

BRIAN (O.S.)
Second zone.

BACK TO SCENE

DAVIDSON
(losing it)
Sorry, sorry, *sorry*!

Davidson stops playing and lets his frustration out on poor Brian.

DAVIDSON
(continuing)
Goddam it! What the hell do you *want* from me? It took me twenty years to learn to play violin right the first time and now you expect me to learn it all over in a few months!

Brian takes this outburst calmly.

BRIAN
You're doing just fine.

DAVIDSON
No, I'm *not*. It's like I'm five years old again. I can't do *anything* anymore! Jesus Christ, I was *crazy* to believe your damn promises!

Davidson puts the violin and bow down, and starts for the door.

BRIAN
(calling after)
If you walk out that door ... you're a
dead man.

Davidson whirls around.

DAVIDSON
You gonna put out a contract on me?

BRIAN
You'll be putting out a contract on yourself.
If you don't kill yourself with drugs—or in a
car—you'll give yourself a heart attack.

Davidson pauses for the longest moment of his life, then goes back and picks up the violin and bow again.

BRIAN
Bowing second zone.

Davidson begins playing, with his bow stroking an inch away from where it was before ... and we're now hearing a perfect scale of ascending chords.

BRIAN
Very good. Now. Did you practice the Bach?

Davison laughs, breaking the tension.

DAVIDSON
Yes, Grandpa.

Brian looks at him questioningly then shrugs—Davidson isn't going to explain the joke.

ON DAVIDSON

as he flips pages on his music stand then begins playing the Bach Air on the G String ... but only adequately. As he's playing, we

DISSOLVE TO

CLOSE ON DAVIDSON PLAYING

as he's playing the Bach Air more smoothly ...

DISSOLVE TO

CLOSE ON DAVIDSON PLAYING

SLOW MOVEMENT BEETHOVEN VIOLIN CONCERTO as he's playing a section requiring more sophisticated technique ...

DISSOLVE TO

CLOSE ON DAVIDSON PLAYING

FIRST MOVEMENT TCHAIKOVSKY CONCERTO as he's zipping through the Auer cadenza ... And

DISSOLVE TO

BRIAN WATCHING DAVIDSON PLAYING

PAGANINI TWENTY-FOURTH CAPRICE which we heard him play in his orchestra audition ... and he's playing it as well on the electronic violin as we heard him play before his injury.

Davidson reaches the extremely difficult conclusion and finishes with a flourish. Brian applauds.

BRIAN
Bravo!

Davidson takes a modest bow, grinning from ear to ear.

CUT TO

INT. RECORDING STUDIO ENGINEER BOOTH - DAY

showing Dearsmoke—and Davidson—other side of the glass, making final adjustments to instruments. A full RECORDING STAFF is present, the ENGINEER being given final directions by Alex. The ENGINEER'S SECRETARY is writing in her log book.

ALEX
—and we'll mix that down later.

ENGINEER
I'm lost. Where are we again?

SECRETARY
Ain't Gonna Help Me, mix three, take one.

The Engineer punches a sequence of numbers into his board and turns to Alex.

ENGINEER
Ready, Alex, and—
(starts tape)
—*Rolling*.

ON ALEX

as he hits the intercom button to the band.

ALEX
Five seconds, people!

INT. STUDIO

as we see the band members adjusting headphones. Cambridge hums a few notes near her standing mike.

ON DAVIDSON

wearing headphones and playing the same electronic violin, plays a few notes then looks at Cambridge.

CAMBRIDGE AND DAVIDSON

as they smile at each other.

BAND'S POV - ENGINEER BOOTH

as they hear several repeating *beeps* then see Alex lower his hand and the red *Recording* sign comes on.

ON DEARSMOKE AND DAVIDSON

as—after a medium tempo intro led by Cambridge on heavy metal guitar, Cambridge begins singing, all the others except Davidson singing back-up.

CAMBRIDGE
I'll make it through this in one *piece*
I gotta take this on alone
I have to *go* the extra mile
Not *say*in' won't be hell
But it'll take me *home*.

DAVIDSON AND CAMBRIDGE

as they do a short duet of guitar and violin, leading into Cambridge and the band singing the first chorus:

POV FROM ENGINEER'S BOOTH

as we see the Engineer adjusting levels and we hear the band on speakers.

CAMBRIDGE AND BAND
So honey you can wait for me
But don't wait by the phone
'Cause your not livin' your life, pal

Ain't gonna help me live my own.

CAMBRIDGE AND DAVIDSON

as they smile at each other while playing another duet, leading into the second verse:

CAMBRIDGE
I can't *live* your life for you
An' you *can't* live mine for me
You gotta take your highs
It stings me but it's my
Responsibility.

ENGINEER'S BOOTH - POV ON BAND

On Alex, looking happy.

Another guitar/violin duet, then a repeat of the chorus:

CAMBRIDGE AND BAND
So honey you can wait for me
But don't wait by the phone
'Cause your not livin' your life, pal
Ain't gonna help me live my own.

CAMBRIDGE AND DAVIDSON

smiling at each other, playing duet, then the final chorus:

CAMBRIDGE AND BAND

CAMBRIDGE AND BAND
So sweetheart you can wait for me
But don't wait by the phone
Yeah, your not takin' your own bows
Ain't gonna help me win my own.

Instrumental lead out, and the band finishes together.

BAND POV - ANGLE ON ENGINEER BOOTH

as *Recording* sign goes out.

STUDIO

ALEX
(on Intercom)
Fantastic, people! Just fantastic!
Good. Two minutes while we set up the
next mix.

As everyone starts taking off earphones and putting down their instruments, Davidson walks over to Cambridge, who grins broadly.

CAMBRIDGE
So you like how we're doin' your song?

DAVIDSON
Great, just great. But it's not really
my song. It was your idea. I think your
name should be on it.

CAMBRIDGE
(delighted)
That's real sweet of you, honey, but it
wouldn't feel right sharing credit just
for writing down what you said.

DAVIDSON
No, really, Cambridge. The song was your
idea. I think your name should be on it
... not mine.

Cambridge suddenly understands and she turns to ice.

CAMBRIDGE
(aside to Sasha)
Right. I get it. We're not *good* enough

No Strings Attached 345

for a classical musician from *Juilliard*.

Davidson backs off immediately.

DAVIDSON
Hey, that's not what I meant! I just
thought it'd be more honest if—

CAMBRIDGE
—if you didn't have your name on a rock
song, 'cause it might embarrass the hell
out of you.

DAVIDSON
Okay, okay! We'll keep *my* name on it.
Jesus, try and be *fair*!

Cambridge glares at him, not buying it.

ALEX
(on Intercom)
Let's do it once more, people!

DAVIDSON AND CAMBRIDGE

as they get ready, the tension between them still high.

CUT TO

INT. FARRER'S RESEARCH & DEVELOPMENT LAB - NIGHT

working late, as Davidson has his Stradivarius under his chin, bow in hand, and Brian, seated at the computer as usual, has a set of carefully-padded pick-ups affixed to the violin, leading to the terminal. Davidson is playing the Bach Air on his violin.

CLOSE ON BRIAN'S COMPUTER MONITOR AND KEYBOARD

as an analysis of the sound the Stradivarius is producing is being displayed on Monitor in real time. Brian hits a key and an instant of the analysis *freezes* on the top half of the monitor

BRIAN AND DAVIDSON

as he turns around and signals Davidson to stop.

BRIAN
That should do it, I think.

Davidson smiles weakly.

DAVIDSON
Jeez, I'm so used to the new fingerings,
I barely know what to do with a real
fiddle anymore.

BRIAN
Good. After what you've put me through,
I don't want you to revert. Now try it
on her clone.

DAVIDSON

as he places his Stradivarius onto a padded table.

PAN OVER TO

ANOTHER VIOLIN NEXT TO IT

which looks to be an identical twin of the Stradivarius ... only this one doesn't have the padded pick-ups. It doesn't need them because a cord is running out from under chin rest, also into Brian's computer. The chin rest is open, showing electronic controls and displays inside.

DAVIDSON

as he picks up the electronic violin ... and begins playing the same Bach ... and it obviously sounds good to him, because he's smiling like the cat that swallowed the canary.

CLOSE ON BRIAN'S COMPUTER MONITOR AND KEYBOARD

as a moving sound analysis of the electronic violin appears on Monitor underneath the Stradivarius analysis. Brian hits a key, freezing on the new sounds.

BRIAN

as he turns around and again signals Davidson to stop. Then he types in several commands and watches.

CLOSE ON THE MONITOR

The two freeze-frames of wave-forms move together ... and match perfectly.

BACK TO SCENE

BRIAN
As promised ... a Stradivarius to the
fifth decimal.

DAVIDSON
We did it?

BRIAN
We *did* it.

Then he remembers a similar moment in *My Fair Lady* and sings badly:

BRIAN
Tonight old boy we did it. We did it.
We *did* it. I never thought we'd do it,
but indeed we did.

ON BOTH

as they grin at each other, sharing a moment of special triumph.

DAVIDSON

as he begins playing the *My Fair Lady* song Brian was singing and, after a few phrases, Davidson quickly slides into Handel's *Music for the Royal Fireworks*—the fourth movement, "The Rejoicing," used to celebrate coronations.

At first we hear only Davidson playing alone...then the full orchestra mixes in and we hear the piece in its full symphonic splendor, continuing over

EXT. JET AIRLINER TAKING OFF - DAY

as—Handel continuing—it rises majestically into the air—

INT. FIRST CLASS LOUNGE - DAY

Handel continuing over, as Davidson, Cambridge, the other band members, and Alex head back to the States—

CUT TO

EXT. SYMPHONY HALL - MORNING

the Handel *Music for the Royal Fireworks* continuing, as we see Davidson—violin case in hand—salute the poster once again as he goes in, other musicians preceding and following him—

ON STAGE - FULL ORCHESTRA

as we see that this is a *live* rehearsal of the Handel *Music for the Royal Fireworks*—

ON ERIC SMITH-KENSINGTON

dressed in turtleneck and slacks—conducting the Handel—

PAN TO

THE CONCERTMASTER

Aaron Silverberg, first stand of the violins, leading the section—

PANNING THROUGH VIOLINS

as we pass row after row of violinists playing the Handel, until finally we're to the last stand of the second violins, and sitting without a stand mate is

DAVIDSON

playing his violin indistinguishably from the rest of the orchestra, and looking damn happy about it.

ON SMITH-KENSINGTON AND ORCHESTRA

as the conductor gestures the orchestra to stop playing. They stop.

    SMITH-KENSINGTON
    (to Concertmaster)
    I'd like to change that so we start the
    phrase with an up-bow *here*—
    (he sings phrase he means)
    —then go back to the down-bow *here*.
    (sings again)

Smith-Kensington sings so well that the orchestra gives him an ovation, the strings knocking bows on music stands.

    SMITH-KENSINGTON
    (laughing)
    If you think I'm cancelling the afternoon
    rehearsal, forget it.

The orchestra laughs. The concertmaster then addresses the section.

SILVERBERG
From letter *D*.

Silverberg stands up and demonstrates the change that the conductor has called for, then sits to mark his part. Smith-Kensington allows a few seconds for the violins to mark parts.

ON DAVIDSON

as he changes the bowings on *his* part.

SMITH-KENSINGTON AND ORCHESTRA

as the conductor raises his hands again.

SMITH-KENSINGTON
Starting at Letter *D*.

The conductor gives the down beat, and the orchestra begins again.

ON DAVIDSON

playing with them.

CUT TO

INT. BACKSTAGE SYMPHONY HALL - DAY

as Davidson is putting his violin in its case, when he's approached by another violinist about his age, FREDDIE SCHWARTZ.

SCHWARTZ
Not gonna find it easy meeting your new
classmates if you insist on sitting all
alone in the back.

DAVIDSON
(laughs)
Maybe ... but it's the only way I know to
make sure you don't get called on.
(extends hand)
Igor Davidson.

SCHWARTZ
(shaking it)
Freddie Schwartz. Listen, Igor—

DAVIDSON
Friends call me Davidson—

SCHWARTZ
Don't rush things, *bubeleh*.
(beat)
As I was saying, Igor, a lot of us head
over to a chili joint called Dr. Kato's
between rehearsals. Wanna join us?

DAVIDSON
(ironically)
Sure ... if you don't mind the loud rock
and roll.

INT. DR. KATO'S - DAY

as Davidson, Schwartz, and a couple of other violinists their age—
RUSSELL and Sylvia—are consuming chili. (We've seen both of them
way back on the String Audition Committee—Sylvia is the woman
who was first and loudest calling for Davidson's disqualification.)
Loud rock music is playing on the juke box. Davidson is careful to
favor his right hand and keep his left out of sight as much as possible.

DAVIDSON
—and I free-lanced in New York after
Juilliard 'cause that's where my contacts

were. It was tough, but touring with the
ballet for two seasons helped a lot.

SCHWARTZ
I guess I was luckier. Never had to
free-lance. Made it into the symphony
right out of Curtis ... and I plan on
staying in it until I retire.

RUSSELL
I don't even see how a violinist can
survive free-lancing anymore, what with
synthesizers drying up all the outside
recording work for us.

SYLVIA
Yeah ... and it's gonna get worse and
worse until the union steps in and puts
contractors who use synthesizers on the
Unfair list.

Davidson realizes prejudice against synthesizers could blow up on him.

DAVIDSON
What can the union do about it? There
are unions members makin' money playin'
synthesizer too, ya know.

Dr. Kato goes to the juke box, and puts in money for another song.

SYLVIA
That's exactly what we have to work on
... getting the union to declare
synthesizers a mechanical device—like
that juke box—instead of an
instrument.

Before Davidson can try answering this, Dr. Kato comes up to their table and addresses Schwartz.

DR. KATO
Everything all right here today, Freddie?

SCHWARTZ
Yep. Great, Doc.

The next song comes on the juke box... and it's Dearsmoke's recording of Davidson's song, "Ain't Gonna Help Me." Davidson tries not to let the others see him react.

SYLVIA
Hey, Doc—when you gonna get rid of that
junk box of yours and bring in a string
quartet for lunch?

DR. KATO
You kiddin', Sylvia—in this place?
The violins would be drowned out by the
music coming from the customers.

Sylvia snickers.

DR. KATO
(continuing)
Besides, you want to deprive Davidson
here of his royalties?

Davidson knows it's coming now.

SYLVIA
(to Kato)
He wrote this song?

DR. KATO
You bet. Matter of fact, it was on *my*
stage that he first played with the band.

DAVIDSON AND OTHER VIOLINISTS

as the others glare at Davidson, and he tries to disappear under the table. The revelation is merely embarrassing at the moment ... but Davidson knows it could also be dangerous to his career.

INT. CAMBRIDGE'S APARTMENT - BEDROOM - DAY

Morning. Instead of a bed there's a futon on the floor, wooden crates serve as a bed table, and there are rock music posters covering almost every square inch of wall and ceiling. Cambridge and Davidson are just awake, but still in bed in each other's arms, yawning.

DAVIDSON
Checkin' out a house in the 'burbs today.

CAMBRIDGE
(yawning)
Great. Be ready in a half hour.

DAVIDSON
You don't have to come if you don't want to.

CAMBRIDGE
I want to. Gimme a chance to check on the album's distribution.

DAVIDSON
(almost reluctantly)
Okay.

CUT TO

INT. PARKING GARAGE - DAY

as Davidson opens the passenger-side door for Cambridge, then gets behind the wheel, of a brand-new BMW.

INT. BMW - OUT OF GARAGE

as Davidson pulls the car out, and shoves in a cassette of a solo violin playing unaccompanied Bach.

INT. BMW - ON CITY STREETS

the recorded Bach continuing.

CAMBRIDGE
That violinist is terrific. You, by any chance?

DAVIDSON
This guy's good ... but I play it better.

CAMBRIDGE
God ... musicians and their egos. Okay, who's the competition?

DAVIDSON
Me ... before my injury. I play it better now.

Cambridge laughs, caught by the second oldest gag in the book.

EXT. REALTOR OFFICE - DAY

as Davidson gets behind the wheel of the BMW again, jingling house keys in his hand.

EXT. COUNTRY ROAD - THE BMW - DAY

on a beautiful fall day, foliage in full majesty, as the BMW pulls into the driveway of a Frank Lloyd Wright-ish and obviously *expensive* home set way back off the road.

IN FRONT OF HOUSE

as Davidson pulls the BMW up and cuts the engine.

INT. HOUSE - HUGE ROOM WITH HIGH CEILING

completely furnished, as Davidson is showing Cambridge around.

DAVIDSON
—And I figure *this* room is perfect for
quartets, soon as I get one going again.

CAMBRIDGE
Quartets? You could put your orchestra in this
room. Just how big is this place, anyway?

DAVIDSON
Thirty-eight hundred square feet ... not
counting the extension to the garage.

CAMBRIDGE
I know your insurance settlement was
big...

As they head toward a connecting door into

THE KITCHEN

CAMBRIDGE
—but you sure you can afford to rent a
place like this?

DAVIDSON AND CAMBRIDGE

Davidson leans against a kitchen counter.

DAVIDSON
Probably not.
(beat)
So guess it's a good thing I bought it.

Cambridge laughs, caught by the *oldest* gag in the book. She throws her arms around Davidson, kissing him.

Somehow, Davidson isn't as enthusiastic as she is.

CUT TO

EXT. SYMPHONY HALL - NIGHT

as we see a dressed-to-the-nines symphony audience going in for the season's opening night.

INT. SYMPHONY HALL

showing the audience as lights go down.

CAMBRIDGE AND ALEX

as they take seats in the audience.

REVERSE ON STAGE - FULL ORCHESTRA

the orchestra in full dress—women in black gowns, men in black full dress with tails—adjusting stands, running through musical phrases.

ON DAVIDSON

as he pulls his stand back a little to put his hands out of sight of the other violinists.

FAVORING THE CONCERTMASTER, INCLUDING ORCHESTRA

as Aaron Silverberg stands. Symphony Hall falls immediately silent, and the Concertmaster nods to the FIRST OBOIST for an A.

The Oboe plays an extended A. The Concertmaster tunes his violin, then nods to the strings to tune ... and a few seconds later the entire orchestra tunes.

THE STAGE

as the Concertmaster sits down again and the orchestra falls silent.

A few seconds of expectation, broken only by audience coughing, pass then

ERIC SMITH-KENSINGTON

also in full dress with tails, walks on stage to audience applause, shakes hands with the Concertmaster, bows to the audience, turns to the orchestra ... and raises his hands to begin.

INCLUDING AUDIENCE AND STAGE

The applause stops.

The conductor's downbeat, and the orchestra begins the symphony season with the Handel *Music for the Royal Fireworks*.

ON ERIC SMITH-KENSINGTON

conducting the Handel, and looking very royal indeed.

PANNING THROUGH VIOLINS

as we again pass row after row of violinists playing the Handel—including Freddie Schwartz, Russell, and Sylvia—until again we're to the last stand of the second violins, and

DAVIDSON

is playing.

CUT TO

INT. BACK STAGE SYMPHONY HALL - NIGHT

at the end of the concert, as Davidson is changing out of his full dress into street clothes. (Women orchestra members are changing elsewhere.)

His electronic Stradivarius clone is sitting in his open violin case on a table a few feet away from him.

Freddie Schwartz walks by, already changed, and sees Davidson's open violin case. He looks at the violin, almost in awe.

Davidson is starting to get *very* nervous ... he knows what's coming.

Schwartz continues looking at the violin.

SCHWARTZ
Mind if I see what your Strad feels
like?

FAVORING DAVIDSON

in a moment that seems in slow motion for him. This is the sort of request that it's almost impossible for one violinist to deny another professional politely. Then Davidson figures a way out.

DAVIDSON
Some other time, Freddie ... I've got my
girlfriend and my brother waiting for me.
(faking new thought)
Tell you what. You're coming to my
house-warming on the 20th, aren't you?
Drag me aside you can try it out then.

SCHWARTZ
Okay, thanks.
(beat)
You inviting the entire orchestra, or
what?

DAVIDSON
Just the strings. Don't want a bunch of
low-lifes, do we?

Schwartz laughs.

CUT TO

INT. RECORD STORE - DAY

the equivalent of Tower or Sam Goody—as Cambridge and Davidson are looking through the new compact disc releases for the *Dearsmoke* album...but can't find it.

The store MANAGER notices their disappointment and comes over to them.

MANAGER
Whatcha lookin' for?

CAMBRIDGE
Dearsmoke. First album by a city band.
I guess you don't have it in yet.

MANAGER
(shakes head)
Had in a few copies but it sold out.
I'll have it back in Saturday if you want
me to hold one for you.

ON CAMBRIDGE

thrilled by the news.

CAMBRIDGE
It sold *out*?

ON MANAGER

MANAGER
(matter of factly)
One of the single's—"Ain't Gonna Help Me"—is gettin' a lot of major market airplay. Matter of fact, next Monday's *Billboard* has the album hitting the charts at forty-one with a bullet.

CAMBRIDGE

as she looks as if she's just been told she's won the lottery.

CAMBRIDGE
Forty-one with a bullet? Are you *sure*?

ALL AGAIN

MANAGER
Just saw a Telex on it an hour ago. Head office always notifies local managers whenever a band in their city hits the charts. Dee-jays'll be playin' it all weekend.

DAVIDSON
Forty-one with a bullet is very good?

MANAGER
Better than very good for an unknown regional band. Just short of amazing.

CAMBRIDGE

as it's *her* turn to jump in the air with an earsplitting:

CAMBRIDGE
Ya-hooo!

ALL THREE AGAIN

as Cambridge throws her arms around Davidson and kisses him... then figures what the hell and kisses the store manager, too.

> MANAGER
> (to Davidson)
> She always this civic minded?

Davidson nods.

> CAMBRIDGE
> (manic)
> You got a phone I can use? It's an emergency!

The Manager gestures her to follow him.

MANAGER'S OFFICE

as Cambridge is on the phone, Davidson and the Manager standing by.

> CAMBRIDGE
> Sasha? ...
> (beat)
> Yeah, I just found out!
> (to Davidson)
> Alex *told* him already.
> (to phone)
> Yeah, we'll be right over!

INT. SASHA'S APARTMENT - DAY

as the entire band, Alex, and Davidson are drinking champagne, eating junk food, and celebrating. The *Dearsmoke* album is propped up near the stereo and the album is on, playing in the b.g.

> SASHA
> (raising glass)
> —and while we're at it, here's to Igor,

who wrote the single that drugged us onto
the charts.

CAMBRIDGE
Alex's the one that drugged you, Sasha—
Igor don't touch the stuff.

Everybody including Davidson groans, grabs a handful of popcorn, and throws it at Cambridge. While she's picking popcorn out of her hair:

FAVORING ALEX

ALEX
First thing we've got to do now is have
the company throw you a party—give the
industry people a chance to meet you.
(heads toward phone)
I better check hotels for facilities
right away.

CAMBRIDGE AND DAVIDSON

As Cambridge has an obvious—but perhaps not too fortuitous—idea.

CAMBRIDGE
Listen, Davidson 'n me are throwin' a
house-warming party next week. What say
we turn it into a celebration for the
band, too?
(to Davidson)
That all right with you, honey?

DAVIDSON
(slowly)
I don't know if that's such a good idea.
Half the orchestra's invited already.

CAMBRIDGE
(sarcastic)
And they might not like slumming, right?

DAVIDSON
That's not what I meant! I just thought
it might get crowded.

Cambridge gets up, furious, and heads for the door.

CAMBRIDGE
You're so full of crap!

Cambridge slams out of the apartment. Davidson chases after her.

INT. HALL - DAY

as Cambridge starts walking fast toward the elevator ... Davidson trying to keep up to her. Cambridge speeds up ... realizes he'll reach her before the elevator arrives, and starts down the stairs.

INT. STAIRCASE

as Davidson chases Cambridge down, taking two steps at a time, and finally grabs her.

DAVIDSON AND CAMBRIDGE

CAMBRIDGE
Let *go* of me, you bastard!

Davidson doesn't let go, and Cambridge keeps trying to pull away.

DAVIDSON
Willya give me a second to explain?

CAMBRIDGE
(still struggling)

Explain what? You been tryin' to keep us
in two separate worlds ever since you
found out you can still play classical!

DAVIDSON
You think I *want* to?

CAMBRIDGE
Then you're *admitting* it!

DAVIDSON
Listen to me, goddammit! Bad enough they
know I play rock! You know what happens
the second they figure out I'm playin' a
synthesizer!

CAMBRIDGE
So what else is new? You said all you
needed was a month before they could find
out! It's almost two months now!

DAVIDSON
It's not that goddam predictable!

CAMBRIDGE
Well neither is how long I can stand
bein' shoved to one side of your life!

This sinks in.

DAVIDSON
Okay. (beat) Okay.

As Cambridge and Davidson hug each other, we

CUT TO

EXT. DAVIDSON'S HOUSE - NIGHT

as a car pulls up and parks. Loud rock music can be heard playing inside.

INSIDE THE HOUSE - LIVING ROOM

the party is in full-swing, people dancing to the music, shmoozing, eating, drinking ... the usual. The crowd is a mixture of all sorts and—perhaps—it's not *immediately* obvious who are from the world of rock music and who are the classical types.

Among the people dancing, we see Cambridge and Davidson.

The party is being catered by Dr. Kato's, and radiation-suited waiters and waitresses are walking around with trays of hors d'oeuvres and drinks.

AT BAR - DR. KATO

himself—in his usual lab coat—as Sylvia sidles up.

SYLVIA
How 'bout a Coke, Doc?

DR. KATO
Sure thing, Sylvia. With or without caffeine?

SYLVIA
Without.

DR. KATO
Regular or diet?

SYLVIA
Diet.

DR. KATO
Sweetened with saccharin, cyclamates, or aspartame?

SYLVIA
(amazed)
What's the difference?

DR. KATO
Saccharin causes cancer in predisposed rats, cyclamates cause cancer in predisposed rats, and aspartame causes increased intelligence in predisposed human beings.

SYLVIA
Make that a Pepsi.

CUT TO

KITCHEN - ON RUSSELL

the other violinist Davidson had lunch with. Russell is dressed like—and without doubt is and always has been—a nerd. He goes up to a radiation-suited WAITER putting hors d'oeuvres on a tray.

RUSSELL
Excuse me, but could you please tell me where the bathroom is?

WAITER
Sorry, don't know. Try upstairs.

The waiter heads off with a loaded tray.

FOLLOWING RUSSELL

as he climbs a staircase and comes to

A LONG HALLWAY

where he starts searching for a bathroom. Russell sees a closed door and opens it.

RUSSELL'S POV - LOOKING INTO BEDROOM

as we see a couple of record-industry types doing lines of coke. They look up at Russell and glare.

Russell closes the door. He continues down the hall and comes to a second door. He opens it.

RUSSELL'S POV - A SECOND BEDROOM

as he sees a MAN lying back on the bed, pants at his feet, and a young, scantily clad girl kneeling between his legs.

The man being serviced looks over to Russell.

MAN ON BED
She'll be through with me in a minute,
sport ... ya mind waiting outside?

Russell closes the second door and continues down the hall.

AT END OF HALL - ANOTHER CLOSED DOOR

as Russell—having no idea what he'll find next, and perhaps interested to find out—decides to try his luck again. He opens the door to find

RUSSELL'S POV - THE BATHROOM

as a very skinny woman is alone in there on her knees, her head over the toilet bowl.

Russell closes the door again.

CUT TO

DOWNSTAIRS AGAIN - LIVING ROOM

as a song ends. Davidson and Cambridge leave the dance floor.

As soon as Cambridge is off the floor, Alex comes up to her.

ALEX
Cambridge? There's a stringer here from
Rolling Stone who's *dying* for a few
minutes with you.

Cambridge goes off with Alex. As soon as she's gone, Davidson is approached by Freddie Schwartz.

SCHWARTZ
Davidson ... you busy now? You said I
could try out that Strad of yours.

DAVIDSON
I didn't forget, Freddie. Come on ...
it'll be quiet in the garage extension.

As they head out back, they pass near the bar, where Sylvia is still standing with her Coke.

SYLVIA
What're you gents up to?

SCHWARTZ
Davidson's gonna let me try out his
Strad.

SYLVIA
You have a *Stradivarius*?

DAVIDSON
It was my grandfather's.
(reluctantly)
Okay, Sylvia, you can try it, too.

ON DAVIDSON, FREDDIE SCHWARTZ, AND SYLVIA

as they enter

THE KITCHEN

and walk outside through a back door.

EXT. BACK OF HOUSE - NIGHT

as—on their way to the extension—they pass Russell ... who's relieving himself into the bushes.

SYLVIA
(without stopping)
You're pissing on your shoe, Russell.

They keep walking. Russell looks down.

RUSSELL
Damn.

He quickly zips up.

RUSSELL
(calling after)
Hey, wait up!

INT. FURNISHED DEN

as Davidson, Schwartz, Sylvia, and—a few seconds later—Russell enter.

Davidson flips on the light, goes to a locked closet, unlocking it, and takes out his Stradivarius case, laying the case on a desk. He takes out the violin—making sure his back is to the others—and tunes the violin.

Carefully, he extends the Stradivarius to Freddie Schwartz.

SCHWARTZ
You first.

Davidson has anticipated this.

DAVIDSON
(shakes head)
I have a paper cut on my first finger.
(beat)
Enjoy yourself.

Schwartz shrugs and takes the violin.

He begins playing Saint-Saens' Introduction and Rondo Capriccioso—a piece with some Gypsy soul in it ... and he's terrific. As the others listen, we

DISSOLVE TO

SYLVIA PLAYING THE VIOLIN

a fast section of the Mendelssohn Violin Concerto...and she's also first rate.

DISSOLVE TO

RUSSELL PLAYING THE VIOLIN

some Fritz Kreisler, perhaps *Tambourine Chinois*...and he's also a very good violinist.

As Russell is playing, the door opens...and

CAMBRIDGE

ducks her head in.

CAMBRIDGE
Davidson ... so *here's* where you've been hiding.

INCLUDING THE VIOLINISTS

Russell stops playing.

CAMBRIDGE
(continuing)
The band's goin' on in five minutes.
Wanna play with us on your song?

Davidson hesitates, but there's no graceful out.

DAVIDSON
Sure thing.

Cambridge ducks out.

RUSSELL
(reluctantly)
Guess you'll be needing this back.

Russell hands the Stradivarius to Davidson.

SCHWARTZ
Tell me, *bubeleh*. How can you waste a
violin like *this* on music like *that*?

DAVIDSON

as he starts putting the Stradivarius back in its case.

DAVIDSON
I *don't* waste it, Freddie.

CUT TO

INT. HOUSE - ON DEARSMOKE

as they're performing, Art on lead vocals, in the room Cambridge said was big enough for the orchestra. Could be—the place is jam-packed and this crowd is *live*.

As the band comes to a big finish, the crowd of guests throws an enthusiastic blast of applause and shouting toward them.

CAMBRIDGE

She waits out the applause, then:

CAMBRIDGE
All *right*. And now the one you've been waitin'
for, number *nine* on the charts this week ...

ON GUESTS

Enthusiastic hoots and more applause.

ON BAND

CAMBRIDGE
Davidson, get your *fiddle* on up here.

ON DAVIDSON

as—amid a roar of hoots and applause—he climbs up on stage with his electronic violin.

SYLVIA AND RUSSELL

as they're standing near the front, watching as Davidson passes close ... and can't miss the fact that the violin Davidson's carrying looks exactly like the Stradivarius.

RUSSELL
Didn't we see him put his Stradivarius away?

Sylvia shrugs, but she's already suspicious, too.

ON DEARSMOKE AND DAVIDSON

as before—after a medium tempo intro led by Cambridge on

heavy metal guitar, Cambridge begins singing:

CAMBRIDGE
I'll make it through this in one *piece*
I gotta take this on alone
I have to *go* the extra mile
Not *say*in' won't be hell
But it'll take me *home*.

DAVIDSON AND CAMBRIDGE

as they do their first duet of guitar and violin—

SYLVIA AND RUSSELL'S POV - CLOSE ON DAVIDSON'S LEFT HAND

as they *watch* Davidson closely, and *see* that he's not playing like any violinist they've ever seen.

CAMBRIDGE AND BAND

CAMBRIDGE AND BAND
So honey you can wait for me
But don't wait by the phone
'Cause your not livin' your life, pal
Ain't gonna help me live my own.

CAMBRIDGE AND DAVIDSON

they smile at each other going into their second duet—

SYLVIA AND RUSSELL

as they exchange completely bewildered looks.

ON FREDDIE SCHWARTZ

as he pushes his way through the crowd until he reaches Russell and Sylvia.

ON THE THREE VIOLINISTS

watching Davidson, astonished.

SYLVIA
(to others)
Watch his left hand.

ON BAND AGAIN

CAMBRIDGE
I can't *live* your life for you
An' you *can't* live mine for me
You gotta take your highs
It stings me but it's my
Responsibility.

VIOLINISTS POV ON DAVIDSON AND BAND

The third guitar/violin duet.

SCHWARTZ
(to the others)
What the hell are his fingers *doing*?

Sylvia and Russell shrug, looking as if they're seeing a U.F.O.

CAMBRIDGE AND BAND
So honey you can wait for me
But don't wait by the phone
'Cause your not livin' your life, pal
Ain't gonna help me live my own.

CAMBRIDGE AND DAVIDSON

smiling at each other, playing duet—

ON DAVIDSON

as he suddenly looks down—

DAVIDSON'S POV

as he *sees* the expression on the violinists faces as they watch.

CAMBRIDGE AND BAND

CAMBRIDGE AND BAND
So sweetheart you can wait for me
But don't wait by the phone
Yeah, your not takin' your own bows
Ain't gonna help me win my own.

Instrumental lead out, and the band finishes together.

THE CROWD OF GUESTS

as they explode into applause.

CAMBRIDGE AND DAVIDSON

as she kisses him full out, then pushes him forward to take a bow on his own-

DAVIDSON

as he takes his bow, trying to be cool outside ... but not quite convincing himself as he wonders how much his orchestra colleagues can figure out.

CUT TO

INT. SYMPHONY HALL - ON STAGE - DAY

during a rehearsal of "Montagues and Capulets" from Prokofiev's *Romeo and Juliet*. A particularly dramatic and *portentious* piece of music.

ON DAVIDSON

as he's sitting in his usual seat, closest to the wings, playing.

WATCHING FROM WINGS - SYLVIA AND RUSSELL

as they're double-checking and see that Davidson is playing violin in the same impossible way he was doing with the rock band.

CLOSE ON SYLVIA AND RUSSELL

as they nod to each other.

CUT TO

INT. SYMPHONY HALL - BACK STAGE - DAY

after rehearsal, as Davidson is checking his notice box. He flips through a stapled sheaf of papers, then finds an envelope. He opens it, reads it ... and knows that his cover's been blown. He leans against a wall and sighs.

CUT TO

SYMPHONY OFFICES - DAVIDSON

as he knocks on the door to the personnel manager's office. Winston answers from behind door.

WINSTON (O.S.)
Come in!

INT. WINSTON'S OFFICE

as Davidson enters.

DAVIDSON
Mr. Winston? I got a note in my box you
wanted to see me.

WINSTON
Right. Have a seat, Mr. Davidson.

Davidson takes the chair opposite the desk.

WINSTON
Mr. Davidson, I'll be blunt about this.
You made your argument, won your bet ...
whatever it is—I don't care. But a
symphony orchestra is no place for
stunts. You want to play violin in this
orchestra, you play a *real* violin. Not
some electronic gadget. Understand me?

DAVIDSON
Is there some *rule* sayin' what sort of
violin I gotta play?

WINSTON
No. It can be an Amati, Guadanini, Lamy,
Fagnola, Gagliano, Bergonzi... or three
dozen other makers ... anything that
plays up to symphonic standards.

DAVIDSON
My violin plays up to symphonic
standards.

WINSTON
A Strad? It certainly does. A great
asset to the orchestra.

DAVIDSON
I wasn't talkin' about my Stradivarius,
sir. I mean my new violin, which just
happens to be electronic. It's a Farrer.

WINSTON
When I said *anything*, I wasn't talking

about electronic toys. Your contract
calls for you to play *violin*. You want
to play this electronic—er—thing of
yours anywhere else, that's up to you.
But in *this* orchestra you play a *violin*.

DAVIDSON
Who's to say mine isn't?

WINSTON
What *is* this to you, anyway? Your
Stradivarius is one of the finest
instruments ever made. Why would you
ever want to play anything else?

DAVIDSON
I *don't*.

WINSTON
Then, damn it, why are we *having* this
discussion?

Davidson knows the whole story will have to come out now.

DAVIDSON
'Cause I can't *play* my Stradivarius any
more. Matter of fact, I can't play any
ordinary violin any more. I had to get a
special violin made I *can* play.

ON WINSTON

as he finally understands.

WINSTON
(slowly)
You lied to me about your hand being
better.

BOTH AGAIN

DAVIDSON
No, sir. I never mentioned my hand. I
told you that because of a miracle, I
could start the season on time. The
miracle was finding a special violin that
my two good fingers can use.

WINSTON
Oh, hell.
(beat)
All right, son. I see now. Your doctors
told you that your hand won't be better
by the time your probationary contract
expired ... and you didn't want to lose
the position.
(beat)
Consider yourself on the disabled list as
of now. The symphony will continue
paying you full salary until such time as—

DAVIDSON
Mr. Winston, that's real nice of you, but
it's not a matter of money. And the best
doctors around don't give me much hope my
hand will *ever* be better.

WINSTON
Mr. Davidson ... I—uh—sympathize
with your tragedy, but I can't change a
dreadful—but simple—fact of
reality. No one can play violin in a
symphony unless he can play *violin*.

DAVIDSON
Sir, I don't find any rules sayin' what's
a "violin" in my orchestra contract ...
or in any union regs. My contract says

I'm playin' *second* violin ... but it
doesn't say a word about *acoustic* violin.

WINSTON
Perhaps not ... It doesn't make me happy
to say this, but your orchestra contract
also says that while you're on probation,
the orchestra may judge you unfit at its
own discretion *without* specifying a reason.

Davidson decides to go in for his best shot.

DAVIDSON
Then let the *orchestra* decide, sir—the
String Audition Committee.

Winston considers it.

DAVIDSON
(continuing)
Let me go behind the screen again. If
any one can pick out that I'm not playin'
a regular violin, I'll walk away leavin'
the orchestra free and clear ... no
trouble ... no strings attached.

WINSTON

as he takes a few seconds to decide...then picks up his phone.

CUT TO

EXT. WINSTON'S OFFICE

Eavesdropping at Winston's door ... are Sylvia and Russell. Sylvia motions Russell away.

SYLVIA
C'mon ... we've got to make some phone

calls ourselves.

RUSSELL
What for?

SYLVIA
Don't you understand? If they can make a synthesizer that sounds like *one* violin, what's to stop them from making one that *really* sounds like twenty...or sixty?

Russell nods, but he's not happy.

CUT TO

EXT. SYMPHONY HALL STAGE DOOR - DAY

as Davidson emerges after his meeting with Winston, violin case in hand.

ON STREET

A TV News truck is parked at the curb, a CAMERAMAN and TV Reporter DEARBORN SCRUBB, standing next to it. Davidson begins walking down the street.

ON SCRUBB AND CAMERAMAN

SCRUBB
(to Cameraman)
There he is!

The Cameraman hefts the camera to his shoulder and starts the tape rolling. Davidson is walking briskly.

SCRUBB
(chasing after)
Mr. Davidson ... Dearborn Scrubb ...
Channel 4 News at Six ...

Davidson looks over but talks while he continues walking.

DAVIDSON
Hi, how's it goin'?

SCRUBB
(chasing after)
Mr. Davidson ... is it true you've been
playing a synthesized electronic violin
as a member of the Symphony Orchestra for
the past month ... and nobody noticed?

DAVIDSON
(still walking)
Somebody noticed all right... but guess
it took a while.

SCRUBB
But *nobody's* ever played an artificial
violin in a symphony orchestra before,
have they?

DAVIDSON
Can't say I know another case.

CUT TO

CLOSE ON A TV SET - DAVIDSON AND SCRUBB

as the interview is being broadcast. Scrubb is still chasing Davidson.

SCRUBB (ON TV)
It's also true, isn't it, that you're the
composer of—and play violin for—a
song high on the rock music charts right
now, aren't you?

WIDER - TV SET BEING WATCHED BY SYLVIA AND RUSSELL

DAVIDSON (ON TV)
That's right.

SCRUBB (ON TV)
Well isn't it unusual for an orchestra
violinist also to be a rock musician?

Davidson has reached his BMW and is unlocking it.

DAVIDSON (ON TV)
Doesn't happen much ... but it happens.

SCRUBB (ON TV)
Is that why the Symphony is trying to
fire you?

CUT TO

ANOTHER TV SET BEING WATCHED BY EVERETT WINSTON

and he looks concerned.

DAVIDSON (ON TV)
Who's givin' you this stuff? The
Symphony is being completely decent about
this ... they're gonna let me audition
again.

SCRUBB (ON TV)
Well ... how do you feel about the
orchestra making you audition a second
time?

On TV, Davidson gets into his car.

DAVIDSON (ON TV)
I'd feel a lot better if I could be at
home right now, practicing for it.

Davidson slams the car door and starts his engine.

ON EVERETT WINSTON

as his telephone rings and he answers.

WINSTON
Hello? ... Yes, Mr. Tavistock ... Yes, I
saw it, too ... Yes, sir ... I know that
very well, Mr. Tavistock ...

CUT TO

INT. SYMPHONY HALL - ON ALMOST EMPTY STAGE - DAY

In an almost exact repeat of the opening sequence. The stage is lighted but empty except for the screen. This time, however, there's no piano on stage.

REVERSE ON AUDITORIUM SEATS

And the Orchestra String Audition Committee is again seated about ten rows back. In addition to the conductor, Eric Smith-Kensington, we again see the concertmaster, Aaron Silverberg.

Sylvia and Russell are once more among the other string players on the committee.

SMITH-KENSINGTON
(calling out)
Number one, please.

CONCEALED BEHIND SCREEN - FREDDIE SCHWARTZ

as he walks out ... raises his violin ... and begins playing Bach.

OFF STAGE - WATCHING FROM THE WINGS

Davidson is standing, nervously, along with several other violinists from the orchestra.

ON THE COMMITTEE

SMITH-KENSINGTON
Thank you. Number two, please.

BEHIND SCREEN

as an ORCHESTRA VIOLINIST walks on stage and begins playing the same Bach.

ON THE COMMITTEE AGAIN

as they listen for a short while.

SMITH-KENSINGTON
Very good. Number three next.

BEHIND SCREEN

as Davidson walks out, but he doesn't raise his violin ... he takes out a cassette.

CLOSE ON THE CASSETTE

and it reads: IGOR DAVIDSON DEMO TAPE - JUILLIARD SCHOOL OF MUSIC.

BACK TO SCENE

Davidson inserts the cassette into a first-class stereo ... and it's the recording of himself playing—before his injury—that he was playing for Cambridge in his BMW.

ON COMMITTEE AGAIN

SMITH-KENSINGTON
Thank you, number three. Number four.

BEHIND SCREEN

as Davidson hits the pause on the recording quickly ... waits about the same interval as between the other violinists ... then raises his electronic violin and begins playing the same Bach.

ON SYLVIA AND RUSSELL - AS DAVIDSON PLAYS

as they look at each other and nod.

ON SMITH-KENSINGTON AND AARON SILVERBERG

as they exchange looks also. They'll continue with this, but they know.

BEHIND SCREEN

on Davidson, playing his heart out and sounding far better than we've ever heard him before... until he hears:

SMITH-KENSINGTON (O.S.)
Very good, number four. Number five
please.

ANOTHER VIOLINIST walks behind the screen and begins playing the Bach.

DISSOLVE TO

THE COMMITTEE AND EVERETT WINSTON

as the Committee Members are tallying up their votes ... and we see the Number *four* on almost all the ballots.

SMITH-KENSINGTON
It's clear, I think, we have a consensus.
(to Winston)
Number four, Everett.

WINSTON

as he nods ... and he doesn't look happy about it.

ALL AGAIN

SMITH-KENSINGTON
(to Committee)
Very well. The rest of you may go now
... not you, Aaron.

The Concertmaster remains seated. Winston also stays. They wait until the Committee is out of hearing range.

ON SYLVIA AND RUSSELL

as they walk out, shaking each other's hand.

AGAIN ON SMITH-KENSINGTON, SILVERBERG, AND WINSTON

SMITH-KENSINGTON
(continuing)
It's a remarkable achievement, actually.
Difference *is* almost too subtle to
notice.
(to concertmaster)
Aaron, how did *you* know?

SILVERBERG
To tell you the truth, it just sounded
too easy. Almost superhuman. No
ordinary violinist can sound that good
... at least not since Heifetz.

SMITH-KENSINGTON
Is it really a detriment to the orchestra
to have a violinist who can sound like
Jascha Heifetz? No matter *how* he does it?

SILVERBERG
I have no real objection to him sitting
behind me.

WINSTON
Well I hate to be the bringer of bad news
... but this orchestra's board of
directors does.

ANGLE FAVORING WINSTON

as he takes a seat and looks at the other two intently.

WINSTON
(continuing)
Do you have any idea how the inevitable
publicity on this this could blow up in
our faces? The precedent regarding
synthesized instruments we'd be setting
for every other orchestra in the country?
The long-term effect on this orchestra's
fund-raising ability?

Smith-Kensington pays close attention.

WINSTON
(continuing)
If the boy stayed because we feel sorry
for him ... this orchestra could very
well end up the laughing stock of the
entire classical music industry. Do
either of you *really* wish to risk that?

SMITH-KENSINGTON AND SILVERBERG

as they realize that the matter has been settled.

CUT TO

BACK STAGE - DAVIDSON PACING

as Everett Winston approaches him. Winston doesn't need to say anything. Davidson just nods.

CUT TO

INT. DAVIDSON'S HOUSE - NIGHT

as he enters, finding the house empty.

INT. KITCHEN

as Davidson finds a note on the refrigerator from Cambridge: "Planning session with Alex tonite. Be back late. Plenty of chili left in freezer. Love, C."

CUT TO

INT. LIVING ROOM

as Davidson is playing violin ... his outlet for all pain and stress. Something slow and sad ... an old Rachmaninoff song.

Emotionally exhausted, he puts his violin down in its case and flops onto his couch. He closes his eyes for a moment ... then hears some rustling and opens them again.

STANDING IN FRONT OF DAVIDSON - MISCHA RUDLENSKY

as an old man in his eighties, the way Davidson remembers him— tall, thin, with elegantly swept back white hair.

Davidson does not react the way a man does when seeing a ghost in a haunted house ... he just takes it for granted that it's his grandfather. He sits up on the couch.

DAVIDSON
Grandpa?

RUDLENSKY
(thick Russian accent)
You expect someone else, maybe?

DAVIDSON
But ... you're dead. How ... how did you get here?

RUDLENSKY
I tell you, not very easily. I have to take bus ... filthy, seats cut open, terrible people who smell bad.
(waving finger)
Not like it use to be.

Rudlensky walks over to Davidson's violin case and looks at his grandson's electronic violin.

RUDLENSKY
This is violin all fuss is about?

Davidson nods.

RUDLENSKY
You permit me try it?

DAVIDSON
Sure, Grandpa, sure.

RUDLENSKY

as he picks up Davidson's violin and bow ... and starts playing ... but the notes are all wrong.

BACK TO SCENE

Rudlensky stops playing.

RUDLENSKY
Notes are crazy ... how you play this,
sonny?

Davidson laughs, gets up, and takes the violin from his grandfather for a second. He opens up the chin rest, hits a control, and hands it back to his grandfather.

DAVIDSON
I had to have it specially fixed because
of my hand. It'll play normally now ...
try it again.

DAVIDSON'S POV - RUDLENSKY

as he lifts the violin under his chin again, and begins playing the lyrical second movement of the Tchaikovsky Violin Concerto.

Rudlensky plays it beautifully, with a satisfied expression on his face. After a few seconds he smiles.

RUDLENSKY
Is first class violin. Sound just like
my Stradivarius.
(thoughtful)
I must tell Antonio Stradivari when I see
him.

BOTH AGAIN

Davidson laughs.

DAVIDSON
It's electronic, Grandpa. It's not a
real violin.

Rudlensky hands the violin back to Davidson.

RUDLENSKY
It walk like duck, it quack like duck ...
it *duck*. This *real* violin.

DAVIDSON
That's not the way the symphony saw it.
They threw me out because of it.

Rudlensky nods.

RUDLENSKY
It not first time happen. Sit down, Igor
... I tell you story.

Davidson puts his violin back in its case and sits on his couch. Rudlensky remains standing.

RUDLENSKY
Back when I your age, I play in orchestra
in St. Petersburg ... this Russia, not
place with old people in Florida.

DAVIDSON
I know.

RUDLENSKY
You know. Back in those days, violin
strings made out of cat gut ...
intestines of sheeps. Not made from
pussy cat, way people think.

Davidson nods.

RUDLENSKY

as he paces back and forth while he talks.

RUDLENSKY
(continuing)

Anyway ... cat gut strings not strong.
Break all time. Hard to keep in tune.
Violin shop get in shipment of new
strings from Paris ... instead of cat
gut, E-string made of steel, other
strings cat gut wound with metal.

CLOSE ON DAVIDSON

listening.

RUDLENSKY (O.S.)
(continuing)
I buy them, put them on violin ... they
sound *good*, they play good. Stay in
tune, don't break so much.

BACK TO SCENE

RUDLENSKY
(continuing)
Hurt my fingers for little while, but
soon I have calluses, it don't hurt no
more.

DAVIDSON
Uh-huh.

RUDLENSKY
To make long story short—conductor of
orchestra find I not using cat gut
strings. He tell me I get rid of metal
strings. I don't want to ... tell him
they play *better* than cat gut ... stay in
tune ... better for orchestra. He say *he*
know what best for orchestra—not me—and
throw me out of orchestra. You know what
I do then?

DAVIDSON
You left Russia and came to America.

RUDLENSKY
I leave Russia and— I tell you this
story already? ... Could have save
myself long bus trip.

Davidson smiles.

RUDLENSKY
(continuing)
Da ... I come to America ... and lucky
thing, because soon all Europe fighting
First World War. Soon, in America, I big
hit as soloist. Playing violin with
metal strings. I never thrown out of
orchestra, I never become soloist ...
probably get drafted, maybe get killed.

Rudlensky takes an old fashioned pocket watch out of his pocket.

RUDLENSKY
I got go now. I late. Twenty years
late.

DAVIDSON
Grandpa ... before you go. You've heard
me play?

RUDLENSKY
You kidding? I go every time you play,
starting with Beethoven Concerto when you
nine.

DAVIDSON
I thought you missed it ... 'cause you'd
died the year before.

RUDLENSKY
Being dead better deal than senior
citizen discount. Senior citizen got pay
half price ... I get in everything free.
Igor, you one terrific musician, I tell
you. Good violinist ... good composer.
Make me very proud. Your hand, it don't
matter if music come from your soul.
Music made by mind and heart, not hand.
Hand just tool.

ON DAVIDSON

as he rubs his eyes for a second, exhausted.

DAVIDSON'S POV

When he removes his hand, Mischa Rudlensky is standing there not as an old man ... but as a vibrant, dark-haired young man about Davidson's age, looking like he did on the old 78 record box ... but in full color.

REVERSE ON DAVIDSON

as he looks with awe ...

DAVIDSON'S POV AGAIN

and nobody is in the room at all.

ON DAVIDSON

as he lies down on the couch again ... then sits up with a start.

DAVIDSON'S POV AGAIN

and he's still alone. Perhaps this *has* just been a dream.

ON DAVIDSON

as he doesn't have time to wonder about this because an idea has suddenly hit him.

DAVIDSON
(to himself)
Not a *world* war, Grandpa...a *musical* war.

He gets up, searches around the room for a piece of paper and a pen ... and starts scribbling furiously.

While he's writing, we see the lights of—and hear the engine of—a car pulling into the driveway.

Davidson keeps on writing, oblivious.

ON FRONT DOOR

as Cambridge comes in.

DAVIDSON AND CAMBRIDGE

as she looks at his face ... and he smiles at her.

CAMBRIDGE
(excited)
They're letting you stay?

Davidson grins from ear to ear.

DAVIDSON
(almost laughing)
Nah, they threw my ass the hell out.

Cambridge tries to figure this out. Davidson goes up to her, kissing her excitedly.

CUT TO

INT. KITCHEN - NIGHT

as Cambridge is having a bowl of chili, and Davidson's having a cup of coffee, telling her about his new idea.

DAVIDSON
(really animated)
So it comes to me while I'm wakin' up from this dream about my grandfather, right? It's like rock music is fightin' a *war* against classical music ... and neither side really knows whether they can trust me or not.

Cambridge is paying close attention.

DAVIDSON
(continuing)
As far as rock music goes, classical is dead from the waist down, and as far as classical goes, rock is dead from the neck up.

CAMBRIDGE
Okay, keep goin'.

DAVIDSON
So it hits me ... that's why nobody's been able to compose anything puttin' rock and classical together that really *makes* it. Rock and classical are complete opposites. You try turnin' them into the same thing, you know what you get?

CAMBRIDGE
(swallowing first)
Elevator music ... right? You get elevator music.

DAVIDSON
Right. It comes out too simple to be classical music ... and too soft to be rock.

DAVIDSON
(continuing)
And I start thinkin' that I already *have* it half written, 'cause I can use my violin concerto ... which nobody wants 'cause it sounds like it was written a hundred years ago. And what I gotta do is, I write in a *rock* band tryin' to *beat* the *musical shit* out of the *violin.*

CAMBRIDGE

as she nods, considering the possibilities.

CAMBRIDGE
Okay, you compose it. Dearsmoke plays the rock part ... But how are you gonna get the *classical* music world to take you seriously?

DAVIDSON

as he smiles.

DISSOLVE TO

EXT. ERIC SMITH-KENSINGTON'S HOUSE - WINTER - DAY

a large, spacious estate ... a wealthy man's home, now covered with snow.

DAVIDSON

as he climbs out of his BMW, carrying his violin, and rings the bell.

AT FRONT DOOR

as Davidson rings. He waits a few minutes, then the door opens and a maid answers.

> MAID
> Yes?

> DAVIDSON
> My name is Davidson ... I'm a violinist.
> Could you please ask the Maestro if he
> can spare a few minutes with me?

> MAID
> Does Mr. Smith-Kensington know you?

> DAVIDSON
> Yes, he does.

> MAID
> Won't you come in, please?

INSIDE LIVING ROOM

as Davidson enters. The place is furnished with the elegance of selection ... there is sparse furniture, but what furnishings are there are impeccable. There is also a full-size grand piano.

> MAID
> Please wait here. What did you say your
> name was again?

> DAVIDSON
> It's—
> (beat)
> Tell the Maestro that it's Mischa
> Rudlensky's grandson.

The maid nods, then heads out toward the back.

IN LIVING ROOM

as Davidson looks around the living room. Then:

SMITH-KENSINGTON
Mr. Davidson, yes?

Davidson turns around to see Smith-Kensington, dressed in a casual sweater and slacks.

DISSOLVE TO

LIVING ROOM - A LITTLE LATER

Davidson and the conductor—drinks nearby—as the conductor is sitting at the piano looking through music, and Davidson sets his violin case on the arms of a chair, and takes out his violin and bow.

SMITH-KENSINGTON
(sardonically)
I don't suppose you need to plug that thing in?

Davidson shakes his head, smiling.

DAVIDSON
Batteries are good for months.

SMITH-KENSINGTON
Hell of a thing if they run out during a performance.

DAVIDSON
(shrugs)
Faster to change than a broken string.

SMITH-KENSINGTON
Perhaps.
(beat)

Shall we give this a try?

ON DAVIDSON

as he raises his violin and begins playing the composition with a lyrical, solo opening statement on his violin.

INCLUDING THE PIANO

as, about sixteen bars into it, Smith-Kensington enters with the piano, playing the orchestral accompaniment.

So far, it's much like Davidson's beautiful ninetenth-century-style violin concerto, which we heard earlier.

As they continue playing, we

DISSOLVE TO

DAVIDSON AND SMITH-KENSINGTON

as they are approaching the end of Davidson's composition, racing to a smash finish.

They both nod at each other, as the music ends with a flourish.

SMITH-KENSINGTON

as he flips back a few pages.

BOTH AGAIN

As Davidson is anxiously awaiting the conductor's verdict. Smith-Kensington motions Davidson over and points to the score.

SMITH-KENSINGTON
I think we need to build up the woodwind
line here a bit, doubling the oboe with
bassoon. Let me show you.

Smith-Kensington plays the music the way Davidson has written it.

DAVIDSON

as he almost can't pay attention to the music, because he realizes that Smith-Kensington is already talking as if it's an accomplished fact that they'll be performing it together.

BOTH AGAIN

SMITH-KENSINGTON
Now here's how I'd change it.

Smith-Kensington plays the music again, demonstrating his point.

SMITH-KENSINGTON
(continuing)
See the difference? You must bear in
mind—all the way through—that the
tendency of the amplified instruments to
drown out the orchestra will have to be
compensated for on the orchestral side.

DAVIDSON
Well, I *did* consider marking in
amplification for the orchestra. But
it'd destroy the tonal purity of the
acoustical instruments.

SMITH-KENSINGTON
Then *destroy* it. This is supposed to be
a war. Let tonal purity be the first
battle casualty.
(beat)
When did you say your rock-and-roll group
is available for this?

Davidson smiles, putting his violin and bow down.

DAVIDSON
Until June, the band'll be touring as an
opener for Springsteen.

SMITH-KENSINGTON

as he gets up from the piano, and motions Davidson to follow him.

SMITH-KENSINGTON
If this means war, let's see if we can
get some reinforcements.

INT. SMITH-KENSINGTON'S STUDY

as the conductor is on the phone, Davidson standing by.

SMITH-KENSINGTON
(to phone)
Well then the programs haven't actually
been printed, have they? ... You can
bloody well tell them to look at my
contract ... they'll find that I *do* have
the right. ...

Smith-Kensington smiles at Davidson, covering the mouthpiece.

SMITH-KENSINGTON
(to Davidson)
That always does it.
(to phone again)
Let the critics howl—that's their
job ... Yes, for SummerFest, first half
of the program for July 18th. ...

Smith-Kensington points to the music, waving Davidson to bring it over to him. When he has it in hand:

SMITH-KENSINGTON
It's titled *Concerto Grosso for Violin, Rock Band, and Orchestra,* Opus 9, by Igor Davidson ... Yes, the same one ... No, he hasn't ... but you can put in the program notes that he's Mischa Rudlensky's grandson ... that should keep the board quiet.
(beat)
The rock-and-roll group? At the moment they're touring with Springstine ...

DAVIDSON

as he smiles.

SLOW DISSOLVE TO

EXT. ORCHESTRAL STAGE - NIGHT

It could be the Hollywood Bowl, Tanglewood, or Saratoga. It's the Symphony's SummerFest ... it's outside ... and the crowd is *huge.*

ON AUDIENCE

people are finishing up picnic suppers, drinking wine and beer... having a good time.

ON LIGHTED STAGE

as the orchestra is just starting to seat itself. In addition to seats for the orchestra, there are preparations going on for much more than just an ordinary concert—special effects are being made ready.

CUT TO

BACKSTAGE IN GREENROOM

as we see Davidson, Sasha, Art, Leo, Vic, and Lenny ... all in full dress and tails—Cambridge in a full length black dress. Alex is also there but wearing only a normal suit and tie.

We don't need any dialogue to know they they've all got butterflies for this one.

There's a knock at the door. Alex answers it.

STAGE HAND
Five minutes, ladies and gentlemen.

ALEX
Thank you.

OUTSIDE GREENROOM - FREDDIE SCHWARTZ

as Davidson sees him walking by in full dress, but without his violin.

DAVIDSON
Hey, Freddie ... wait up!

Davidson grabs his violin and heads after Freddie.

BACKSTAGE - ON DAVIDSON AND FREDDIE SCHWARTZ

as Davidson catches up to him.

SCHWARTZ
(smiles)
So, *bubeleh* ... how's life in the fast lane?

DAVIDSON
Fast ... we go on in a couple minutes.

SCHWARTZ
And what's so important that it can't wait until after your premiere?

Davidson extends his violin to Freddie.

DAVIDSON
I thought you might like to play a Stradivarius tonight.

Freddie looks shocked.

DAVIDSON
Matter of fact, Freddie ... I've been thinking who might be able to give this honey a foster home ... that is, until medical science figures out nerve regeneration.

SCHWARTZ
(still in shock)
You are honest-to-God offering to put your Strad on loan to me?

DAVIDSON
(nods)
I can't play it the way it needs, Freddie. And fine violins need to be played or they go bad.

SCHWARTZ
(choked up)
I—

DAVIDSON
Go on...take it. We'll sign papers later.

Freddie is just short of in tears.

DAVIDSON
(beat)
Go on.

FREDDIE SCHWARTZ AND DAVIDSON

as the violin passes from Davidson's hand to Freddie's. Davidson pats Freddie on the shoulder, then starts back toward the green-room.

DAVIDSON
Take good care of her for me, will ya?

Freddie can only nod.

CUT TO

EXT. STAGE

The orchestra is now fully seated.

Eric Smith-Kensington walks on stage, followed close order by Davidson, carrying his violin.

The conductor, then Davidson, shakes hands with the concert-master, then join Smith-Kensington in bowing.

The concertmaster, Aaron Silverberg, stands, signals to the Oboe for an A. Davidson tunes his violin.

Then the concertmaster tunes, followed by the violins, the rest of the strings...the rest of the orchestra. The concertmaster sits. Davidson remains standing.

STAGE WINGS - ALEX

Watching everything closely, and looking nervous.

SMITH-KENSINGTON

as he looks to Davidson.

DAVIDSON

as he nods.

ON FULL STAGE

as everyone is ready. The conductor turns to Davidson and nods.

DAVIDSON

as—completely alone—he begins a solo violin introduction, without any accompaniment. It is lyrical, completely romantic in character. A song of unfettered joy ... joy in being able to soar completely free of gravity.

ON DAVIDSON AND ORCHESTRA

After some seconds, Smith-Kensington gives a down beat to the orchestra ... which joins in with a full, lush accompaniment.

The violin and orchestra continue, sending this melody that Davidson has introduced on violin through the orchestra ... into a beautiful duet between violin and oboe.

Suddenly, as the duet continues,

CLOSE ON LEO

somewhere—we don't know where yet—from a synthesizer keyboard hanging from shoulder straps—the sound of martial bagpipes appears as if from a distance, and gets louder and louder, countering the melodic material of the violin/oboe duet.

ON DEARSMOKE - INVADING STAGE

Softly, at first—as if they are marching closer—Vic on drums, then Lenny on bass guitar, and finally Cambridge, Sasha, and Art on electric guitar get closer and Closer and *Closer* until—finally—they are *there*, musically invading the orchestra with a heavy metal, hard rock melody of their own.

Like an invading army the members of the band spread out into the orchestra like an attack squad.

ON THE ORCHESTRA

as—in a vain attempt to defend the violin and oboe from this onslaught—

THE STRINGS AND THE WOODWINDS

join in, adding the full weight of their instruments on the side of the violin and oboe.

But it is no contest. The louder and more intense the strings and woodwinds become ... the louder

THE ROCK ENSEMBLE

becomes.

Suddenly:

OFF STAGE - MISCHA RUDLENSKY

materializes out of empty air. He sees the rock band invading the orchestra and knows it needs help ... and dead or not, he's just the violinist to do it.

Rudlensky grabs an extra violin and starts toward the stage.

ALEX'S POV

as he *sees* a violin float in the air past him onto the stage.

RUDLENSKY

as he takes an empty seat next to Russell in the second violins and begins playing.

ON DAVIDSON

as—just for a second while he's not playing—he thinks he sees his grandfather in the orchestra.

THE ORCHESTRA

In a second attempt at defense,

THE VIOLINS

throw their melody to the

BRASS

—trumpets and trombones—who fire it back at

DEARSMOKE

but even these sallies are easily countered by the rock band ... as it swipes them out of the way with ease.

In a final, desperate attempt,

THE ORCHESTRA

calls on its big guns—

THE KETTLE DRUMS AND TIMPANI

to fight off the rock band.

SMOKE AND LASERS

starts shooting onto the stage, and laser blasts pierce the smoke. The enemy has conquered. Territory has been taken. The orchestra has been defeated.

THE ORCHESTRA AND BAND

And the first movement of the concerto ends with the rock band celebrating its victory and

DAVIDSON

the solo violin, sadly giving surrender.

ON SMITH-KENSINGTON

as he lowers his hands.

ON THE AUDIENCE

who don't know—or don't care—about the custom of not applauding between movements ... and they're screaming their heads off and applauding.

SMITH-KENSINGTON, DAVIDSON, AND DEARSMOKE

as—according to custom—they give a very *brief* acknowledgement to the audience, then immediately turn back to work.

ALEX

in the wings, watching the audience, forgetting for the moment the mystery of the violin, and kvelling.

SMITH-KENSINGTON

as he raises his hands again, to begin the second movement.

ON DAVIDSON

as the solo violin introduces the opening statement of the second movement.

It is slow and sorrowful, a song of subjugation, bondage, and occupation.

ON DAVIDSON AND THE CONCERTMASTER

as the two violins commiserate in a back-and-forth solo.

as the entire orchestra picks up the melody, first

THE STRINGS

as they toss it back and forth between

VIOLINS, VIOLAS, AND CELLOS

and the melody becomes grander and more sorrowful.

MISCHA RUDLENSKY

as he turns the page on the music.

RUSSELL

as he *sees* the music turn, without any stand mate he can see.

THE REST OF THE ORCHESTRA

as it joins in with the strings. Then:

VIC

with a martial drumbeat, enters, followed by

SASHA, ART, LEO, LENNY, AND CAMBRIDGE

the conquerers, as they walk among their conquered slaves, tossing out melodic orders which are quickly picked up by

VARIOUS ORCHESTRA MEMBERS

and obeyed quickly ... or punished.

CAMBRIDGE

as she tosses a melody—from heavy metal guitar—at

DAVIDSON

who picks up the melody ... and turns it into a lively little melody, with a colorful bow-hand pizzicato. The plucking of violin strings is tossed back to

CAMBRIDGE

who picks it up from Davidson, and throws it back, loaded with energy again.

CAMBRIDGE AND DAVIDSON

in a guitar/violin duet, as she attempts to give orders ... and he attempts to win her over with seduction ... and the result is that the violin begins winning. The melody started on the violin is now carried by

CAMBRIDGE

as she drops back two hundred years into a classical guitar rendition of the melody. The melody is picked up by

LENNY

on bass guitar, and carried over to the

DOUBLE BASSES

in the orchestra.

LENNY AND DOUBLE BASSES

as *they* now join in a duet. Then,

THE TIMPANI AND ORCHESTRA PERCUSSION

seize their opportunity and

A PERCUSSION DUET

is tossed back and forth between Vic and the Orchestra percussion.

But this sort of thing can't be allowed to go on for long.

SASHA

acting as general of the occupying forces, starts pulling his own people back into line, first

VIC

who returns to the fold, taking

THE ORCHESTRA PERCUSSION

with him, as defectors from the symphony. Then

LENNY

returns to rock music, taking

THE DOUBLE BASSES

who defect over to the rock side as well.

SASHA

gives melodic orders to the

BRASS

—trumpets and trombones—who also defect to the rock band. But

CAMBRIDGE

is reluctant to leave the world of classical guitar for rock ... and a violin/guitar duet establishes that a firm inroad has been made into the conquerers by

DAVIDSON

on violin.

CAMBRIDGE AND DAVIDSON

in a final, almost secretive duet, before

CAMBRIDGE

picks up the rock theme again, and

DEARSMOKE

plays as a whole again, joined by their

ORCHESTRAL DEFECTORS

—the brass, percussion, and double basses.

ON SMITH-KENSINGTON

as he conducts a musical bridge into the concerto's third movement, without break.

A secret defense project has been developed by

DAVIDSON ON VIOLIN

introducing a new martial melody as

THE ORCHESTRA

all of them, on a single musical *command*, put on ear protectors—the sort used on shooting ranges.

Suddenly:

IMMENSE AMPLIFIERS

rise up out of the stage and

BOOM MICROPHONES

rise, aimed at the different orchestra sections..

THE FIRST VIOLINS

go along with it, but

SYLVIA AND THE SECOND VIOLINS

at first resist the melodic material offered by the now amplified

DAVIDSON

and

FIRST AND SECOND VIOLINS

send the theme back and forth, arguing bitterly. The argument is overcome, however, when

THE ROCK BAND

enters again.

SASCHA ON GUITAR

as he issues melodic orders to

DAVIDSON AND THE VIOLINS

and the violins, led by Davidson, resist the melody.

SASHA ON GUITAR

as he repeats the orders, louder, and

DAVIDSON AND THE VIOLINS

as they resist again.

SASHA ON GUITAR

as he calls out the enforcers—

DEARSMOKE, BRASS, AND PERCUSSION

to lay down the law to the resistant

VIOLINS

and the violins, now *amplified*, send back a blast to the shocked

BAND AND DEFECTORS

who melodically reel, at the resistance power.

DAVIDSON

as the violins lead a melodic counter-attack.

CAMBRIDGE

as *she* defects to Davidson's side and

DAVIDSON ON VIOLIN AND CAMBRIDGE ON GUITAR

join together, almost as one instrument, in issuing battle orders to

THE ORCHESTRA

Slowly but surely, the defectors are won back, first

THE DOUBLE BASSES

as they pick up the violin melody, then

THE BRASS

as they return to the symphonic mode, then

THE TIMPANI

as they defect once again, back to the orchestra.

SASHA ON GUITAR

as he issues melodic orders ... but the troops aren't listening.

CAMBRIDGE

as the guitar defies the

GUITAR

and refuses to follow its orders anymore. Finally,

LEO, ART, AND VIC

as they run for their musical lives, abandoning Sasha to fight the orchestra alone.

LENNY

as he takes off his bass guitar, picks up a bassoon, and joins the bassoon section of the orchestra.

SASHA AND FREDDIE SCHWARTZ

As Freddie leaves his chair, captures Sasha, and handcuffs him.

DAVIDSON ON VIOLIN AND CAMBRIDGE ON ELECTRIC GUITAR

and—in a magnificent triumph—the violin and guitar toss melodies back and forth, then to

THE ORCHESTRA

and—in a moment of luminescent glory

VIOLIN, ELECTRIC GUITAR, AND ORCHESTRA

play together, in a march of hope and glory.

MISCHA RUDLENSKY

playing violin as part of the victory

ON DAVIDSON

and he can *see* his grandfather, clearly, in the orchestra.

ON ALEX

as *he* can sees his grandfather, also.

DAVIDSON AND HIS BROTHER

as we can see them looking at each other, and at their grandfather.

MISCHA RUDLENSKY

as, the battle won, he puts down the violin on the seat and disappears.

ON ERIC SMITH-KENSINGTON

as he lowers his arms ...

ON THE AUDIENCE

as it rises to its feet as one, exploding into screams of ovation.

ON STAGE

as the conductor, leads

DAVIDSON AND DEARSMOKE

then

DAVIDSON AND CAMBRIDGE

to take their bows, then

DAVIDSON ALONE

to take his.

CLOSE ON DAVIDSON

as he bows, and we see his sudden intense surprise at seeing

DAVIDSON'S POV - MISCHA RUDLENSKY

standing next to him, bowing.

ON DAVIDSON AGAIN

as he looks again.

DAVIDSON'S POV AGAIN

and where Rudlensky was is now empty space.

ERIC SMITH-KENSINGTON AND ORCHESTRA

including Freddie Schwartz, as they take their bows.

The sound of wild screaming and applause fades, and we hear, over, a reprise of Dearsmoke singing "No Strings Attached."

END CREDITS ROLL and we

FADE OUT.

The Mars Story

It didn't take finding what might be, and might not be, evidence of bacteria on Mars for people to want to go there. No matter how inhospitable to life the Red Planet seems—and that assessment changes year to year—it still seems one of the likeliest prospects for human exploration and eventual colonization.

When "Profile in Silver" was aired for the third time on CBS, my agent received a call from Tom McDermott, a veteran TV producer who had a deal with the network to develop a TV movie about the exploration and colonization of Mars. It was intended to be a serious scientific approach about how such an enterprise might actually be accomplished, and what we might find when we got there.

This was the first time in my life that someone I didn't already know had seen my work and had approached me with a writing project, rather than my beating the bushes for work—so I took the meeting with enthusiasm.

For a science-fiction writer who grew up on Heinlein, it was sheer fun writing a serious near-future science-fiction story about the colonization of Mars. This isn't as flashy with special effects as science fiction usually has to be; it's just a pretty good story that takes science and technology seriously, and uses just enough farther-out speculation to make it entertaining.

For you Heinlein fans who know every word he wrote by heart, look for an homage to a classic Heinlein story, right near the beginning.

Not long after I delivered this to McDermott, I took a lease on a Los Angeles area apartment, so I could be bicoastal and start pursuing more work out here. Difficulties I'd had doing story conferences by telephone for *Twilight Zone* made it abundantly clear that if I was going to pursue more work in Hollywood, I had to have a local address again.

Three days after I signed the lease, The Writers Guild voted to go out on strike. The strike lasted for six months—and resulted in the Guild members getting a deal they could have had on the first day.

Lots of writers lost their houses over that strike. I lost this project, which died during it.

Kids, take the advice I never took from my parents.

If you're bound and determined to become a writer ... don't quit your day job.

—JNS

The Mars Story
by J. Neil Schulman

Prologue

This is not fantasy.

While these situations, developments, and discoveries haven't happened yet, this story is a serious projection based on the latest scientific data and engineering plans. Some of it may seem fantastic ... but is any of this more fantastic to us than a story showing men exploring the moon would have been to someone three short decades ago, in 1958?

That was the year I started school.

Children starting school in 1988 will grow up to live and work in deep space, in lunar villages, in settlements on Mars. Their spaceships will travel to the outer reaches of our solar system in the same time it took steamships to travel from England to America. They will work on space engineering and planet- development projects that will be, to their generation, what the transcontinental railroads and migration west were to a previous generation.

But is any of this surprising? It isn't if we remember what the world was like a mere generation ago. When *our* parents started school, *their* parents were barely used to airplanes, radio, talking movies, and medical X-rays. Yet they grew up to see robot spaceships send back color TV pictures from Saturn, computers that do everything from cooking their dinner to correcting their spelling, and laser surgery that can make the blind see again.

The child starting school today might very well have a job as incomprehensible to us in 1988 as the explanation "I'm in software" would have been to parents in 1958.

But no matter where the children of today will live, no matter what their work will be, they will grow into men and women very much like us. We will recognize them by their dreams and their fears, by their passions and their frustrations, by their triumphs and their tragedies.

And miracle of miracles, they may even teach us something about ourselves...

Countdown to Mars

We first meet GEORGE O'NEAL at a quiet table in a cocktail lounge, where he's having a drink with two old business associates. George is a large man in his forties with both brains and brawn enough to have bossed the biggest engineering jobs of his time and still retire relatively young.

The men George is drinking with are trying to convince him to take one more job ... as boss of the Environmental Development team on Mars. Mars has almost no air, most of the water is frozen deep underground, and the climate is abominable. If people are going to live there permanently, Mars will have to be "terraformed": engineered to an ecology that can support life.

George isn't jumping at the chance. What the heck does he want on Mars? He's gotten used to easy living. Why the heck would *anyone* want to leave the comforts of home for a frozen wasteland like Mars?

George's associates press him to think about it—telling him he's the only man for the job. The Martian Development team has gotten bogged down with endless problems: machinery isn't working the way it's supposed to, they're reporting "unexpected" atmospheric effects and "weird" electrical phenomena, and biochemical experiments are producing puzzling "anomalous results" reminiscent of the Viking probes in the 70's.

The entire settlement schedule is getting loused up, holding up other projects ... and the Martian Development Corporation needs someone with George's experience to take over, figure out what's wrong, and put everything back on schedule.

They're offering George a fortune in cash, stock, and Martian land options to take the job.

George agrees to consider the offer, and they leave the cocktail lounge. As they get up, we catch a glimpse of a brilliant Earth hanging outside a thick window ... and we realize this discussion has been on the moon.

We follow George home, through the mall-like underground streets of Luna City, to his condominium, where we meet his 15-year-old son, MARK. George and Mark have lived alone for two years, since George's wife (and Mark's mother) died.

George discusses the offer with Mark. As far as Mark is concerned, there's just no question: his father has been miserable ever since his wife died. It's time for him to get back into action, and this Mars job sounds like the exact thing he needs.

All right, George says, Mark can stay with friends until his high school class graduates, before starting classes at Luna University or heading off to a college on Earth.

Or, Mark points out, he can complete his high school work on Mars, where he'd have access to some of the top specialists alive, fill in with courses taught on computer, and easily ace the college entrance exams.

He'd *better* ace them, George tells his son, or Mark can *walk* back from Mars.

A blue summer sky, a green back yard, a suburban house with swimming pool, and a barbecue grill let us know we're without a doubt on Earth. DR. BARBARA SCHNEIDER, and her husband JACK, a top advertising executive, are hosting a weekend party with their teenage kids CYNDI and DOUG, for friends, neighbors, business associates of Jack's, and university colleagues of Barbara's.

Barbara is a renowned bio-historian accepted as a top expert in fields ranging from the origins of life to the origins of civilization: her academic credentials include a medical degree, a doctorate in archeology, supporting degrees in biochemistry and geology; her professional credits include publication in top professional journals, in encyclopedias, as well as having written several bestselling books popularizing her ideas.

Barbara has been considering a foundation grant to join researchers on Mars that have just made a startling discovery: fossilized leaves. This is the first proof that plant life once existed on Mars—the first *extraterrestrial* life ever found.

As Jack is flipping a hamburger on the grill, he overhears Barbara telling another professor that she's decided to accept the grant.

Jack glares at his wife, telling her she has wonderful timing. What an absolutely marvelous afternoon to break up a twenty-year marriage.

A family conference later resolves that Doug is remaining on Earth to stay near his girlfriend and college. Cyndi, however—planning a scientific career of her own—has decided that she's going with her mother to Mars.

The Trip Out

For travellers departing from Earth such as Barbara and Cyndi Schneider the trip to Mars starts with a day-long passenger rocket flight from the Mojave Desert to Fortnight Station, an orbiting spaceport halfway to the moon, complete with hotels, restaurants, and shopping center.

Travellers from Luna City, such as George and Mark O'Neal, also take a shuttle to Fortnight, but the trip is much faster.

Fortnight Station is where the spaceliner *Ares* is docked for its fifth voyage on the Earth-to-Mars run. Unlike earlier spaceships to Mars, which took as long as a year sailing through space, the *Ares*' "Forward Drive" can maintain constant acceleration for most of the trip, making the journey in less than a week.

With some differences, the trip to Mars isn't all that different from an ocean voyage today. Sleeping facilities are more like Pullman railroad cars than staterooms. Instead of lifeboat drills there are "solar flare" drills. There are stomach-wrenching periods of free-fall only at the beginning of the trip, at mid-point "ship's turn-over," and at the end: because the ship is usually under constant acceleration, there is a normal feel of gravity.

Normal for Earth dwellers like Barbara and Cyndi, that is. For George and Mark, who have lived for years in the moon's one-sixth gravity, the periods of free-fall are their only relief: the rest of the time they have a hard time walking to the dining room, because everything—including themselves—weighs six times what they're used to. They look forward to Mars, where everything will weigh only *twice* as much as they're used to.

It's on the *Ares*' activity deck, where George and Mark are exercising to acclimate themselves to their higher weight, that they meet Barbara and Cyndi Schneider. Mark and Cyndi hit it off right away, but George and Barbara don't do as well. They immediately get into an argument.

Barbara argues that Mars should be left as it is for scientific research, while George argues that Mars is a worthless stretch of frozen wasteland waiting for people to turn it into farmhouses, factories, and forests.

For Barbara, the discovery of plant fossils on Mars means that

Mars is a treasure trove of information for scientists studying the origins of life. For George, the discovery of plant fossils on Mars is reason to start prospecting for oil and coal.

George's ego also takes a beating when Barbara has to help in lifting a barbell off his chest.

It's not exactly love at first sight.

Arrival

The *Ares* guides itself into orbit around Mars close to the outer of Mars' two moons, Deimos, where a rocket shuttle for passage down to the planet waits for them. Deimos is so small that it has hardly any gravity at all, and so makes for a perfect site for an orbital space platform—a space harbor. But like so many harbors before it, this one has labor difficulties.

The *Ares* arrives just after the declaration of a harbor workers' strike, and the strikers have blocked off the main docking passageway, demanding that their terms be met before they'll allow passengers or baggage transferred to the shuttle.

The *Ares'* CAPTAIN, learning of George's success in settling previous labor disputes, asks George to talk to the strike leaders on his behalf.

The strikers agree to talk to George ... but they refuse to allow the *Ares* to dock. George will have to come in by a small auxiliary airlock.

George "floats" over in a space suit, pulling himself from airlock to airlock along a tether.

Once inside with the strikers, George spots a man who he worked with on a previous job, HANK NASH, and asks him what the beef is. Hank outlines the problem: the harbor management hasn't made good on promised improvements in workers' living quarters.

George also talks to the HARBOR MANAGER, and gets his side of the story. It's not a deliberate management policy, just delays caused by endless snafus on Earth.

Management is saying go back to work and we'll meet the demands. The strikers are saying meet the demands *first* then we'll go back to work.

George plays Solomon. He tells the workers that since they won't allow ships to dock, obviously this strike can't be settled on Mars.

George will have to tell the *Ares*' Captain to take his ship all the way back to Fortnight Station, and the strikers will have to send representatives to negotiate with the harbor company officials on Earth. Of course with the ship full there's no room for them to travel in the *Ares*. Labor's negotiators will have to arrange for their own transportation ... which might take a while, considering that there won't be any economic incentive for them to send out another ship.

Or, the strikers can allow the *Ares*' passengers to transfer to the shuttle, and a labor negotiator can hitch a ride back.

This is *blackmail*, one of the strikers suggests.

Yep, George agrees—it's blackmail *both* ways. Each side has its hands around the other guy's throat, and both are strangling. They either start cooperating with each other or *both* sides are dead in space.

Another striker asks what guarantee they have that if they go back to work, the harbor management will make good on its promises.

George says he'll guarantee it personally. If management doesn't make good, George promises that he'll use the Martian Development Corporation's discretionary fund to pay for the workers' facilities, then sue the harbor facility for failing to meet *their* contractual obligations to provide working harbor facilities to the Development Corporation.

With Hank Nash's assurance to the other strikers that George's word is as good as gold, the strike is over.

The *Ares* docks and George and the other passengers transfer to the shuttle, and begin their sojourn on Mars.

Mars

Our characters disembark from the shuttle at Marsport, the largest city on the planet—population just under 500. We follow them as they arrive at their various new homes and jobs and learn their way around.

Marsport is a private development—a residential and commercial park—put together by a consortium of American and Canadian investors including major corporations, foundations, and universities. There are other settlements on Mars—the Soviets have several, as do the Chinese, the European Common Market, and the

Japanese—but Marsport is the only one that is completely privately owned and operated.

Marsport is made up of bubble-buildings—pressurized, insulated, and radiation shielded—connected by underground tunnels. The thin Martian atmosphere makes the Martian surface dangerous for extended human exposure, not only failing to protect against the sun's deadly radiation the way Earth's air does, but giving off "secondary particles" deadly to living things. People go outside only when absolutely necessary, and have to wear radiation dosimeters keeping track of their exposure.

The United Nations charter under which Mars was opened for human migration allows any country, organization, corporation, or private individual to homestead Martian land and stake claim to natural resources, but they can claim only the land and resources which they are usefully developing. The radiation problem outside makes this difficult, thus the Development Corporation has a top priority in thickening the Martian atmosphere—the project George has come to Mars to facilitate.

The major project for thickening the atmosphere, which George takes over, involves chucking H-bombs into ancient Martian volcanoes, blowing off the volcanic caps, and making them active again. Volatile gasses and water vapor will be outgassed, thickening the atmosphere and creating a "greenhouse effect."

Volcanic ash will increase the ground's ability to absorb sunlight, warming the planet. Permafrost locked under the Martian soil will melt, releasing more water vapor into the atmosphere, clouds will form ... and it will rain on Mars for the first time in billions of years.

The problem is, the project just isn't progressing the way it's supposed to. There are unexplained "natural" voltage surges fouling up electrical equipment, jamming radio links, and causing repeated mechanical breakdowns.

George's investigations into the causes of these problems lead him to cooperate with the investigations being made by Barbara Schneider, who's trying to solve some scientific mysteries of her own. The main mystery is that some of the plant remains she's finding appear to be in locations which geological features prove have been waterless for millions of years ... and they're plant varieties *found on Earth.*

As George and Barbara follow a trail of scientific clues, sometimes assisted by Cyndi and Mark, they stumble onto an archeological find far greater than Schliemann's discovery of Homer's Troy.

Near the base of one of the Martian volcanoes lie *human artifacts* encrusted in 50,000-year-old volcanic lava.

And the "anomalous effects"—the electrical phenomena, atmospheric interference, etc., are centered *here*.

Excavations in the area begin to uncover an ancient human settlement covered by volcanic eruption, just as Pompeii and Herculaneum were buried in A.D. 79 by the eruption of Vesuvius.

Further investigations discover that *some* of this 50,000- year-old colony are intact, and some ancient equipment is still operating. It is the automatic operations of this ancient electronic equipment that is causing the interference that's been fouling everything up.

This is not the first time that human beings have tried to colonize Mars.

To Barbara, this is the greatest scientific find of all time raising a million new questions: who *were* these ancient space travellers? Do their descendents still live on Earth? Why has none of this ancient technology been found on Earth? And will evidence of their travels be found on still other planets?

To George, these questions are fascinating but of no immediate consequence. What *is* of immediate consequence is that his "interference" problem is solved. Now that he knows what's causing the problems that have been delaying the Development project, the engineers can work away from the ancient city—leaving the site to the flood of scientists that will soon be coming to investigate it.

The engineering problem solved, George goes ahead with preparations to set off the first H-bomb charge in the volcanic caldera.

Barbara, meanwhile, works with her own scientific team to decipher electronic records—a technology similar to videodiscs—found in the ancient ruins.

But even though the written language is impenetrable, there are pictures and diagrams that are easier to understand ... and hours before George's team is supposed to set off the first nuclear blast, Barbara comes to a horrifying conclusion: the ancient colonists had been attempting an atmosphere development project of their own ... and tried the exact same technique of reigniting volcanoes that George is about to try now.

Their entire colony may very well have been destroyed when they set off their *own* nuclear blast to activate a Martian volcano.

And George might be hours away from repeating history with disastrous consequences.

Immediately Barbara tries to get in touch with George by radio, but atmospheric conditions prevent radio contact.

The clock is ticking now, as Barbara frantically drives a Mars buggy across the Martian desert to tell George what she's learned ... and only minutes before the scheduled nuclear explosion, she manages to get through to him.

George takes Barbara's warning seriously and—overruling the protests of another Corporation engineer with a right cross—he cancels the scheduled blast.

Later, George recommends to the Corporation that the volcanic ignition plan be put on indefinite hold until further investigations can be made by scientists ... including his future wife, Barbara.

And while Barbara investigates the ancient city, George will remain on Mars to work on engineering an alternative way to make Mars more livable.

Figure 8

Before *Back to the Future* changed the face of time-travel in the movies ... before *Sliders* gave us tripping into alternate earths as weekly fare, there was a big hole on the big screen waiting to shoot a decent time-travel cross-dimensional story into.

This was mine.

It was my intention to write the script of this with Léon Bing, a former top fashion model who I'd met through my agent, Joel Gotler, and who subsequently became a good friend. Léon has since gone on to become a top writer of books about troubled teens, with books such as *Do or Die*, and *Smoked*.

But time and chance happeneth to us all, Léon and I both got busy on other projects, and it just never happeneth.

—JNS

Figure 8
by J. Neil Schulman

We open, in 1976, at the World Science Fiction Convention in Kansas City.

Sixteen-year-old science-fiction fan JOEL LINDER is attending the convention with his friend WALTER when, impossibly for any adolescent to believe, Joel is pursued through the convention hotel by the stunning 32-year-old world-famous model, DANA LANGLEY.

An adolescent fantasy is played out as Dana takes him up to her hotel room, shows him that she is wearing the identical twin of a moon rock which Joel has and which, by all logic, must be the *only* one ... then she seduces him.

After they make love, Dana disappears into the bathroom, and Joel hears what sounds like a gunshot. Scared she's killed herself, he opens the bedroom door to find ... she's disappeared. And there's no way she could've gotten out.

There is, however, a package addressed to Joel. He opens it to find a note from Dana addressed to him that says, "WHEN YOU SEE ME AGAIN I WON'T KNOW YOU," and with it a used paperback book—a bestselling novel titled *RECOUNT*, which is about what would have happened if Nixon had beaten JFK in the 1960 presidential election.

There are a few odd things about this novel. The first is the author's name: JOEL LINDER. The second is the author's picture—which shows Joel as he'll look in ten years—and an author's bio sketch that matches Joel's background and continues forward ten years.

The third oddity is the copyright date: 1987—eleven years in the future.

Joel sits down to read the book, having lost interest in the convention.

It takes Joel a while, but he does manage to track Dana Langley down ... and as the note promised, she has no idea who he is or that they've ever met before, much less made love. But when he shows her the note, she is intrigued by the fact that it is written in her handwriting, and she invites Joel up to her apartment.

They start as Platonic friends, and, over time, he eventually becomes her lover—whether it's again or not is an open question; but he definitely falls head ovr heels in love with her.

Joel goes on to college at MIT and graduate school in physics at UC Irvine, getting a Ph.D. Joel and Dana's relationship continues but not as lovers, just as friends. The paperback book he was mysteriously given is lost in an apartment fire; he rewrites it—mostly from memory—then submits the novel manuscript to a publisher, and it's accepted. It becomes a hardcover bestseller.

When it comes out in paperback, it looks exactly like the book he'd found in the hotel bathroom eleven years earlier.

In 1988, at age 44, Dana commits suicide. Joel is mourning her death and has the job of closing her apartment thrust upon him by her relatives. As he does, he finds her diary, begun when she was a child, telling her life story. She had wanted to become a writer but instead was thrust into a career in modelling, at the age of sixteen, when a photographer took her picture with Richard Nixon at his election headquarters on election eve. Nixon lost the election but she won a modelling contract ... and was pushed into it by her mother. She's always felt it was the wrong choice ... age has left her with no career and only a marginal living.

Shortly after Dana's death, Joel—now a prominent author at 28—attends another World Science Fiction Convention, where he is approached by a man in his fifties with a full beard and mustache. He seems familiar to Joel—he looks like a family relation—but Joel can't place him. The man has a paperback copy of Joel's novel on him.

The man tells Joel that he has a time machine in his hotel room ... and Joel can try it out if he wants to.

Having already had one profoundly weird life experience sixteen years earlier, Joel decides to investigate.

In the man's hotel room is a machine holding open a portal to SOMEPLACE ELSE.

The man tells Joel that the door leads to 1960, and Joel can walk through that door, find Dana Langley at age 16, and prevent her from having her picture taken with Nixon. She'd never become a model, become a writer instead, and never reach the stage of despair that leads to suicide.

Joel asks if he can get back to the present. The man says, "I guarantee it. The time machine will take you back to this exact moment. You and I will meet again right now, in this hotel room."

Joel steps through the time portal ... and, as promised, he's back in 1960. But, not quite as promised, the time machine burns out ... and Joel finds himself stranded back in 1960 with nothing much from his own time other than his moon rock, some money and personal effects with the wrong dates, and a copy of his novel in paperback.

He seeks out Dana and manages to get into the hotel with the Nixon-for-President election eve headquarters. He pursues the young Dana in almost the precise way the older Dana once pursued him ... and uses the same gambit on her she used: he's read her diary and knows her secrets.

Then, in an empty hotel room, he convinces her not to have her picture taken with Nixon by telling her about the future that she'll live through if she does. He tells her about how Kennedy will win this election by a few electoral votes, the JFK assasination, the War in Vietnam, about Watergate and the Nixon resignation. He tells her how, if she has her picture taken with Nixon, she'll become the most famous model in the world ... live an unhappy life, and kill herself in her early forties.

Incredibly, the scene between Dana and Joel happens in reverse, as this time the older Joel seduces the 16-year-old Dana.

Incredibly, Dana believes what Joel tells her about her future.

Incredibly, so does Richard Nixon, who's been in the bathroom, relieving himself, and overhearing everything.

And, when Nixon demands a recount in the election the next day, history is changed, and Nixon is declared the victor over Kennedy.

We follow Joel and Dana, as they marry and live through a changed history—a history where the war is in Cuba, not Vietnam; where there's never an American program to go to the moon; where the Beatles never come to America; where music in the 60's is a continuation of the protest folk music of the 50's; and where Martin Luther King is still living in the seventies to fight for civil rights legislation that a President Johnson never got passed in 1964.

We follow Joel's attempts to rebuild the time machine from his knowledge of theoretical physics and what he can deduce from the remains of the machine.

We follow Dana's career as she becomes not a model but a best-selling writer with a speculative novel, based on Joel's knowledge of the alternate history he lived through, telling what would have happened if *Kennedy* had won the 1960 election.

We follow the day when Joel gives his wife his moon rock in a pendant on a gold chain ... even more valuable in this time-line, where *nobody* has ever walked on the moon.

We follow Joel and Dana's sorrow as they discover that Joel's time voyage has somehow left him with a sperm-count too low to give them children.

And, in 1976, when Joel finally gets the time machine rebuilt, we follow Dana, age 32, as she takes the machine across the dimension of an alternate time-line to the World Science Fiction Convention of 1976 ... where she meets and seduces a sixteen-year-old Joel Linder, hoping the encounter will leave her pregnant with her future-husband's child. This time we follow her into the bathroom as she leaves the package with the paperback book, *RECOUNT*, which Joel had brought with him sixteen years earlier, then she steps through the time portal, and steps across time and dimension into the arnms of her husband, Joel, now 44-years-old.

We are still there, nine months later, when Dana gives birth to their daughter, Gillian.

And, in 1988, we are there when Joel—56-years-old with a full beard, Dana—now 44—and Gillian, now age 11—use the time machine to step from the world in which Nixon won in 1960 to the world where Kennedy won.

While Dana and Gillian wait, Joel-with-beard seeks out his younger, 28-year-old beardless self, and the older Joel convinces his younger self to take the machine back to 1960 to talk Dana out of having her picture taken with Nixon.

And the older Joel is absolutely truthful when he tells the younger Joel that they will, absolutely guaranteed, meet again here-and-now in this hotel room.

When Joel steps through the time portal, the door to the past closes up with a bang, and 56-year-old Joel, his wife, the still-living 44-year-old Dana, and their daughter Gillian leave the hotel to live the rest of their lives happily ever after.

"To Err Is Humanoid"

This is the one script I almost decided not to include in this collection.

Unlike the others, I didn't originate the story—my ex-wife, Kate O'Neal, did. Kate and I wrote it using the "bible" of an existing episodic TV series, which makes the work even less original.

So why include it?

Well, there are several reasons.

The first is that I've always been pissed off about how this script was treated. When Kate and I wrote this spec script for *Star Trek: The Next Generation,* Melinda Snodgrass was story editor. Melinda was a libertarian whom I knew through her close neighbor at the time, fellow Prometheus-award-winner Victor Milan. Hollywood is a community dominated by the left, and there just aren't that many libertarians of our generation with TV screen credits. I felt having a couple of *Twilight Zone* sales under my belt, writing a spec script would at worst get Kate and me a meeting to pitch other stories, even if they didn't like this one.

Melinda not only didn't lobby for this script at *ST:TNG*, she turned us down for a pitch meeting.

"Libertarians" like that remind me of Humphrey Bogart as the police drag Peter Lorre away in *Casablanca*: "I stick my neck out for nobody."

The other reason I'd like people to be able to read this script is that it was ahead of its time in a lot of ways.

"To Err Is Humanoid" was written to the second-season bible for *ST:TNG*, but it incorporated plot elements that the series, and its spin-offs *Deep Space Nine* and *Voyager* wouldn't get to for years. A major character (Riker) is shown royally screwing up and feeling lousy about it. You just didn't do that when Gene Roddenberry was the showrunner. And, in the second season, the Ferengi were never portrayed as anything but scumbags with no redeeming qualities. The multi-faceted Quark and his family were years away from being developed.

Finally, with the exception of "Profile in Silver," which was produced, all the other scripts in this collection require the reader to imagine all the production values. With a spec script for any episodic series whose characters everyone knows by heart, you can just plug a spec script into a universe you already know, then just sit back and enjoy the ride.

Even though this script includes second-season *ST:TNG* story elements that annoy the heck out of some fans (Dr. Pulaski's bigotry against Data, Wesley always having to save the day), I still think it's a pretty decent script.

I tried to get the legal eagles at Paramount to clear the script, as originally submitted, for publication; they refused, citing "legal and business considerations." So, I have removed all Paramount trademarked characters, devices, and settings from the script, and replaced them with satirical names, devices, and settings. The current version of the script, as published here with these substitutions, is now *legally a satire* of a typical second-season episode of *Star Trek: The Next Generation*.

That's my story and I'm sticking to it.

To Err Is Humanoid
Story by Kate O'Neal
Teleplay by Kate O'Neal & J. Neil Schulman

FADE IN

TEASER

EXT. THE ASTROSHIP ENTROPY

as it approaches a planet, towing a huge barge-like container.

Picardo's voice over

PICARDO
Captain's diary, Astrodate 43174.3. We are on a maintenance and research mission to deliver a chlorine barge to the planet Vivaria. A Confederacy wildlife sanctuary since the 22nd century, Vivaria is populated by many fantastic and otherwise extinct creatures and the Rangers who care for them. A select team from the Entropy will monitor wildlife activities, in addition to replenishing supplies and upgrading and repairing the Confederacy provisions system.

CAPTAIN'S READY ROOM

as Picardo sits in Captain's chair, viewing images of strange looking animals. He changes the images with the touch of a panel.

CONN
(on communicator)
Captain Picardo, we are within fifteen minutes of Vivaria.

PICARDO
Good. Close orbit, Mr. Valdez.

Picardo gathers his materials and rises.

CUT TO

GAME ROOM

where Rusher and Biker play a chess-type strategy game.

RUSHER
(to Biker)
But how can such different and highly sensitive species live together without conflict on Vivaria?

BIKER
It's a delicate balance. The Confederacy sanctuary system was designed to provide the exercise and food to fulfill each species' predatory needs. The wildlife can live there in safety, without worrying about becoming someone else's next meal.

RUSHER
And have the Rangers been successful in encouraging the species to reproduce in this environment?

BIKER
They haven't needed any encouragement. I understand the population on Vivaria has tripled since I was there one summer as a cadet.

RUSHER
(confidentially)
What's the strangest mating process you ever saw on Vivaria?

BIKER

as he pauses thoughtfully. He is saved when his communicator calls.

PICARDO'S VOICE
Commander Biker, report to bridge immediately.

BIKER (rising)
I'll tell ya some other time.

ANGLE ON RUSHER

as he makes a face as if he's been cheated.

INT. BRIDGE

Biker enters, with Rusher in tow.

PICARDO
First Officer, you can take over now while I prepare for our research trip. After you've emptied the carton into the Arganean Ocean we'll stream down.

BIKER
No problem, Captain.

PICARDO
I'll be in the library if you need me. Commander Beta, I could use your help.

Picardo and Beta exit.

RUSHER
(to Biker)
I'll go assist Jorge in Engineering.

Biker nods permission. Rusher exits.

CUT TO

ENGINEERING

Rusher enters and approaches Lafayette, who sits at the control console.

LAFAYETTE
Hey, Welles. Have a seat.

RUSHER
(with mock wistfulness)
Gee, my first chlorine deposit. That carton must be five times the size of the Entropy. How do you handle something so gigantic?

LAFAYETTE
It's really very controlled. As long as the four tractor streams stay consistent, the carton slips right into the receptacle.

RUSHER
What do we do now?

LAFAYETTE
Just sit here and wait for the word "go".

CUT TO
BRIDGE

where Biker sits in command chair.

BIKER
(to Computer)
Get me Ranger Okano on the screen.

FRONT MONITOR

where image of Asian female appears onscreen. She has a

strange creature perched on her shoulder.

BIKER
Glad to see you, Katy. How's life on Vivaria?

OKANO (on screen)
(teasing)
Everything calmed down after you left, Biker. The Screaming Blue Widni has finally stopped screaming.

BIKER
(laughs)
Look, you could've warned me never to approach one from behind.

OKANO (on screen)
You were still pulling blue fuzz off yourself three weeks later.

BIKER
Well, now I'm getting a chance to redeem my reputation. Several of us from the Entropy will be streaming down for research and repair.

OKANO (on screen)
I remember when R and R used to mean "Rest and Relaxation."

BIKER
We'll try to do some of that as well.

OKANO (on screen)
I'll look forward to a demonstration of those leadership qualities I hear you've developed in fifteen years.

BIKER
I'll give you a sample right now. I'm delivering the chlorine carton for your Arganean Ocean.

OKANO
Our hatch is set to "Receive."

BIKER
(to Engineering and to Okano)
Prepare to transfer chlorine container. Jorge
set stream 1 at 45 degrees, stream 2 at 135...

CUT TO

ENGINEERING

where Lafayette programs panel, with Rusher assisting him.

BIKER'S VOICE OVER
...Beam 3 at 225, and stream 4 at 315.

LAFAYETTE
(into communicator, to Biker)
Parameters set. Tractor streams ready.

CUT TO

BRIDGE

BIKER
Enact tractor streams, begin transfer.

BRIDGE, FAVORING MONITOR

where Biker sees chlorine carton disengage from the
Entropy and be tugged towards receiving tank on Vivaria.

BIKER
Take stream 3 power to 22 gigagrams.

CLOSE ON MONITOR

where the carton tilts as one stream's power reduces.

BIKER'S VOICE
Beam 2 to 24 gigagrams.

CUT TO

EXT. ENTROPY

showing container in the process of transferring from ship to Vivaria.

CUT TO

BRIDGE

where we see Biker checking his power monitor and seeing no power registering for indicator 4. He moves some dials, gets no response and becomes alarmed.

BIKER
Jorge, no power on stream 4!

CUT TO

ENGINEERING

where Lafayette looks puzzled and gets up and checks some wall indicators, nodding to Rusher to take the controls.

LAFAYETTE
That's an odd insertion he's using.

RUSHER
(to Biker)
Are you sure, sir?

BIKER'S VOICE
(on intercom)

I'm sure, ensign. No power on 4.

Rusher looks to Lafayette, who gives him an affirmative nod. Rusher shrugs and cuts power off from Beam 4.

RUSHER
(offhandedly, laughing)
For a minute I thought he meant he had no power on 4.

LAFAYETTE
How could that be? We're showing power on 4.
(checking indicator)
Commander Biker, what's the reading on your number four indicator?

BIKER
I just told you. It says no power.

ANGLE ON LAFAYETTE

as it dawns on him. He leaps up.

LAFAYETTE
Welles! Power back on stream, then get to the bridge!!

ANGLE ON RUSHER

as his head shoots up in alarm as he realizes the mistake.

CUT TO
BRIDGE

where Biker sees chlorine carton suddenly tilt and crush.

CUT TO

EXT. THE ASTROSHIP ENTROPY

as carton buckles and greenish gas begins to seep
out through cracks.

CUT TO

INT. BRIDGE

where Biker looks at monitor in alarm.

CUT TO

BRIDGE MONITOR

where we see gas pour out of carton and envelop the
atmosphere of Vivaria.

END OF TEASER

Act I

BRIDGE OF ENTROPY

with alarms sounding, general commotion.

MONITOR

where Okano's face appears. As she speaks, we can hear
alarms on Vivaria in the background.

OKANO
(onscreen, to Biker)
What the hell is going on?!

ON BRIDGE

Before Biker has a chance to respond, Picardo comes
running onto bridge.

PICARDO
What the hell is going on?!

Rusher runs onto bridge.

BIKER
(angrily, to Rusher)
I said I needed power on stream 4! What happened?

RUSHER
What you said was "no power on 4". We took that as an order to cut off power.

BIKER
No power means I'm getting no power. How could Jorge—

PICARDO
(interrupting)
Commander, we'll hold an Inquiry later.
(to Communicator)
Dr. Tchaikowsky, report to bridge on the double.

Biker looks to Rusher for support, but receives a hot, mistrustful glare. This exchange is noticed by Picardo.

PICARDO
Beta, give me a current report on the effect the release of liquid chlorine can have on Vivaria.

BETA
There should be no immediate effect on wildlife or humans. However, the gas was released into the planet's exosphere.

Tchaikowsky enters bridge.

BETA
(continuing)

The chlorine will gradually seep down into the ozonosphere, react chemically with the ozone, and create a hole in the protective ozone layer.

PICARDO
Commander Biker, prepare to stream down with emergency medical support. And take Ensign Rusher with you.

BIKER
Aye, aye, sir.

TCHAIKOWSKY
The effects of ultraviolet radiation aren't immediately apparent. The burn will increase day by day until the chlorine can be contained.

OKANO (onscreen)
How long will that take? Some of the species here are extremely delicate.

PICARDO
We don't know yet. Beta, how about matter conversion to combine oxygen with the chlorine and change it into ozone?

BETA
Captain, I do not believe this would be a viable solution. At maximum power, the Entropy would be able to convert a gas cloud of this size within...

Beta makes some calculations.

BETA (continuing)
...approximately 35 years. This extended timeframe is due to the unusually large volume of the gas.

PICARDO

as he frowns.

PICARDO
Is there another element into which chlorine can be converted in a shorter time constraint?

WIDER AGAIN

as Beta calculates.

BETA
Only one, sir, but applied to Vivaria's exosphere, it would result in severe acid rain.

PICARDO
Ranger Okano, we're not going to be able to do a matter conversion. We're going to have to contain the gas somehow. In the meantime, you should take precautions against ultraviolet exposure.

TCHAIKOWSKY
Try to shelter the animals as much as possible. All your Rangers should wear protective clothing and headgear.

BIKER
(to Okano)
Katy, I'll stream down right away to help you get the wildlife under cover.

OKANO (onscreen)
These are outdoor creatures! You know they can't be kept inside.

BIKER
(at a loss)
I can't tell you how sorry...

OKANO (onscreen)
Then don't tell me. Just do something!

PICARDO
We'll do everything in our power, Ranger. I take full responsibility for the damage the Entropy has caused.

OKANO (onscreen)
But it's the creatures who'll pay the price.

CLOSE ON BIKER'S FACE

as he registers dismay.

CUT TO

TRANSPORTER ROOM

where Tchaikowsky briefs her emergency medical team. Morph, Rusher and Biker stand in back and react to the following descriptions of the destruction their actions caused.

TCHAIKOWSKY'S VOICE OVER
Medical Diary, Astrodate 43175.4. We are preparing to stream down to Vivaria to administer emergency treatment for ultraviolet burns. The hole in the ozone continues to grow, and with it the intensity of the burning. I only hope that we are equipped to deal with the varied effects this will have on the rare species of animals on Vivaria.

TCHAIKOWSKY
Group One, you will be working with Dr. Simpson, on the amphibian class animals. They will require oral therapy, as their skins are impervious to topical treatments.

BIKER
Group Two will work with me, treating avians and small mammalians, starting with the application of topical burn ointments.

TCHAIKOWSKY
Groups three and four will treat large mammalians, under the guidance of Ranger Okano and Lieutenant Morph. The leaders of each group will distribute specific medical data on the creatures.

Leaders distribute data cards for crew's tricorders.

TCHAIKOWSKY
We have to be ready to treat severe burns to many tissue types. The initial reaction will be similar to a first degree sunburn. As the burn intensifies in the following twelve to fourteen hours, some creatures may require epidermal grafts.

Medical crew members exchange uneasy glances.

TCHAIKOWSKY
After twenty four hours, we could see what the twenty third century saw after the War on Baindera. I expect each of you to exhibit professional detachment.
(to Biker)
Commander?

BIKER
(to crew)
We have very little idea of what reactions to expect from the wildlife. All of you are to diary your findings with me or Dr. Tchaikowsky. You are to work with Vivaria Rangers in attempting to restrain any wildlife.
(to bridge)
Beta, are we clear for transport?

BETA'S VOICE
Commander, long-range perceptors indicate a large
astroship in sector five. It appears to be a Durangi
cruiser.

BIKER
Can you give me more information on its
orientation and intent?

BETA'S VOICE
It seems to pose no threat to our mission. It is
in orbit around one of the outer planets, Class C.

BIKER
I don't think they'll bother us. Let me know if
the Durangi ship's orientation changes.
(to medical team)
Prepare to stream down.

Crew takes positions on teleporter platform.

BIKER
(to operator)
Energize.

The crew dematerializes.

CUT TO

EXT. THE PLANET VIVARIA

where the crew reappears. They are met by Okano.

OKANO
The Canolupa have been the hardest hit.

CLOSE ON OKANO'S HAND

as she holds out her palm, upon which is a whisp-like

creature, collapsed into a heap.

WIDER AGAIN

OKANO
I've hoisted a make-shift tent and started
treatment.

As they walk, Morph is surprised when a small monkey-like creature jumps up and sits on his shoulder.

MORPH
What is this on my shoulder?

OKANO
A Krehoe.

MORPH
Why is this on my shoulder?

OKANO
I guess it likes you.

Morph looks at the Krehoe with disdain. He tries to shrug it off, but it only nestles closer.

EXT. TENT

Okano leads the crew to a tarpaulin, which shelters a variety of small creatures starting to show signs of pain.

INT. TENT

as they enter.

OKANO
Doctor, I have applied a topical burn treatment, but the Striped Bondos seem to be more severely affected.

TCHAIKOWSKY
I'll have a look at them right away. Nurse?

Tchaikowsky and nurse crouch down and get to work.

BIKER
Let's get started constructing a recovery room.

He motions to accompanying crew, who start assembling shelter and equipment.

TCHAIKOWSKY
(looking up at Biker)
It's going to get worse before it gets better.

The medical team starts examining the wildlife.

CUT TO

CLOSE ON SLIGHTLY LARGER ANIMAL

out in brush, as it scuttles under a bush, beginning to suffer.

EXT. THE ASTROSHIP ENTROPY

near Vivaria, where we see gas cloud continuing to spread.

CUT TO

INT. BRIDGE

PICARDO
(speaking to Astrofleet Command, onscreen)
I need every vessel that you can get to me on the double—planetary vessels, commercial freighters, anything.

ASTROFLEET OFFICER
There is no Confederacy vessel of that size or power requirement anywhere near your quadrant.

PICARDO
Then send me smaller cruisers, and we'll link them together.

ASTROFLEET OFFICER
Captain Picardo, there's not another ship in your sector.

PICARDO
There's got to be a Astrofleet fuel tanker that can pick up this chlorine spill. What about the Hector?

ASTROFLEET OFFICER
She's nowhere near you. I'm telling you, there's not an available ship within three weeks of Vivaria, Captain Picardo.

ON PICARDO

as he starts to get really worried.

PICARDO
If we don't get help before three weeks are up, there won't be life on Vivaria!

CUT TO

EXT. ENTROPY

where gas cloud grows larger over Vivaria.

END OF ACT I

Act II

EXT. VIVARIA

where larger and larger animals are being treated for burns. The temporary shelter has reached capacity, and the medical team is treating wildlife stranded out in the open.

Morph walks along, the Krehoe still on his shoulder.

MORPH
(to Krehoe)
You are cute. Klingers hate "cute".

Morph shrugs and this time the animal falls off and lies weakly on the ground. Morph starts to walk away, but stops when he notices the Krehoe is hurt. He picks it up and brings it to Okano, who is caring for other creatures near tent.

MORPH
This animal is not well.

OKANO
I'm not surprised. Krehoes don't have much of an immune system to start with, and the ultraviolet is completely wiping it out.

MORPH
Can you help it?

OKANO
I can try. Leave it with me.

Okano examines the Krehoe, and Morph exits.

Biker enters, very upset and haggard looking. The Entropy crew members have begun to display heat blisters and flaking skin on their hands and faces.

ON BIKER AND OKANO

as Biker kneels down next to Okano.

BIKER
You look beat.

Biker massages Okano's neck. She shrugs him off.

OKANO
Not compared to him.

She shows Biker the Krehoe she is treating.

BIKER
Hey, isn't this a Krehoe? I remember when they were nearly extinct.

OKANO
(giving him a look)
They still are.

ON BIKER

as he goes outside.

ON TCHAIKOWSKY

helping an animal in the bush.

TCHAIKOWSKY
Commander, I need your help!

ON BIKER

as he rushes to her side.

TCHAIKOWSKY
Help me to raise its head! It's going into
coronary arrest.

ON BOTH

as Biker struggles to lift the creature, while Tchaikowsky
tries to give it an injection.

TCHAIKOWSKY
Higher! I can't find an artery.

Biker wrenches the creature off the ground. Tchaikowsky
injects it. She checks under its eyelids and sighs.

ON TCHAIKOWSKY

TCHAIKOWSKY
(sadly)
You can put it down. It's dead.

ON BIKER

as he looks at the dead animal in his arms. He stares at
it for a moment before gently setting it on the ground.
He gets to his feet, beaten. His eyes well up as he looks
to the skies for an answer.

ON OKANO

under tarpaulin, as she sees Biker outside and goes to
him. She puts a hand on his shoulder.

ON BOTH

OKANO
I'm sorry I was angry with you before.
Everything seemed so terrible, and I guess I was
looking for someone to blame.

BIKER
What a coincidence that you chose me.

OKANO
Bill, stop beating yourself up about this.
Everything happened so fast.

BIKER
You can stop trying to make me feel better. Just come out and say it: It was my fault.

OKANO
Nobody blames you.

ON BIKER

as he turns away from Okano.

BIKER
Well, I do.

He staggers away from the medical unit, to a spot out of hearing distance of the others. He touches his communicator to call Picardo.

BIKER (to Picardo)
Captain Picardo, the situation here is pretty bad.

PICARDO'S VOICE
What seems to be the problem, Commander?

BIKER
Captain, it's a shambles down here...creatures dying everywhere...at the rate the ozone is breaking down, we can't keep up. (He pauses). I need help.

CUT TO

BRIDGE OF ENTROPY.

TOY
Captain, I get the sense that Commander Biker is feeling depression, guilt and utter fatigue.

Picardo gets the idea that Biker needs help.

PICARDO
I'll stream down a fresh medical team right away. Send up those from your team who most need relief.

ON TOY

as she interprets Biker's condition.

BIKER'S VOICE
(rambling, distraught)
There are so many kinds of animals, and they need different kinds of attention. We can't fill all their needs.

TOY
Commander Biker is in an extremely agitated condition, Captain. It is possible that he is currently incapable of fulfilling his duties as commanding officer.

ON BRIDGE

BIKER'S VOICE
It's different than treating humans. Humans can say what they're feeling, what they need. We have no way of communicating with these creatures, and they're dying. Dr. Tchaikowsky can't work fast enough.

TOY
Captain, I think I could be of assistance on

Vivaria. If I could feel the needs of the particular species there, perhaps I could recommend their treatment.

PICARDO
(to BIKER)
First Officer, Lieutenant Toy and Commander Beta will stream down to replace you.

BIKER
But, Captain!

PICARDO
You have your orders. Prepare to stream up. You are relieved of your command.

Toy and Beta rise and exit toward the teleporter room.

CUT TO

EXT. VIVARIA

where Biker is even more crestfallen after being relieved. He looks up.

ON BIKER

BIKER
Ready to stream up.

He is dematerialized.

CUT TO

INT. ENTROPY

as Biker enters bridge, looking upset.

PICARDO
You're off duty, First Officer. I suggest you get some rest.

BIKER
Captain, I am perfectly capable of commanding that landing party.

PICARDO
That's for me to decide.

BIKER
While you're at it, why don't you assign me to work in Maintenance, since you've relieved me of my command of the landing party.

PICARDO
Bill, you're understandably upset, but this is neither the time nor the place to discuss it.

BIKER
Captain, I—I need your help.

PICARDO
You need your rest. There will be an informal Inquiry about the cause of this accident at 08:00 hours tomorrow. I want you to be at your best.

BIKER
I have never been worse. I don't know how I can go on after what I did.

PICARDO
Listen, Bill, I can't discuss this incident with you before the Inquiry!

The bridge crew members look up from their work and take notice of this discussion.

BIKER
Everything and everyone on the planet is burning up!

PICARDO
You will not stand here and disrupt bridge operations. Report to sickbay immediately.

Biker looks around and sees that he has made a spectacle of himself. He bolts from the room.

CUT TO

PASSAGEWAY

Biker careening down hallway. He enters sickbay.

CLOSE ON BIKER

as he surreptitiously takes a bottle marked "Grain Ethanol, For Medicinal Purposes Only."

DOCTOR
Can I help you, Commander?

BIKER
No thanks, you just did.

ON PASSAGEWAY

as Biker exits sickbay and heads for the Officer's Club.

CUT TO

INT. OFFICER'S CLUB

where Gwinne is carrying a tray of drinks across room, and as Biker rushes in, they collide.

ON BOTH

GWINNE
Oof! This is the closest encounter I've had all
week.

BIKER
I'm sorry, Gwinne. I'm in no mood for company.

GWINNE
Well, I need someone to listen to. Have a seat.
I'll be right back.

Gwinne hands Biker a drink from her tray. She goes to
deliver remaining drinks while Biker takes a seat in
a corner of the bar.

ON BIKER

as he takes the bottle out of his clothes and secretly
adds alcohol to his glass of alanol.

ON GWINNE

as she approaches the table and takes a seat.

She raises her glass in a toast.

GWINNE
To the Durangi!

ON BIKER

as he looks into his drink.

BIKER
Not this time.

GWINNE
Hey, they're not my favorite lifeform either, but at
least they invented Alanol.

ON BOTH

BIKER
What good is euphoria if you can just turn it off at will?

GWINNE
I bet you're wishing you were somewhere else.

BIKER
I can't believe this is real. It feels like a nightmare.

He drinks.

GWINNE
You know, you're a human being, not a machine. We're all allowed to make mistakes sometimes.

BIKER
A First Officer can't afford to make mistakes of this size. I shouldn't be in Astrofleet if I can't be entrusted with command of the Entropy.

GWINNE
Are you accusing Captain Picardo of poor judgment in choosing you?

BIKER
It's my fault for signing up in the first place.

Biker drinks, getting more and more depressed.

GWINNE
You're not acting like the Bill Biker I know. You sure that's one of mine?

Gwinne takes his drink before Biker can stop her. She sniffs it.

GWINNE
That's not alanol—it's alcohol! What're you trying to do, destroy yourself with that stuff?

BIKER
I want to get away.

GWINNE
Sorry, honey, but this is life, and there's no escape. You belong in sickbay.

BIKER
(referring to his drink)
That's where I got this.

Gwinne shakes her head.

BIKER
I'm letting everyone down. I can't get my focus off my error and on toward a solution.

GWINNE
All right. Tell me what's the worst that could happen down there.

Biker sighs.

BIKER
Worst outcome would be the destruction of all life on Vivaria and the extinction of hundreds of rare species.

GWINNE
Now how can we improve that situation?

BIKER
Well, we're already administering burn treatments, but the liquid chlorine is continuing to dissolve the ozone layer. Everything will keep on burning unless we can contain the spill and regenerate the ozone.

GWINNE
And how are we going to stop that chlorine?

CLOSE ON BIKER

BIKER
The only way is to contain the spill in a tractor net until we can repair the holding tank. But we'd need to coordinate our efforts with another astroship.

BOTH AGAIN

GWINNE
Hmmm. Where are we going to get another astroship?

BIKER
That's the problem! There are no Confederacy ships available. The only astroship within range is a Durangian ship.
(gets an idea)
The Durangi are traders. I wonder if we could strike a bargain....

Biker leaps up.

BIKER
(continuing)
I've got to get to Sick Bay for an alcohol antidote!

ON GWINNE

as she smiles and nods.

GWINNE
You sure do.

OFFICER'S CLUB

as Biker hurries out of the lounge.

END OF ACT II

Act III

EXT. ENTROPY

PICARDO'S VOICE OVER
Captain's diary, Astrodate 43176.3 Forty-eight hours have passed since liquid chlorine exploded into Vivaria's atmosphere, causing me to cancel my plans to stream down. There is now a hole in the protective ozone the size of the the planet's largest continent, Mersa. The ultraviolet rays are taking a toll on increasingly larger wildlife.

CUT TO

SICKBAY

where Biker is being treated by Doctor.

BIKER
(to medic)
I need to get sober in a hurry.

DOCTOR
What have you had?

BIKER
About a hundred milliliters of ethanol.

DOCTOR
Ethanol! I didn't know anyone still drank that.

Doctor shines a light in Biker's eyes.

DOCTOR
(continuing)
The fastest thing would be to convert the alcohol in your blood to sugar.

BIKER
Let's get started.

Doctor applies matter conversion instrument to Biker. We see his alcohol level decreasing steadily on meters on monitoring equipment.

ON BIKER

as he touches his communicator to speak to Picardo.

BIKER
Captain, I have an idea. I think we can get that nearby Durangian ship to help us net the spill while we siphon back the chlorine.

PICARDO'S VOICE
They're a rough bunch to negotiate with. They don't speak our language.

BIKER
I was thinking of using the universal language: profit.

PICARDO'S VOICE
You have a point. I've never known a Durangi to pass up a bargain.

BIKER AND MEDIC

as Medic scans Biker's body.

RIker is made to follow an object with his eyes.

BIKER
My thoughts exactly. What do you say?

PICARDO'S VOICE
That would require an expert negotiator, and unfortunately my First Officer is in sickbay.

CLOSE ON BLOOD ALCOHOL INDICATOR

as it drops steadily.

ON BIKER

as he watches his alcohol level drop to zero.

CUT TO

BRIDGE OF ENTROPY

where Picardo listens for Biker's response.

BIKER'S VOICE
(on communicator)
I just got well.

Picardo looks pleased.

PICARDO
Prove it.

BIKER'S VOICE
Peter Piper picked a peck of pickled peppers.

PICARDO
Report to bridge immediately, First Officer.

CUT TO

INT. BRIDGE OF ENTROPY

where Picardo and Biker are in the midst of negotiations with Durangi Commander on monitor.

BIKER
We need your help, or all life on Vivaria will be destroyed.

DURANGI COMMANDER
It's a shame your stupid mistake has ruined such an otherwise valuable planet. You see, the Durangi also have an interest in Vivaria now that we have discovered Sneging Root there.

BIKER
Is it so important that you get the root now?

DURANGI COMMANDER
It's a pricey commodity, Commander. The Durangi have used it for hundreds of years for its calming properties. It helps us to unwind.

PICARDO
Can't you get it somewhere else? In case you hadn't noticed, we're having a crisis here.

DURANGI COMMANDER
Vivaria is the only planet in this part of the galaxy where Sneging Root still grows. Besides, we find that a crisis is sometimes the best time to negotiate terms.

BIKER
The longer we wait, the more destruction there will be. We would be grateful for your assistance and expertise.

DURANGI COMMANDER
You should be. It's possible that we could help with netting the gas, in exchange for exclusive

mining rights to Sneging Root on Vivaria. It is our intention to commence global strip mining for Sneging Root.

BIKER
But collecting the root would put the future of the sanctuary creatures in jeopardy. Many of the species are extremely sensitive and require a stress-free breeding environment. Industry is what threatened them in the first place.

DURANGI COMMANDER
Our motto is: Survival of the fittest. If these animals are so fragile, you're opposing nature by keeping them alive in a hostile environment.

PICARDO
That was the point of making Vivaria a sanctuary! The Confederacy sought to preserve species that would otherwise die out on an industrial planet.

DURANGI COMMANDER
I don't think you're in any position to argue, since the whole planet may be ruined if we don't help you clean up the mess you made.

BIKER
Perhaps we can work out collection rights for limited areas.

ON DURANGI COMMANDER

DURANGI COMMANDER
Just to show you what good sports we are, we'll hash out the details later. We're ready to connect to our tractor net to yours at any time.

ON BIKER AND PICARDO

BIKER
With any luck, we should be able to repair the container and siphon back the chlorine within twelve days.

DURANGI COMMANDER
Eleven days.

Biker looks to Picardo.

PICARDO
We'll do our best. Let's begin the containment in two hours.

DURANGI COMMANDER
We'll be ready.

CUT TO

EXT. VIVARIA

where Entropy medical team treats burn victims.

ON TOY AND TCHAIKOWSKY

as they bend over an injured creature. Toy lays her hands on it lightly.

TOY
The burn is responding to the ointment, but this animal is still dying.

TCHAIKOWSKY
I've applied topical treatment as well as injections. I don't know what else to do for it.

TOY
Doctor, more than anything else, it seems to be severely dehydrated.

TCHAIKOWSKY
But all the animals have received constant supplies
of drinking water.

TOY
What I'm sensing is a dryness in its glands.

TCHAIKOWSKY
Of course, glandular dehydration! Its ducts must
be nearly empty. I'll irrigate them immediately.

Tchaikowsky administers intraveinous treatment and the
creature responds immediately.

CUT TO

ANOTHER PART OF THE EMERGENCY MEDICAL CARE
INSTALLMENT

where Beta carries a large animal to Rusher for treatment.

ON BETA AND RUSHER

BETA
I hope Commander Biker is recovering.

Rusher attends to creatures.

RUSHER
I hope he's sorry.

BETA
Wellesley, I do not understand your statement just
now. It seems inconsistent with your...(He thinks
of the expression)...hero worship—of Commander
Biker.

RUSHER
(snorts)

From now on I'm going to start picking my heroes more carefully. I trusted Bill. I don't know how he could have let me down.

BETA
(eager to be helpful)
I can explain. Although Commander Biker has an unusually low error rate, his performance record reveals that he has made mistakes in approximately .0072% of his command decisions.

RUSHER
No, Beta. I meant that I'm disappointed because I had thought Bill was a perfect example of a commanding officer.

BETA
Now I understand why you are disappointed. You have set up an unattainable ideal. To paraphrase one of your poets, to err is humanoid.

ON RUSHER

as he realizes he has been unfair in expecting too much from Biker. He smiles.

RUSHER
You know, Beta—you're right.

BETA
(puzzled at what seems obvious to him)
I know.

Rusher exits.

CUT TO

BRIDGE OF ENTROPY

PICARDO
Commander, we'll commence the netting operation now. Are you ready, Lafayette?

CUT TO
ENGINEERING

where Lafayette sits ready at console.

LAFAYETTE
Ready, Captain. Tractor nets are positioned to capture the outermost boundaries of the spill.

CUT TO

BRIDGE

PICARDO
(to Durangi)
At my signal, activate tractor nets.

Entropy crew looks at monitors.

PICARDO
Activate.

CUT TO

EXT. ANGLE ENTROPY

where computer-imaged tractor nets issue from the Entropy and the Durangi ship. The nets surround the gas cloud and interlock, holding the chlorine.

CUT TO

BRIDGE OF ENTROPY

ON PICARDO

LAFAYETTE'S VOICE
Tractor nets are secured, Captain.

PICARDO
Begin siphoning.

CUT TO

EXT. TWO ASTROSHIPS

as the Entropy begins to siphon the chlorine, while the Durangi ship draws in its net like a spider as the cloud is slowly consumed.

BRIDGE OF ENTROPY

BIKER (to Durangi)
A perfect catch, Commander. (to Lafayette) Good work, Lafayette. If all goes well, the greater part of the spill will be contained soon.

END OF ACT III

Act IV

INT. TENT

Morph enters tent, carrying medical supplies.

BETA
(to Morph)
Humans are quite confusing.

MORPH
I have often thought so. We are much alike, Beta.

Beta considers this and grimaces.

MORPH
(continued)
How is the Krehoe doing?

BETA
It does not appear to be responding to our treatment.

They look at Krehoe.

BETA
(continuing)
It is succumbing to infection. Dr. Tchaikowsky projects only a one in five survival rate for this species.

Morph's face softens as he looks compassionately at the Krehoe.

MORPH
Is there nothing else that can be done?

BETA
A bone marrow transplant would greatly increase its chances, but there are no healthy Krehoes to act as donors.

Morph gets an idea.

MORPH
Would any other creatures do?

BETA
Since the Krehoe has virtually no immune system, rejection is not a problem. Almost any healthy mammalian could donate.

MORPH
Would it be painful?

BETA
Extremely.

MORPH
I volunteer.

CUT TO

EXT. VIVARIA

where Durangi team streams down with equipment. They begin surveying land and putting markers in the ground.

TCHAIKOWSKY
(to Durangis)
Welcome, Doctors. Thank God you're here. Please follow me.

DURANGI 1
We're not doctors. We're engineers.

DURANGI 2
We've come to survey Vivaria for root mining.

TCHAIKOWSKY
What in the—

DURANGI 2
Please don't interfere, Doctor. We're under orders.

ON TCHAIKOWSKY

TCHAIKOWSKY
This is absurd. This is an emergency medical unit, treating wildlife which may die. This is not a mining site!

ON TCHAIKOWSKY AND DURANGIS

DURANGI 1
That depends.

Durangi holds an instrument against the ground and checks meter.

DURANGI 1
This area shows extremely high concentrations of Sneging Root. You'll have to take your medical unit elsewhere.

TCHAIKOWSKY
(to communicator)
Captain Picardo, we've encountered a problem.

PICARDO'S VOICE
The creatures aren't responding to your treatments, Doctor?

TCHAIKOWSKY
It's not that, Captain.

Tchaikowsky is interrupted as the Durangis try to remove medical equipment to stake out sections of ground. Okano comes running out of the medical tent.

OKANO
Take your hands off that equipment! These creatures will die if I don't treat them.

DURANGI 2
We are under orders to prepare this site for mining.

OKANO
If you prevent me from performing first aid, the inhabitants of this planet will all be corpses. (Into communicator) Captain Picardo! We need help!

We see one of the Durangi start drilling holes and taking
soil samples.

PICARDO'S VOICE
(on Tchaikowsky's communicator)
What's going on down there, Doctor?

TCHAIKOWSKY
Captain, we seem to have become a Durangi strip
mining camp.

CUT TO
INT. ENTROPY

in conference room, where Picardo, Biker, Lafayette and
assorted officers sit around a table.

BIKER'S VOICE OVER
Personal Diary, Astrodate 43181.3. Today the inquiry
on my actions in the Vivaria incident will be held.
I am not looking forward to having to relive this
event, but no amount of questioning could be more
painful to me than my own feelings of guilt.

ON PICARDO

PICARDO
As this inquiry is informal, I will use a simple
question and answer format. If any question is
unclear to you, or you wish to convey additional
information not asked of you, please feel free to
do so. The first witness will be Lieutenant Lafayette.

ON ENTIRE ROOM

as Picardo addresses Lafayette.

PICARDO
Lieutenant, in your own words, tell us about the

events leading up to the liquid chlorine spill.

Lafayette looks uneasily at Biker, who gives him a reassuring glance. Lafayette takes a deep breath.

LAFAYETTE
The liquid chlorine carton was being transferred as usual, until Commander Biker gave what I thought was an unusual command to cut power on stream 4.

PICARDO
Why did this command seem unusual to you?

LAFAYETTE
My first thought was that cutting power on stream four would throw the carton into an odd trajectory.

PICARDO
Did you convey your projection to Commander Biker?

LAFAYETTE
No, sir. I believed that Commander Biker knew what he was doing.

PICARDO
Did Ensign Rusher express any confusion to Commander Biker?

LAFAYETTE
He asked the Commander if he was sure.

PICARDO
How did Commander Biker respond?

LAFAYETTE
He repeated the same command, "No power on 4".

PICARDO
What did you do?

LAFAYETTE
I nodded to Rusher to obey the command. Then
all hell broke loose.

PICARDO

PICARDO
Yes, we know that part. When did you realize
that a grave error had been made?

ON BOTH

LAFAYETTE
When Ensign Rusher said that for a moment he
had thought the Commander had asked for a power
boost on 4. By that time, it was too late.

PICARDO
Why did you obey the command, against your
initial judgment?

LAFAYETTE
I trusted Commander Biker's judgment. I assumed
he had more data than I had.

PICARDO
Thank you, Lieutenant. The next witness will be
Commander Biker. Commander, are you in
agreement with the Lieutenant's statement of the
sequence of events?

ON ALL

BIKER
I am, but I would like to state for the record that
I was unaware of Lafayette and Rusher's

misunderstanding of my statement. My intention was to report a power loss, not to issue an order.

PICARDO
Can you tell us what you meant when you said, "No power on 4".

BIKER
My number four indicator dropped to zero, while all the others remained constant. We know now that I experienced a meter failure due to a faulty bus, but at the time I thought the number four stream had been cut off.

PICARDO
At what point did you become aware that your "report" had been taken wrongfully?

BIKER
Not until it was too late, when Rusher came onto the bridge. It never occurred to me that my statement had been acted upon as if it was a command.

PICARDO
I see. Do either of your wish to make a closing statement?

LAFAYETTE

as he shakes his head "no".

ALL AGAIN

BIKER
I would like to say that I assume complete culpability for—

PICARDO
(interrupting)

Your position here is not to judge yourself. That's what I am here for.

FAVORING PICARDO

as he pauses to collect his thoughts.

PICARDO
I'm ruling that the miscommunication between the bridge and engineering was caused by a technical malfunction which caused different interpretations of the same statement.

FAVORING LAFAYETTE AND BIKER

as they listen.

PICARDO

PICARDO
But it is vital to remember that in an intense operation such as this, it is of utmost importance for all communication between the bridge and engineering to be crystal clear, and redundant if necessary. You must put yourself in the other's place and consider every possible interpretation of your words.

Biker looks at his lap.

PICARDO
Bill, Jorge, it's not that either of you was wrong—it's that you weren't right enough.

BIKER

as he faces Picardo.

BIKER
I understand. I thank you, Captain.

ON ENTIRE CONFERENCE ROOM

PICARDO
This Inquiry is adjourned.

END OF ACT IV

Act V

INT. TENT

TCHAIKOWSKY'S VOICE
Medical Diary, Astrodate 43181.5. We are so
overworked on Vivaria that I have had to delegate
some surgical duties to Beta. I would say that
Beta's excellent motor skills and perfect memory
would make him a natural-born surgeon—if he
had been naturally born.

Beta is performing a tricky bone marrow transplant, instructed by Tchaikowsky. She withdraws donor marrow from Morph while Beta withdraws contaminated marrow from the Krehoe in preparation for the transplant. Morph and the Krehoe lie next to each other on parallel tables.

TCHAIKOWSKY
After you bore a hole in the pelvic crest, carefully
withdraw 10cc's of red bone marrow.
Beta does this. Morph winces with the pain.

BETA
I have withdrawn the marrow, Doctor.

TCHAIKOWSKY
Now do the same to the Krehoe. Good. Now
unscrew the syringe end and replace it with the

donor marrow.

BETA
Done.

TCHAIKOWSKY
All right. Slowly release the new marrow into the hole in the Krehoe's pelvic crest.

Beta does this. Everyone is rigid with tension.

BETA
The donor marrow is in place.

Everyone gasps with relief.

TCHAIKOWSKY
Fine work, Beta. I never thought I'd be saying this, but we couldn't have done it without you.

BETA
(correcting her)
We couldn't have done it without a marrow donation from Lieutenant Morph.

MORPH
(in pain)
It was my pleasure.

The Krehoe squeaks and reaches toward Morph.

Morph starts to smile at the Krehoe, then realizes he is watched and resumes his gruff expression.

CUT TO

BRIDGE OF ENTROPY.

PICARDO'S VOICE OVER

Captain's Diary, Astrodate 43182.6. Eight days have passed since our cleanup operation began. Three quarters of the chlorine spill has been siphoned into the repaired barge, but the crisis is far from over.

PICARDO
Captain, your engineers are interfering with the well-being of a Confederacy sactuary.

DURANGI COMMANDER
(onscreen)
Nonsense. Your medical team may continue treating your wildlife as they wish.

PICARDO
The animals cannot be properly treated if my crew is unable to utilize sophisticated medical equipment.

DURANGI COMMANDER
Captain, it was necessary for us to relocate your medical operations—at our expense, I might add. Your landing party kept interfering with our mining engineers. I assure you, your operation will be undisturbed once we're firmly installed on Vivaria.

PICARDO
Vivaria is under Confederacy jurisdiction, by interplanetary agreement. You cannot plunder this defenseless planet. If you can't understand it any other way, we own it.

DURANGI COMMANDER
Acquiring real estate is a Durangi specialty.

PICARDO
You people have left Vivaria alone for two hundred years. What took you so long?

DURANGI COMMANDER
Since it was a sanctuary, the Confederacy seems to have hidden the fact that Vivaria is riddled with Sneging Root. It's a perfect site for a massive strip mining operation. Of course, if you don't agree, we can disconnect our tractor net and leave.

PICARDO
But the Durangi are already a wealthy people.

DURANGI COMMANDER
Ah, Captain, we always say you can never be too rich or too short. Why should we settle for what we have, when we could have so much more?

BIKER
But if you strip mine for Sneging Root on Vivaria, many creatures may be unable to survive there. Most of them are quite sensitive and require an undisturbed environment.

DURANGI COMMANDER
Sometimes progress must roll forward, even if some history is crushed beneath its wheels.

BIKER
But who can say whether Sneging Root or rare animals are more important?

DURANGI COMMANDER
I always say, "Let the market decide." It comes down to Economy.

BIKER
At the expense of Ecology.

CUT TO

VIVARIA

where medical personnel have resumed treating the injured.

ON RUSHER

as he playfully "lifts" a Durangi communicator from one of the mining engineers.

RUSHER
(into communicator)
I know you can hear me on the Durangi ship.
You're making a big mistake.

CUT TO

BRIDGE OF ENTROPY

where we see Entropy crew and Durangi (onscreen) hearing Rusher.

RUSHER'S VOICE
At the rate you plan to excavate, the Sneging Root resources on Vivaria will be exhausted in less than a century.

DURANGI COMMANDER (on screen)
What's this young boy babbling about?

PICARDO
Rusher is one of my best men.

DURANGI COMMANDER (on screen)
(To his crew)
Disconnect!

CUT TO

VIVARIA

where, to Durangi Commander's annoyance, Rusher reactivates the Durangi communicator and continues.

ON DURANGI BRIDGE

RUSHER'S VOICE
The Sneging Root supply is so plentiful here because Vivaria is volcanic. Ash from the volcanic activity draws Sneging Root down into fissures in the rocks.

VIVARIA

DURANGI COMMANDER'S VOICE
I don't have time for elementary botany lectures.

RUSHER
You must listen to me. If you extract the Sneging Root at the rate you're planning, the fissures will shift and possibly collapse. This would redirect volcanic output, and might wipe out Sneging Root on the planet for all time.

ENTROPY BRIDGE

Picardo and Biker exchange glances, as do the Durangi Commanders. All are impressed.

DURANGI COMMANDER'S VOICE
Continue.

RUSHER'S VOICE
If you abandon the idea of strip mining in favor of water or forced air extraction at a slower rate, Vivaria would go on producing Sneging Root for at least 2 to 3 thousand years.

CUT TO

VIVARIA

where medical personnel have resumed treating the injured.

ON RUSHER

as he playfully "lifts" a Durangi communicator from one of the mining engineers.

RUSHER
(into communicator)
I know you can hear me on the Durangi ship.
You're making a big mistake.

CUT TO

BRIDGE OF ENTROPY

where we see Entropy crew and Durangi (onscreen) hearing Rusher.

RUSHER'S VOICE
At the rate you plan to excavate, the Sneging Root resources on Vivaria will be exhausted in less than a century.

DURANGI COMMANDER (on screen)
What's this young boy babbling about?

PICARDO
Rusher is one of my best men.

DURANGI COMMANDER (on screen)
(To his crew)
Disconnect!

CUT TO

VIVARIA

where, to Durangi Commander's annoyance, Rusher reactivates the Durangi communicator and continues.

ON DURANGI BRIDGE

RUSHER'S VOICE
The Sneging Root supply is so plentiful here because Vivaria is volcanic. Ash from the volcanic activity draws Sneging Root down into fissures in the rocks.

VIVARIA

DURANGI COMMANDER'S VOICE
I don't have time for elementary botany lectures.

RUSHER
You must listen to me. If you extract the Sneging Root at the rate you're planning, the fissures will shift and possibly collapse. This would redirect volcanic output, and might wipe out Sneging Root on the planet for all time.

ENTROPY BRIDGE

Picardo and Biker exchange glances, as do the Durangi Commanders. All are impressed.

DURANGI COMMANDER'S VOICE
Continue.

RUSHER'S VOICE
If you abandon the idea of strip mining in favor of water or forced air extraction at a slower rate, Vivaria would go on producing Sneging Root for at least 2 to 3 thousand years.

DURANGI COMMANDER (on screen)
This alternative would make the Durangi empire much richer in the long run.

VIVARIA

RUSHER
And you can restrict your mining to volcanic areas, so the creatures can still live in their habitats in peace.

DURANGI COMMANDER'S VOICE
(wryly)
What a bonus.

BIKER'S VOICE
Captain, it is in both of our interests that we should work together to achieve what we both want.

RUSHER

as he smiles.

CUT TO

BRIDGE OF ENTROPY

PICARDO
If you restrict your mining so it doesn't disturb the habitats, we will help you establish Vivaria as a mining/sanctuary, to our mutual benefit.

DURANGI COMMANDER (on screen)
We agree, Captain Picardo, under one condition.

PICARDO
Which is?

DURANGI COMMANDER (on screen)
Don't let word get around that the Durangi are involved in Ecology!

The Durangi cut off communication and disappear from screen.

CUT TO

INT. BRIDGE

Two days later. Picardo and Biker sit in command chairs.

RUSHER

as he enters and heads for his CONN station.

PICARDO
That was a fine game of chess you played down there, Ensign. You're becoming a valuable member of the team.

Rusher smiles and looks at Biker.

RUSHER
Well, I learned from the best, sir.

ON BIKER AND RUSHER

who smile. Their friendship is restored.

PICARDO AND BIKER

PICARDO
(quietly, to Biker)
Well, First Officer, things are getting back to normal.

BIKER

(quietly)
The worst does seem to be over.

PICARDO
I was gratified to see the Entropy team act with clarity and doggedness in a crisis. The situation on Vivaria is under control and now we can all get on with our lives.

BIKER
Except for one thing.

PICARDO
What's that?

BIKER
How do I live with myself?

PICARDO
By focusing on the next job at hand. Ensign Rusher, set course for Godda Clive.

RUSHER
Course laid in, sir.

PICARDO
Enact.

CUT TO

EXT. ENTROPY

as it pulls slowly away from Vivaria.

THE END

About J. Neil Schulman

J. Neil Schulman is the author of two Prometheus award-winning novels, *Alongside Night* and *The Rainbow Cadenza*, short fiction, nonfiction, and screenwritings, including the CBS *Twilight Zone* episode "Profile in Silver."

His first nonfiction book was *Stopping Power: Why 70 Million Americans Own Guns*, of which Charlton Heston said, "Mr. Schulman's book is the most cogent explanation of the gun issue I have yet read. He presents the assault on the Second Amendment in frighteningly clear terms. Even the extremists who would ban firearms will learn from his lucid prose."

Stopping Power was published in hardcover in June, 1994, by Synapse-Centurion, and sold out its first printing of 8,500 copies. It was quoted from by witnesses on both sides in the March, 1995 hearings on firearms before Congress's House Subcommittee on Crime. An updated edition with new material is being released by Pulpless.Com, Inc., in Spring, 1999.

Schulman's next book, *Self Control Not Gun Control*, picked up where *Stopping Power* left off with an exploration of the uses and abuses of both personal and political power.

Dr. Walter E. Williams, talk show host, newspaper columnist, and Chairman of the Department of Economics at George Mason University, says of *Self Control Not Gun Control*, "Schulman interestingly and insightfully raises a number of liberty-related issues that we ignore at the nation's peril. His ideas are precisely those that helped make our country the destination of those seeking liberty. The book's title says it all: personal responsibility, not laws and prohibitions, is the mark of a civil society."

Schulman's most-recent book is *The Robert Heinlein Interview and Other Heinleiniana*, just released by Pulpless.Com, Inc., which Virginia Heinlein calls "a book that should be on the shelves of everyone interested in science fiction."

Schulman has been published in the *Los Angeles Times* and other national newspapers, as well as *National Review*, *New Libertarian*, *Reason*, *Liberty*, and other magazines. His *L.A. Times* article "If Gun Laws Work, Why Are We Afraid?" won the James Madison Award from the Second Amendment Foundation; and in November, 1995, the 500,000-member Citizens Committee for the Right to Keep and Bear Arms awarded Schulman its Gun Rights Defender prize. Schulman's books have been praised by Nobel laureate Milton Friedman, Anthony Burgess, Robert A. Heinlein, Colin Wilson, and many other prominent individuals. His short story "The Repossessed" was the lead story in *Adventures in the Twilight Zone*, edited by Carol Serling; and his short story "Day of Atonement" appeared in the shared-world anthology *Free Space* edited by Brad Linaweaver and Ed Kramer, a Tor hardcover published in July, 1997.

Schulman is a popular speaker on a variety of topics, and a frequent talk show guest for such hosts as Dennis Prager, Michael Jackson, Oliver North, and Barry Farber. He was on ABC's *World News Tonight* as an expert on defensive use of firearms during the 1992 Los Angeles riots, and was chosen to debate Los Angeles County Sheriff Sherman Block on UPN Channel 13 News Los Angeles on the topic of the repeal of the federal "assault weapons" ban.

J. Neil Schulman is a pioneer in electronic publishing, having founded in 1987 the first company to distribute books by bestselling authors for download by modem. He is currently Chairman and Publisher of Pulpless.Com, Inc., which operates the Pulpless.Com web site—"Pulpless Fiction & Nonfiction, too!"—on the World Wide Web at www.pulpless.com, and his personal web site is at www.pulpless.com/jneil/. His internet address is jneil@pulpless.com.

All of Mr. Schulman's books are available for download from these web sites.

www.ingramcontent.com/pod-product-compliance
Lightning Source LLC
Chambersburg PA
CBHW032012230426
43671CB00005B/63